GRACE ABOUNDING
TO THE CHIEF OF
SINNERS

Engrav'd & Publish'd by *J.an.1.1813, from a Sketch by F.W.L. S.to Elstow.*

ELSTOW CHURCH

JOHN BUNYAN

Grace Abounding to the Chief of Sinners

EDITED BY ROGER SHARROCK

OXFORD

AT THE CLARENDON PRESS

Oxford University Press, Amen House, London, E.C.4

GLASGOW NEW YORK TORONTO MELBOURNE WELLINGTON
BOMBAY CALCUTTA MADRAS KARACHI LAHORE DACCA
CAPE TOWN SALISBURY NAIROBI IBADAN ACCRA
KUALA LUMPUR HONG KONG

© *Oxford University Press 1962*

FIRST PUBLISHED 1962
REPRINTED LITHOGRAPHICALLY IN GREAT BRITAIN
AT THE UNIVERSITY PRESS, OXFORD
BY VIVIAN RIDLER
PRINTER TO THE UNIVERSITY
1972

PREFACE

THIS edition of Bunyan's spiritual autobiography takes its place alongside the revised edition of *The Pilgrim's Progress* in the same series; it is fitting that *Grace Abounding to the Chief of Sinners* should stand beside the allegory both as a classic of spiritual writing and as a record of the experience which Bunyan transforms into imaginative fiction in the story of Christian.

Grace Abounding has received much less attention from modern editors than *The Pilgrim's Progress*, and John Brown's edition in the Cambridge Classics (1907) appears to be the only twentieth-century attempt at a scholarly text. Brown, however, reprinted the text of the sixth edition of 1688, the last to be published in Bunyan's lifetime, adding a small appendix of variants from the earlier editions.

I have gone back to the first edition in the hope that reliance on that text affords the best hope of restoring what Bunyan originally wrote. It has thus been possible to retain a number of colloquial and ungrammatical forms, pleasingly fresh and vigorous, which were pruned away by earlier editors and printers. The history of the text is less complicated than that of *The Pilgrim's Progress*, since of the six editions published before Bunyan's death only four survive, the first, third, fifth, and sixth. A specially interesting problem is raised by the many new paragraphs added in the third and the fifth editions, and these have been restored to the form in which they first occur.

The Introduction gives some account of Bunyan's early life, his sectarian background, and his relation to the tradition of the Puritan spiritual autobiography. Some attempt has been made in the Notes to show the work in relation to the whole ambience of the gathered churches as well as to provide a full explanatory and historical commentary. Extracts from the *Bedford Church Book* dealing with Bunyan's activities, the continuation of his life attributed to George Cokayne and usually printed with *Grace Abounding* in the editions from the seventh onwards, and the relevant portions of the narrative of Agnes Beaumont (from B.M. MS. Egerton 2414) are added as appendixes.

It is a pleasure to own my indebtedness to those who have helped me with either information or criticism. I should like to mention in particular Dr. Arthur Brown of University College, London; Mr. E. S. de Beer; Miss Joyce Godber, Bedford County Archivist; Professor David Hawkes; Professor James Kinsley; Mr. E. T. Milligan of Friends' House Library; Dr. Geoffrey Nuttall; Mr. N. E. Osselton; Dr. E. A. Payne, formerly Librarian of Regent's Park College; Professor Henry Talon of the University of Dijon; Mr. H. G. Tibbutt, F.R.Hist.S.; Mr. Owen Watkins; and the officials of Bedford Public Library; the British Museum; the Huntington Library, San Marino, California; the Pierpont Morgan Library; the Edward Turner Sims Library, University of Southampton; and the Trustees of Bunyan Meeting, Bedford.

ROGER SHARROCK

University of Southampton
October 1961

CONTENTS

REFERENCES AND ABBREVIATIONS

[*The place of publication, unless otherwise stated, is London*]

BUNYAN'S WORKS

The Life and Death of Mr. Badman, edited by John Brown (Cambridge, 1905)
Badman

The Holy War, edited by John Brown (Cambridge, 1905)   *H.W.*

The Pilgrim's Progress, edited by J. B. Wharey, revised by Roger Sharrock
(Oxford, 1960)   *P.P.*

In alluding to or quoting from Bunyan's other works reference is made to *The Works of John Bunyan*, edited by George Offor (Edinburgh and London, 1860–2); the title of the work is followed by volume and page reference to Offor. The following titles are given in an abbreviated form:

Come and Welcome to Jesus Christ (1678)   *Come and Welcome*

The Doctrine of the Law and Grace Unfolded (1659)   *Law and Grace*

The Holy City, or, the New Jerusalem (1665)   *Holy City*

A Few Sighs from Hell, or, the Groans of a Damned Soul (1658)   *Sighs from Hell*

Solomon's Temple Spiritualized; or, Gospel Light fetched out of the Temple at Jerusalem (1688)   *Solomon's Temple Spiritualized*

A Treatise of the Fear of God (1679)   *Fear of God*

OTHER WORKS

The Narrative of the Persecution of Agnes Beaumont in the Year 1674, edited with an Introduction by G. B. Harrison (1929)   *Narrative of Agnes Beaumont*

Victoria County History of Bedfordshire (1908–14)   *V.C.H. Bedford*

John Brown, *John Bunyan: his Life, Times and Work*, revised edition by Frank Mott Harrison (1928)   *Brown*

The Church Book of Bunyan Meeting 1650–1820, a facsimile edition with Introduction by G. B. Harrison (1928)   *Church Book*

Dictionary of National Biography   *D.N.B.*

Journal of George Fox, edited by John L. Nickalls (Cambridge, 1952)
Fox, Journal

Modern Language Review   *M.L.R.*

Oxford English Dictionary   *O.E.D.*

INTRODUCTION

(i) *Bunyan's Early Life*

JOHN BUNYAN was born in 1628 in the village of Elstow a mile outside Bedford. His baptism was recorded in the Elstow parish register as follows:

> 1628. John the sonne of Thomas Bonnionn, Junr. the 30th of Novemb.[1]

Thomas Bunyan described himself in his will as a 'braseyer' or travelling tinker. There were numerous Bunyans in Bedfordshire and the name is recorded at Pulloxhill, about nine miles from Elstow in the early thirteenth century. A William Bunyan held a messuage of land in Elstow in 1548, and the cottage in which John Bunyan was born eighty years later was situated on this land, at Harrowden to the south-east of Elstow. In the sixteenth century the Bunyans were yeoman farmers who were going down in the world, as is indicated by recurring sales of the family lands; Thomas Bunyan's father, also called Thomas, had some property to dispose of and made a will before he died in 1641: in it he described himself as a 'Pettie Chapman'.[2] Thomas, the father of John, was the son of the first of his four wives and was baptized on 24 February 1602/3. The elder Thomas Bunyan was on 21 October 1617 presented at the Archdeacon's Court at Ampthill for telling the churchwardens that they were 'forsworne men',[3] but it is not clear whether his offence sprang from Puritan principles. His son Thomas married as his second wife in 1627 Margaret Bentley, the mother of John; she, too, was a native of Elstow, and had been born in the same year as her husband. The will of her mother, Mary Bentley, dated 27 June 1632, bequeaths

---

[1] *Transcript Registers of the Archdeaconry of Bedford*, based on the returns sent yearly to the Registry under the canon of 1603: the parish register for the period before 1641 has been lost; Brown, pp. 26–27.

[2] Bedford County Record Office, *Bedfordshire Wills*, 1641, No. 202; further evidence of the family's yeoman status is found in Bunyan's father's will: 1675–6, No. 74; Brown, pp. 291–2.

[3] *Act Books of the Archdeaconry of Bedford*.

a number of domestic articles characteristic of the better, well-appointed artisan household, including 'painted cloaths about the house'.[1]

The Bunyans must have had an accepted position in the life of the parish. Their tinkering was not that of disreputable vagabonds, but a settled occupation which involved a regular tour of the neighbouring hamlets, making and mending household utensils whether of metal or pewter. After his conversion Bunyan much exaggerated the low station of his family; he describes himself at the beginning of *Grace Abounding* as 'being of that rank that is meanest and most despised of all the families in the Land'; this is neither false humility nor the defiant class consciousness of the mechanic preacher, but rather an expression of proper Christian humility about worldly matters common in the personal testaments of the age: on the gallows in 1662 Colonel John Okey, the regicide, who came of a well-to-do Bedfordshire county family, spoke in the same strain about his antecedents.[2]

Later statements by Bunyan suggest that for some time at least he was educated either at a petty school or at a local grammar school. He declares 'notwithstanding the meanness and inconsiderableness of my Parents, it pleased God to put it into their heart, to put me to School, to learn both to Read and Write'.[3] He adds that he soon forgot whatever he learnt; and in the Second Part of *The Pilgrim's Progress* the phrase *ex carne et sanguine Christi* is glossed 'the Latine I borrowe'.[4] In *The Doctrine of the Law and Grace Unfolded* (1659) he writes: 'I never went to school to Aristotle or Plato, but was brought up at my father's house in a very mean condition, among a company of poor countrymen';[5] this is simply a disclaimer of the refinements of humane learning, not a statement that he never attended a school. He presumably left early in order to earn his living. The school may have been the one at Houghton Conquest

---

[1] *Bedfordshire Wills*, 1632.

[2] H. G. Tibbutt, *Colonel John Okey, 1606–1662* (Bedfordshire Historical Record Society, 1955), p. 159.

[3] At Houghton Conquest school reading and writing were taught as extras at a special charge, which would explain this statement (F. M. Harrison, *John Bunyan: A Record of Recent Research*, 1940, pp. 16–21).

[4] *P.P.*, p. 229.

[5] *Law and Grace*, The Epistle to the Reader, i. 495.

(opened in 1632), which was designed for boys from the whole county of Bedford, whereas Sir William Harper's foundation in Bedford was exclusively for 'nourishing and educating poor boys in that place'. Houghton Conquest is the next parish to Elstow. At that time the Houghton Conquest school had a better reputation than the grammar school at Bedford.

Grace Abounding to the Chief of Sinners is intended as a record of the inner religious life of Bunyan, not as a narrative of his life in the world. But the tantalizingly meagre facts it contains are almost all the remaining evidence. In the last decade of the seventeenth century some short biographies of a hagiological nature were appended to posthumous editions of his works. One of these, *A Continuation of Mr. Bunyan's Life; beginning where he left off, and concluding with the Time and Manner of his Death and Burial; together with his true Character*, completes the life in the seventh edition of *Grace Abounding*; it is reputed to be by Bunyan's ministerial colleague, another Bedfordshire man, George Cokayne.[1] Another, *The Struggler*,[2] concludes the folio *Works* of 1692 and is by its editor Charles Doe. But neither biographer shows any acquaintance with the period of Bunyan's life prior to his imprisonment, and they are hazy enough about the details of his later activities. Doe does, however, say that Bunyan's father was 'of the National Religion, as commonly men of that Trade are'. Bunyan had to wait for the books and conversation of his first wife before he felt the Puritan influence or began to take an interest in the 'nonconformity-men' of his own locality.

Bunyan speaks in the autobiography of being troubled in childhood by fearful dreams and visions. It may be that there was a pathological side to the nervous intensity of these fears; in the religious crisis of his maturity his guilty terrors took the form of hallucinations and auditory and tactile delusions.

---

[1] A Bedfordshire man who became rector of St. Pancras, Soper Lane, under the Commonwealth, and after the ejection of 1662 was minister of a congregation in Red Cross Street This London congregation maintained connexions with the Bedford separatist Church during Bunyan's membership and pastorate, receiving Bedford brethren into communion by letters of dismission. See *Church Book*, p. 46; *Calamy Revised*, ed. A. G. Matthews, Oxford, 1934, p. 124.

[2] *Works*, iii. 763–8; cf. another narrative by one who had known Bunyan in prison, *An Account of the Life and Death of John Bunyan*, in *The Heavenly Footman* (2nd ed. 1700), pp. 108–32.

Bunyan served in the army in the Civil War, probably on the Parliamentary side. Some have thought the family was for the King because his half-brother, the first son of his father's third wife, was baptized Charles in the summer of 1645, a time when it would have been difficult to have overlooked the loyalist associations of the name. A somewhat unreliable account (1692) speaks of his 'being now in an Army where wickedness abounded',[1] but does not substantiate the statement. On the other hand the muster rolls of the Parliamentary garrison at Newport Pagnell show that a John Bunyan performed his military service there from November 1644 to June 1647.[2] The surname was too common in Bedfordshire at this time for the identification to be accepted as a certainty, as it has too readily been by later biographers; but there is at least a strong presumption that he was mustered in a county levy for the Parliament and served in the Newport garrison: in November 1644 he would be just sixteen, the usual age for recruitment. Also the account of Emanuel's army in *The Holy War* (1682) nostalgically recalls the ardour and discipline of the New Model Army: as well as general features of seventeenth-century military organization there are prayer meetings and preaching captains, and Shaddai's first expeditionary force shows the same orderly behaviour towards civilians which distinguished the Ironsides (they pass 'through the regions and countries of many people, not hurting or abusing any, but blessing wherever they came'[3]). Bedfordshire was solidly in the Parliamentary interest, and Newport was an important garrison, situated on the lines of communication between north and south. If Bunyan was there, though only a member of a raw militia unit himself, he would have ample opportunity of seeing the crack regiments of the Eastern Association passing through.

The garrison commander was Sir Samuel Luke, the model for the hero of Butler's *Hudibras*. The army was the seed-bed for the left-wing Puritan sects, Quakers, Seekers, and Ranters, and the soldiers

---

[1] *An Account of the Life and Actions of John Bunyan* (1692; bound up with the spurious Third Part of *The Pilgrim's Progress*), p. 18.

[2] P.R.O. *Commonwealth Exchequer Papers*, xxviii. 121B; Brown, pp. 46–50; H. G. Tibbutt, *Bedfordshire and the First Civil War with a Note on the Military Service of John Bunyan* (Elstow Moot Hall Pamphlet, 1956).

[3] *H.W.*, p. 220; cf. Sir Charles Firth, *Cromwell's Army* (1912), pp. 45, 150, and his article 'Bunyan's *Holy War*', *Journal of English Studies* (1912–13), i. 141–50.

turned preachers are bound to have influenced an impressionable youth. Henry Denne, who was connected with Lamb's General Baptist Church in Bell-alley, was at this time on an evangelical tour of Bedfordshire and Cambridgeshire;[1] we do not know whether there was any personal contact between him and Bunyan at Newport, but fifteen years later when the latter had become a preacher to conventicles, Denne took up his defence in print. George Fox, at the beginning of his years of wandering, 'stayed awhile' at Newport, remaining there till June 1644;[2] and the firebrand Paul Hobson, who belonged to the Church of the Crutched Friars in Aldgate ward which had seceded from the independent congregation of Henry Jessey, was arrested by the governor for his heresies and sent to be examined before the authorities in London.[3] Living in this atmosphere, it would be difficult not to become acquainted with the prime notion of the enthusiastic sectaries, shared alike by Cromwell and his meanest trooper, that the effort to religious truth meant an obstinate search, often from sect to sect, relying on free grace internally revealed, and condemning all forms of organization as 'legal and dark'; Bunyan, however, dissociates himself from the excesses of the Ranters and from the doctrines of the early Quakers (§§ 44–45, 123–5), but the stress on the supersession of the old law and mere moral conformity in his early writings, and even in the First Part of *The Pilgrim's Progress* (not in the Second) is stronger than the Puritan norm, stopping short, however, on the hither side of antinomianism.

Bunyan relates that during his military service he narrowly escaped being sent on a fatal mission to the siege of a certain town; he characteristically omits any details of time or place, being intent only on the example of a providential deliverance:

I with others were drawn out to go to such a place to besiege it; but when I was just ready to go, one of the company desired to go in my

---

[1] Thomas Edwards, *Gangraena* (3rd ed. 1646), Part I, pp. 22–24, 33–34, of the additional matter.

[2] Fox, *Journal*, p. 3.

[3] B.M. Stowe MS. 190, f. 280, is a letter from Sir Samuel Luke to Stephen Marshall dated 13 Nov. 1644 complaining of the assemblies of sectaries within the garrison; there is no reply from Marshall in the Luke Letter-books: cf. *Calendar of the Letter Books of Sir Samuel Luke*, ed. H. G. Tibbutt (Bedfordshire Historical Records Society, 1957), pp. 144–5.

room, to which, when I had consented he took my place; and coming
to the siege, as he stood Sentinel, he was shot into the head with a
Musket bullet, and died.[1]

The anonymous author of *The Life and Actions of John Bunyan*
identifies the town as Leicester;[2] however, Leicester was besieged
not by Parliamentarians, but by Royalists, and stormed by Prince
Rupert on 14 June 1645, though it is possible that the garrison may
have previously been reinforced from Newport and other places.

In the summer preceding the commencement of his military
service his mother and his sister Margaret died within a month of
each other, and his father married a third wife.

Bunyan's name appears on a list of soldiers belonging to Colonel
Charles O'Hara's regiment who had volunteered for service in
Ireland in June 1647; but the regiment was disbanded in the following month, after a detachment of it had marched as far as Chester;
it may have been here in the Dee that he 'fell into a crick of the Sea'
and experienced another miraculous escape from death (§ 12).

Some time soon after his discharge from the army and before 1649
Bunyan married. His first wife's name and origin are unknown, but
since she used to speak to him of her father's piety as though he
were a stranger to her husband, it may be presumed that she came
from somewhere other than Elstow. Their first child, a blind
daughter Mary, was baptized in July 1650. In a famous passage of
the autobiography he says that he and his wife 'came together as
poor as poor might be, not having so much as a Dish or Spoon betwixt us both' (§ 15). But by the third edition he has moderated the
force of this statement, altering the phrase to 'not so much as houshold-
stuff as a Dish or Spoon': in revising the book he was anxious to
avoid the impression that he and his wife were without cottage,
livelihood, or money; he had returned to the family trade and there
was some assurance for the future. Three more children, Elizabeth,
John, and Thomas, were born to this first wife of Bunyan before her
death in 1658. The record of Elizabeth's birth in the transcript
register of Elstow shows that she, too, was baptized there in 1654,
though Bunyan had himself by this time been baptized by immersion as a member of the Bedford separatist Church.[3]

---

[1] *G.A.*, § 13.   [2] *Life and Actions* (1692), pp. 17–18.   [3] Brown, pp. 222–3.

(ii) *The Bedford Separatist Church*

References to the passage of time in *Grace Abounding* are frequent but vague. His wife's dowry brings to Bunyan the awakening books, Arthur Dent's *The Plain Mans Path-way to Heaven* and Lewis Bayly's *The Practice of Piety*; the former taught him that even a manual of instruction could employ racy colloquialisms and salt its precepts with homely proverbs. Marriage is soon followed by the growth of a serious interest in religion; gradually he gives up his swearing, his dancing, his Sunday sports, and—hardest sacrifice of all—his bell-ringing. Outward reformation is succeeded by a sense of sin and unworthiness. All the central third of the book deals with a period of spiritual temptation leading to his final assurance of grace. We have time references as follows: 'some considerable time' (§ 18), 'about a moneth, or more' (§ 26), 'thus I continued about a year' (§ 31, referring to the period of his outward reformation); then comes mention of the poor women of Bedford who have found happiness in a doctrine of free grace (§ 37) and his encounter with the Ranters and their books (§§ 44–45). The Bedford separatists formed their congregation in 1650 and there were many women among the first members; 1650 was also a year of antinomian activity in the army, in London and the eastern counties; Lawrence Clarkson's *A Single Eye All Light, No Darkness* appeared and was confiscated by the authorities; earlier he had preached in Bury St. Edmunds and may have reached Bedford in his travels with the army.[1] Abiezer Coppe was also active at this time and had published his *Fiery Flying Roll* and *A Second Fiery Flying Roule* in the previous year. After further references to 'many days', 'several days', Bunyan embarks on a period of Bible searching that lasts 'above a year' (§ 65); he then meets John Gifford, the founder of the Bedford Church (§ 77), a meeting which must have taken place after 1650; then comes the first serious temptation to despair of his salvation, lasting 'about a year' (§ 106).

Almost immediately after he has received some relief and token of his election, he is buffeted by another wave of temptations: this is a time of profound mental agony when he fears that he has

[1] Lawrence Clarkson, *The Lost Sheep Found, or, the Prodigal Returned to his Father's House* (1660), pp. 1–16, and see *infra*, pp. 137–8.

betrayed Christ, because he gives in one day to the obsessive internal voices which urge him to 'Let him go if he will' (§ 139). The period of despair begins a year after he first hears these voices (§ 133) and lasts 'for two years together' (§ 142) or for 'well nigh two years and an half' (§ 198). The temptation began one and a half years after the period of his wife's first pregnancy (§ 242); the years covered may thus be dated 1650–3.

He was received into the Bedford congregation about 1655. He had already resorted for spiritual direction to its pastor Gifford. Now he would make a confession of his religious experience before the whole Church, as the custom was; such testimonies in the gathered Churches were the sources of the spiritual autobiographies which followed; and he would be baptized by immersion. His name is the twenty-sixth in a list of members under the year 1655 in the Bedford *Church Book*: there is also a note to the effect that 'Mr Bunyan began to preach some time in the year 1656':[1] and also an entry, the first of many, showing that on 28 June of that year he undertook with other brethren a pastoral visit on behalf of the Church. The evidence of these dates confirms his autobiographical statement that when he was invited to exhort the brethren he had been 'about five or six years awakened' (§ 265); the awakening may be dated either from the sermon on keeping the Sabbath heard in Elstow parish church (§ 20) which so aroused his conscience, or from his meeting with the poor women of Gifford's congregation a little after that.

Bunyan's history was to be interwoven for the next thirty-five years with the history of this small separatist community. Both the man and the Church owed more to the broad stream of English Puritan life than to any special sectarian bias. The Church was open-communion: that is to say, it admitted all who professed 'faith in Christ and holiness of life'; it prescribed immersion as a token of membership; but neither the founders, nor Bunyan himself when he came to be pastor, insisted like the Strict Baptists on baptism as an obligatory mark of Christian fellowship. They considered themselves simply in apostolic terms 'the church of Christ in and about

---

[1] *Church Book*, p. 15; this dating is to be preferred to the vaguer estimate of Doe: 'he lit on to the dissenting congregation of Christians at Bedford, and was, upon confession of faith, baptized about the year 1651, or 52, or 53' (*Works*, iii. 765.).

Bedford'. They grew up around a nucleus of older men, John Grew, Samuel Fenne, and others, who had agreed 'to search after the nonconforming men, such as in those dayes did bear the name of Puritanes'. The leading spirit in the group was John Gifford, a Royalist major who was converted while under sentence of death for his part in the Kentish rising of 1648. He became their first pastor and laid down the broad and tolerant principles by which the Church was to abide:

Now the principle by which they thus entered into fellowship one with another ... was Faith in Christ and Holines of life, without respect to this or that circumstance, or opinion in outward and circumstantiall things.[1]

In spite of this apparent liberality a strict control was exercised over the admission of new members. They were required to have undergone a conversion of the classic Puritan type, following on a conviction of their own unworthiness and the indispensability of the free grace of Christ as Mediator of the new covenant for salvation. Evidence for the genuineness of the experience was provided by their testimony before the meeting. After admission a strict supervision was maintained over the devotional and moral life of the members; as Bunyan became more prominent he was often active in visiting and exhorting lapsed brethren.[2] Marked out as they were, even before the Restoration, from the generality of Bedford citizens, the Church tended to form a social as well as a religious community; after the Restoration, when the penal laws were applied against dissenters, and when the second generation began to grow up, this tendency became more pronounced. The standards of the separated community had to be upheld in the face of a critical outer world; cases of vice and dishonesty were sternly rebuked by Bunyan and his fellow elders, and marriages with 'unbelievers' were frowned upon.

There was a democratic spirit at work in the Bedford Church, as in other gathered congregations. Gifford reminds his people in his last testament that in Christ there is neither bond nor free, and

[1] *Church Book*, p. 2.
[2] Such visits were even undertaken when he was on parole from the county jail: see entries for the period 1660–70 in *Church Book*, pp. 24, 27, 28, 31

warns them against the evil example of offering seats to wealthy members in time of prayer; women played a vital role (two of the most eloquent sectarian autobiographies are by women, those of Anna Trapnel and Jane Turner), stress was laid on outward simplicity, and those brethren who had 'most of the demonstration of the Spirit, and of power' could address the meeting. Grew and John Eston, both aldermen, paid fines in March 1651 for appearing in the council chamber without their gowns of office.[1] General Baptist influence was also present in the area, reinforced by the recent preaching tours of Henry Denne and William Erbury; this made for tenderness towards the individual conscience, and also for an element of political and social radicalism. A passage in Gifford's death-bed letter to the Church breathes millenarian sentiment at a time (1655) when Fifth Monarchy agitators, some of whom were in custody, had begun to regard Cromwell as the Beast of Revelation:

Let the promises made to be accomplished in the latter dayes, be often urged before the Lord in your comings together, and forget not your brethren in bonds.[2]

Members of the Church signed the petition sent from Bedfordshire in 1657 advising Cromwell against accepting the Crown.

In 1653 Gifford had been presented by Bedford Corporation to the living of St. John's, which was in their gift. The separatists thus found themselves a part of the Cromwellian establishment. Gifford died in 1655, and after a dispute over his successor settled by the Protector, his place was taken by John Burton, a young man in weak health who lived only a few years.

Bunyan moved from Elstow to Bedford in 1655. His first published tracts grew out of public disputes with the Quakers in Bedford market-place. Beckrings Park, the house of a county magistrate, Fox's friend John Crook, provided an evangelizing centre, and the movement spread rapidly after the mission of William Dewsbury in 1654. The early Friends were rivals of the independent

---

[1] Cf. 'the rich begun to rejoyce and to show themselves very wicked and hard-hearted to the poor' (*Stevington Church Book*, p. 22 (*c.* 1682)).
[2] *Church Book*, p. 4.

and Baptist Churches for the allegiance of the common people: Fox had gained his first following among a group of 'shattered Baptists', and both sects shared a belief in the freedom of any man to testify in the Spirit. Bunyan's gift of vigorous and simple expression had brought him to the fore as a disputant. The controversy is recorded in his first books *Some Gospel Truths Opened* and *A Vindication of Some Gospel Truths Opened*. The Quaker protagonist was Edward Burrough, whom Bunyan calls 'a grossly railing Rabshakeh'.[1] The errors of the Quakers are mentioned in *Grace Abounding* in a passage which is expanded in the fifth edition.[2] Bunyan's natural approach to religion was literal and objective: when he read in the Bible that the Israel-ites were the peculiar people of God, he besought his father to tell him 'whether we were of the *Israelites* or no'; the orthodox Calvinism he learnt from Gifford and the Bedford elders hardened this literal-mindedness by its dogmatic insistence on the transcendence of God and the inability of the human soul to help itself. Thus the Quaker reliance on an inner light seemed to him both on doctrinal and temperamental grounds a blasphemous rejection of the objective character of revelation.

His next works are *A Few Sighs from Hell, or the Groans of a Damned Soul* (1658) and *The Doctrine of the Law and Grace Unfolded* (1659); these were clearly compiled from sermon material, and they remind us of Bunyan's statement in the autobiography that his spiritual terrors did not fully abate until some time after he had begun to preach and exhort, so that 'I went my self in chains to preach to them in chains' (§ 277).

He married his second wife, Elizabeth, in 1659. There were further public disputes, some of them with university-trained clergy, both Anglican and Presbyterian, to stimulate the self-con-sciousness of the mechanic preacher. One, in a barn at Toft in Cambridgeshire with Thomas Smith, Professor of Arabic at Cam-bridge and University Librarian, is described by Charles Doe; it prompted Henry Denne to intervene on Bunyan's behalf: 'You seem to be angry with the Tinker because he strives to mend souls, as

---

[1] For the controversy with Burrough see George Fox, *The Mysterie of Iniquitie* (1660); W. C. Braithwaite, *The Beginnings of Quakerism* (1932), pp. 285–8; Elisabeth Brockbank, *Edward Burrough, A Wrestler for Truth, 1634–62* (1949).

[2] *G.A.*, § 125.

well as Kettles and Pans.'[1] William Dell, Master of Caius College under the Commonwealth and rector of Yelden, from which he was ejected in 1662, and like Bunyan 'professedly against *Paedobaptism*, and yet he had his own children baptized', allowed him to preach from his pulpit on Christmas Day 1659.[2]

He would have at this time been made a deacon if he had not so constantly been 'taken off by the preaching of the Gospel.'[3] His importance in the religious life of the region at this period is shown by the letter of a local Quaker to Fox describing the Bedford Church as 'Bunyan's people'.[4]

(iii) *Bunyan's Imprisonment*

For ten years the separatists had enjoyed freedom of worship and had exercised a measure of influence on public policy. With the Restoration of Charles II this came to an end. Bunyan was one of the first victims of persecution by the civil power. On 12 November 1660 at Lower Samsell in South Bedfordshire he was brought before a local magistrate and charged with holding a conventicle. Since he refused to give an assurance that he would not preach again, he was imprisoned in the county jail in Bedford. Down to the late eighteenth century the small and picturesque town lock-up on the bridge over the Ouse was pointed out as the place of his confinement. But Bunyan's offence had taken place in the county area and he would therefore be imprisoned in the county prison. Since fresh legislation against Dissenters had not yet been introduced, he had been prosecuted under the old Elizabethan Act against nonconformity.[5] The penalty prescribed was three months' imprisonment in the first instance; if the offender continued to preach or to attend conventicles, and refused to conform to the Church of England, he was liable to transportation. The law was applied to Bunyan in a

[1] Henry Denne, *The Quaker No Papist* (1659), A2.
[2] *Calamy Revised*, ed. A. G. Matthews (Oxford, 1934), p. 162.
[3] *Church Book*, p. 19 (27 Aug. 1657).
[4] Alexander Parker to George Fox, fourth day of the third month 1659, *Swarthmore Transcripts* (Friends' House Library), iii. 45.
[5] 35 Eliz., c. i, 'An Act to retain the Queen's Majesty's Subjects in their due Obedience.' For its application in Bunyan's district see W. M. Wigfield, *Recusancy and Nonconformity in Bedfordshire* (Bedfordshire Historical Records Society, 1938), pp. 145–229.

manner in which severity and leniency were strangely intermingled: instead of being released at the end of three months he was kept in prison a full twelve years, but from time to time he was allowed out to visit his friends and family and even to address meetings—in fact, to repeat his crime. He was originally sentenced by Sir John Kelynge at the quarter-sessions in January 1661. After three months the Clerk of the Peace, Paul Cobb, visited him in his cell, and tried without effect to persuade him to submit. In terms of strict law he should now have been set free, but he was not, and all the efforts of his family to bring his case before later sessions of the justices were unsuccessful. His wife pleaded courageously with the judges at the Midsummer Assizes in August 1661; she moved the pity of one of them, Sir Matthew Hale, but was apparently unable to carry out his advice to sue for a pardon or a writ of error. On the other hand, by keeping Bunyan in prison the Bedfordshire magistrates avoided having recourse to the harsher penalty of transportation.[1]

This was the second great crisis of Bunyan's life; the first was his struggle with the purely inward terrors of spiritual sin and despair, as recounted in the central sections of *Grace Abounding*. The final sections contain a much shorter account of his imprisonment for conscience' sake (*A Brief Account of the Author's Imprisonment*).

But Bunyan also left a series of what are practically verbatim reports of his examinations before the justices and subsequent interviews. These must have been written in prison immediately after the events, and probably in the form of pastoral letters to console and fortify the Bedford congregation. There are five short narratives, each ending with an epistolary formula like 'Farewell'. They communicate the sense of strain and immediacy of a prisoner who does not yet know what is to happen to him (e.g. 'where I lie waiting the good will of God').[2]

This document remained in manuscript until 1765 when it was published by James Buckland as *A Relation of the Imprisonment of Mr. John Bunyan*. This is of special interest since no manuscripts of Bunyan are known to have survived to our day other than those

---

[1] W. T. Whitley, *Trans. Bapt. Hist. Soc.* vi (1918–19), 1–24. Bunyan's continued imprisonment is shown by the Bedford jail calendars of 1665, 1668, and 1669, now in the County Record Office, H.S.A. 44/1; H.S.A. 11/5/3; H.S.A. 12/4.

[2] See 'The Origin of *A Relation of My Imprisonment*', R.E.S. x (1959), 260–6.

pages of the Bedford *Church Book* which are conjectured to be in his hand. The claim of the title-page, 'Written by himself', is substantiated by a contemporary witness, Joseph Gurney. His testimony, which seems to have passed unnoticed by John Brown, his reviser F. M. Harrison, and other Bunyan biographers, is contained in a letter to the *Evangelical Magazine* in 1813:

Rev. Sir,

Having heard that some persons doubt the authenticity of a small publication entitled 'A Relation of the Imprisonment of Mr. John Bunyan', printed in the year 1765, I beg leave to lay before your readers the following circumstances respecting its publication:—I accompanied my late honoured father in his annual visit to his relations and friends in Bedfordshire in the summer of 1765. When at Bedford, my father was informed that a granddaughter of Mr. John Bunyan's had a manuscript of her grandfather's, for which she wished to find a purchaser. She was aged and infirm. My father and I went to her lodging; and she delivered the manuscript to my father in my presence, requesting him to sell it. The manuscript was in Mr. Bunyan's handwriting. The copy was very fair; and it was sewed up in a little book.

When my father returned to London, he offered it to several booksellers; but the late Mr. Buckland was the only person who was willing to purchase it: he gave five guineas for it, which the poor woman joyfully accepted; and Mr. Buckland immediately printed it

Yours etc.

Walworth   JOSEPH GURNEY[1]

Joseph Gurney's father, who negotiated for the book, was Thomas Gurney (1705–70) the inventor of a system of shorthand and the first shorthand writer to the House of Commons. The positive assertion that the work was in Bunyan's hand is noteworthy. The Gurneys may of course have relied on a family tradition, but as one professionally concerned with handwriting Thomas Gurney could have formed his own opinion. If so, he must have seen an authenticated specimen; he had grown up in the Bedford neighbourhood and numbered among his friends and relations members of Bunyan's Church; in 1730 he had married Martha Marsom, the daughter of

---

[1] *Evangelical Magazine* (1813), p. 148.

Thomas Marsom, a fellow prisoner of Bunyan in the county jail.[1] He does, however, make a mistake about Bunyan's descendant: she was Hannah Bunyan, his great-granddaughter, not his grand-daughter, being the granddaughter of Bunyan's son John (d. 1728) by his first wife. She was born in 1694 and died on 15 February 1770 aged seventy-six.[2]

There is an interesting correspondence between the terrors met in his spiritual autobiography and the history of his conflict with the civil power. In either case there is a single, unambiguous decision to be made: in the first, the tempting voices have to be affirmed or denied, and then all is over; in the other, the scene has shifted to the world of external action where a simple decision to preach or not to preach can alter his whole manner of life, reducing him from a re-spectable artisan and father of a family to a prisoner and an outcast. A simple yes or no initiates a whole train of events, mental happen-ings in the former case, and in the latter real actions in the outward life. At any time, merely by undertaking not to preach again to a public assembly, Bunyan might have obtained his release: this is the measure of his courage and of the degree of personal integrity he had achieved once his religious doubts were at rest.

The imprisonment was not a continuous period of solitary con-finement. There were periods of relaxation, when, on the evidence of the *Church Book*, he was able to make journeys on behalf of the Meet-ing, travelling even as far as London. When the new penal legisla-tion became effective in 1664–8, the jail was filled with Noncon-formists, and the prisoner had a congregation to preach to. Visitors were frequent; and throughout his confinement he was able to maintain his family by making 'many hundred gross of long Tagg'd Laces'.[3] He had, however, more time for writing and in these years his production increased rapidly. *Christian Behaviour* (1663) deals with the proper relation between father and family, master and servant; its scheme of values is typical of other conduct books by Puritan (and Anglican) divines, and it illustrates the conservatism of Bunyan's social views. *I Will Pray with the Spirit* (1663) is a defence

---

[1] *D.N.B.*, article on Thomas Gurney.
[2] Brown, pp. 245, 429.
[3] *An Account of the Life and Death of Mr. John Bunyan*, p. 126.

of extempore prayer against the set forms of the Prayer Book: this comes close to the very principle for which he was suffering. *The Holy City* (1665) is an exposition of the heavenly Jerusalem described in Revelation. Less poetic than this visionary work with its millenarian overtones are the rough, salty verses of three other books: *Profitable Meditations* (1661), *One Thing is Needful* (1664?), and *Prison Meditations* (1665).

Grace Abounding is the most considerable achievement of the imprisonment period. It reflects not merely the enforced leisure which enabled Bunyan to write an autobiography, but the turning in of the mind upon itself which obliged him to experience over again the emotions of his conversion. As with Wordsworth, the experience had to be recollected in tranquillity before it could become the focus for an imaginative reappraisal. Nor did the process end here; for the narrative of his introspective pilgrimage through doubts and terrors is intimately linked with the allegorical treatment of the Christian life in *The Pilgrim's Progress*. It was once assumed that the allegory was begun during Bunyan's second, shorter imprisonment, which was assigned to some time between 1672 and 1678 and probably to 1676. Such was the view of Dr. John Brown, Bunyan's Victorian biographer; and it was also that of W. T. Whitley, F. M. Harrison, and more recently Professor Henri Talon. But the discovery of a bond for Bunyan's release in June 1677,[1] after only six months' imprisonment, when considered with the fact of the book's entry on the Stationers' Register in the following December, gives reason to doubt whether it would have been possible for him to complete the First Part of *The Pilgrim's Progress* within so short a time. It is more reasonable to suppose that it was begun during the first imprisonment (1660–72), and that it followed naturally and inevitably on the completion of the spiritual autobiography. Already Bunyan's imagination had fed strongly on biblical imagery in order to render psychological experience; his tendency to turn metaphor into myth may be seen in his dream of the strait gate excluding him from heaven and the saints (§§ 53–55), or in the manner in which the biblical texts speak to him as voices, like the Word of God descending upon the Old Testament prophets. *The Pilgrim's Progress* reveals

[1] Joyce Godber, *Trans. Cong. Hist. Soc.* xvi, no. 1 (1949).

a bolder development of this pictorial instinct: demons and giants, and a fairy-tale narrative of adventure, take the imagery of *Grace Abounding* a stage further. One work attempts the sheer, naked presentation of inner experience; yet into it personal and traditional imagery is introduced; in the other the writer is wholly absorbed in his imaginative fiction, and yet contrives to make it moral and allegorical at every point: both together represent with a beautiful exactness the relation between the dreamer's morbid interior conflicts and their resolution in the integrated personality which led him to play without faltering his part in the world of action.

(iv) *Spiritual Autobiography*

The form of *Grace Abounding* and the principles by which Bunyan selected certain episodes of his life to illustrate his religious progress, belong to a recognizable seventeenth-century genre, the spiritual autobiography, cultivated especially by the Puritans, and developed on more specialized lines after 1640 by the leaders of the radical sects.

To the Puritans the regeneration of the individual soul was the central fact of religious experience. The life of the Christian on earth was seen as in constant movement; progress or deterioration was always taking place. Richard Rogers, a teacher who himself taught many pastors of the next generation, declared: 'Whatsoever good things God's people already have and enjoy; yet he hath more in store for them.'[1] Growth in grace continued throughout the lifetime of the believer in a manner comparable to organic growth; it was therefore possible to trace its progress and to plot the symptoms of regeneration. Even conversion was no sudden storming of the soul by grace, but a gradual process marked by clearly defined stages: first came conviction of sin, when the Christian was convinced of his share in the general depravity of the human race, and sure that his own good works could avail him nothing; then came vocation or calling, when he had evidence of his election by God, and felt that an unmerited

[1] Richard Rogers, *Seven Treatises* (5th ed. 1630), p. 732. See O. Raymond Johnson, 'Growth in Grace in Puritan Theology', *Evangelical Quarterly*, xxv (1953), 131–41.

love had set him on the right hand in the awful scheme of pre-destination; there succeeded to this, justification, the achievement of a saving faith, and sanctification, the growth in holiness of life; finally glorification brought the pilgrim's progress to an end.

The primary task for the Calvinist was then to ascertain whether he was numbered among the elect. This could only be done by searching his heart and minutely examining his daily conduct. From the time of Elizabeth onwards, the English Puritans, forming as they did a minority, though a substantial one, within the national Church, had accepted the challenge set by the doctrine of election and made their appeal practical and pastoral. Instead of formal theology, their concern was for saving souls; and though the general pattern of conversion was the same, the signs of grace and the particular forms taken by temptation might differ from one person to another. The great Elizabethan practical Puritans, Richard Greenham, William Perkins, John Dod, and their successors, laid the foundations of a descriptive psychology of conversion. All their work was conducted through the normal course of preaching the Word and expounding Scripture texts, but their reading of the Bible was always directed towards the spiritual life of the individual. Tyndale, who of the Reformers is most representative of the trend of later Puritanism, exhorts his readers to take 'the stories and lives which are contained in the Bible for sure and undoubted ensamples that God will so deal with us unto the world's end'.[1]

In the eighty years before the Civil War, diaries and confessions abounded in which assurances of grace and occasions of doubt and temptation were recorded; at the same time a method of spiritual guidance and a body of observations about the problems of believers were created. Thus autobiographies tend to conform to a standard pattern. The authors share a common method of introspection. When Bunyan tells how he was awakened to a sense of sin by hearing the vicar of Elstow attacking Sabbath sports he was participating in a classic crisis which produced similar incidents in other autobiographies. The stress laid on what may seem trivialities, bell-ringing and other recreations, is paralleled not only in Puritan literature but in the earliest Christian autobiography: St. Augustine

[1] Tyndale, *Doctrinal Treatises* (Parker Society, 1848), p. 463.

dwells on the implications of stealing pears from an orchard in boyhood, remembering that God is he by whom 'the very hairs of our
head are numbered'.[1]

Before the Civil War the form of autobiography usually met with
is the life of a celebrated minister, generally an academic Puritan,
written by a disciple or fellow clergyman, and published after his
death. The funeral sermon was often a biography, concentrating on
providences, conversion, and fruitful ministry. A similar pattern is
found in those on pious laymen and women, such as Thomas
Taylor's *Profitable Memoriall of the Conversion of Mrs. Marie Gunter*
(1633). The general pattern is as follows:

  (i) Early providential mercies and opportunities.
 (ii) Unregenerate life: sin and resistance to the Gospel.
(iii) Conversion, often ushered in by an 'awakening' sermon.
 (iv) Calling; vocation to preach the Gospel.
  (v) Account of the ministry, often with anecdotes to illustrate
      his pastoral work.

Reticence soon gave way as a publishing convention gradually
became established. It seems likely that Thomas Goodwin intended
eventually to publish the autobiographical memoranda he left at his
death.[2]

There was a new development in spiritual autobiography in the
period of religious ferment between 1640 and 1660. Baptists,
Quakers, and Seekers injected fresh vitality into the form and applied
it to new purposes. Bunyan and his like, socially inferior to the Presbyterian and Independent clergy and without formal education for the
ministry, attempted to justify themselves and to establish their
special calling by detailed accounts of the work of grace upon
their souls. The radical sectaries are less restrained, more introspective and given to psychological detail than their predecessors.
They were accustomed to the self-revelation of the experience-
meeting. John Rogers, introducing a collection of conversion docu-
ments, says: 'Every one to be *admitted*, gives out some *experimental*
Evidences of the work of *grace* upon his *soul* (for the Church to judge

---

[1] Augustine, *Confessions*, II. iv.
[2] Thomas Goodwin, *Works* (1704), V. v–xix.

of) whereby he (or she) is *convinced* that he is *regenerate*, and received of God.'[1]

Many of the sectarian lay preachers, including almost all the Quakers, were persecuted and imprisoned, from the Commonwealth period onwards. The opposition of the world bred a fierce class-consciousness in the preachers. Now a new subdivision appears in the form of such autobiographies: an account of trial and imprisonment. Vavasor Powell, the Welsh evangelist, includes one which is close to Bunyan's in treatment (*The Life and Death of Mr. Vavasor Powell*, 1671). The inspiration of the Acts of the Apostles is at work in both.

(v) Grace Abounding: *Analysis of Contents*

The contents may be grouped according to the conventional divisions of autobiography. It can then be seen how far the selection of incidents and the treatment correspond to the general pattern, and to what extent Bunyan's presentation of experience is original.

Before Conversion: §§ 1–36.
Conversion: §§ 37–252.
Calling: §§ 253–305.
Ministry: §§ 319–39.

> *Additional sections and shorter passages (added in the third and fifth editions)*

12–14	Four providential escapes from death.
32	His new respectability.
33–36	He gives up his bell-ringing.
43–45	His contact with the Ranters and their errors.
70–71	His education in biblical symbolism.
83–85	A passage on the doctrine of imputed righteousness.
88	An expansion of a previous passage: man as the least fortunate of the creatures.
94 ⎫ 105 ⎭	More details of his state of wretchedness.
129–31	The whole episode of his meeting with Luther's *Commentary on Galatians* and its effect on him.

---

[1] John Rogers, *Ohel or Beth-shemesh, A Tabernacle for the Sun* (1653), p. 354.

There are significant departures from the autobiographical norm. Conversion is the most important part of the life-story and takes up almost two-thirds of the book. The divisions devoted to calling and ministry are correspondingly reduced. The account of conversion is devoted largely to his moods of despair, and particularly to a single period of temptation lasting two years (§§ 132–252).

In this central core of the book dealing with his inner conflicts Bunyan is most personal and least influenced by traditional precedents (some of the sections added later show, on the other hand, a desire to embellish experiences artistically, and to draw from his past fresh incidents likely to encourage and evangelize). Other sectaries, too, were morbidly concerned about the chance of their having committed 'the great sin', the sin against the Holy Ghost; the following confession in a collection of experience compiled by Vavasor Powell is not untypical:

Then was I repulsed in all duties by Satan, terrifying my soul to perswade me, that it was in vaine for me to seek for salvation, because I had committed the sin against the holy ghost (which God by his word hath declared shall never be forgiven neither in this world, nor in the world to come) . . .[1]

Nor was the length of Bunyan's struggle exceptional in the ambience of the gathered churches: we hear of 'T.A. converted after three yeares terrour upon his Conscience!' and of 'A.I. awaiting on the ordinances . . . and that in affliction of spirit for neare a yeares time'. Even the peculiar isolation of the sinner from his fellow men which would now be called neurotic finds a parallel in the case of John Crook, who says 'I thought every Man or Woman to be in a better Condition than my self'.[2] This comes close to Bunyan's 'O how happy now was every creature over I was! For they stood fast, and kept their station, but I was gone and lost'. But the uniqueness of Bunyan's treatment lies in its psychological penetration and freedom from rationalization into stock Calvinist formulae. The exactness of his recreation of the life of the soul is the result of his living over again the original experience. As Professor Talon has written: 'Bunyan was haunted by the desire to survey his whole life in one glance, to hold his soul in his hands, the better to possess himself . . . he strove to recapture all the threads of his past at one go, and knot them to a present that was always slipping through his fingers; he wanted to press his past to him, wrap it around him to ensure that it really was his.'[3] This imperious inner need, ultimately stronger than the motive of religious propaganda, has imparted a continuous rhythmical flow to the whole work so that it reads like a single sentence, torrential but not confused, having its changes of tone and tempo that are nevertheless obedient to the overriding music of the whole; the music is that of a speaking voice: it is as if the confession is delivered in a continuous intimate speech to a friend.

Bunyan unites the emotional fervour of the extreme sectaries with a firmer Calvinist framework than they adhered to. All happens in due order as might be approved by a Puritan academic, a Perkins or a Sibbes. Legal Christianity is succeeded by the terror of the Law, conviction and grace grow from reading the Bible; a cardinal principle of reformed theology is upheld: that doubts and afflictions are

---

[1] *Spiritual Experiences of Sundry Beleevers* (1653), p. 145.
[2] *A Short History of the Life of John Crook* (1706), p. 14.
[3] Henri A. Talon, *John Bunyan: the Man and his Works* (English trans. 1951), p. 132.

the test of faith and also the privilege of faith; 'great sins do draw out great grace', as Bunyan puts it. The principle works in reverse, too: Arthur Dent remarks that men of tender skins feel even the lightest feather laid upon the hand;[1] this might serve to describe the mental conflicts depicted in *Grace Abounding* which, though they are real states of the soul, grow out of quibbling misunderstandings about texts. Bunyan himself came to recognize them later as the errors of the inexperienced Christian.

(vi) *The Text*

Six editions of *Grace Abounding* were published in Bunyan's life-time, 'The Sixth Edition, Corrected' appearing in 1688, the year of his death. No surviving copy of the second or fourth edition is known. In the seventh edition (1692) the narrative is completed by *A Continuation of Mr. Bunyan's Life* attributed to George Cokayne, a Bedford man who had been an intimate friend of Bunyan and who became minister of a London independent congregation. But as in the case of *The Pilgrim's Progress*, the text undergoes a progressive deterioration in the editions subsequent to his death, and an editor need concern himself only with the earlier ones.

THE FIRST EDITION

Title-page: GRACE / Abounding to the chief of Sinners: / OR, /A Brief and Faithful / RELATION / Of the Exceeding Mercy of God in Christ, / to his poor Servant / *JOHN BUNYAN*. / Wherein is particu-larly shewed, The man-/ner of his Conversion, his sight and trouble for / Sin, his Dreadful Temptations, also how he / despaired of Gods mercy, and how the Lord at / length thorow Christ did deliver him from all / the guilt and terrour that lay upon him. / Whereunto is added, / A Brief Relation of his Call to the Work / of the Ministry, of his Temptations therein, / as also what he hath met with in Prison. / All which was written by his own hand / there, and now published for the support / of the weak and tempted People of God. /[long fine rule] *Come and hear, all ye that fear God; and I will declare / what he hath done for my soul*, Psal. 66.16. / [long fine rule] *LONDON*: / Printed by George Larkin. 1666. / [fine rule round t.-p.]

---

[1] Arthur Dent, *The Plain Mans Path-way to Heaven* (ed. 1617), p. 242.

Collation: 8⁰. A–F⁸, G⁴, title-page, A1ʳ; blank, A1ᵛ; 52 leaves. A PREFACE, A2ʳ–A5ᵛ; text, pp. 1–94. Lace borders at head of Preface and at head of p. 1. Running title: 'Grace Abounding / to the chief of Sinners'.

From p. 93 to the end (G4: comprising §§ 269–72 and the Conclusion) smaller type, brevier in place of long primer, is used, no doubt to make room for the Conclusion added while the book was going through the press and to compress the text into the allotted sheets.

The copies inspected have the headlines of the running title interchanged on pp. 32 and 33; 'cheif' for 'chief' in recto headline on pp. 9, 13, and 17. There are corrected states of sheets A and B. Of the copies inspected, the Huntington and Pierpont Morgan have the second state of A, the British Museum copy has that of B. The latter corrects 'Gedford' to 'Bedford' at B8; both show only minor corrections and very few changes of punctuation. Sig. D4–5 (pp. 45–48) are missing from the British Museum copy.

Copies collated: British Museum; Henry E. Huntington Library; Pierpont Morgan Library.

THE THIRD EDITION

Title-page: Grace Abounding / To the Chief of / SINNERS / OR, / A brief and Faithful Relation of the / exceeding Mercy of God in / Christ to his poor Servant / *JOHN BUNYAN.* / *Wherein is particularly shewed, The manner of his Conver-/sion, his sight and trouble for Sin, his dreadful Tempta-/tions, also how he despaired of Gods Mercy, and how / the Lord at length through Christ, did deliver him from / all the guilt and terrour that lay upon him.* / All which was written by his own hand, and now / published for the support of the weak and / tempted people of God. / [long fine rule] The Third Edition, Corrected and much enlarged / by the Author. / [long fine rule] / *Come and hear, all ye that fear God, and I will declare / what he hath done for my soul,* Psal. 66.16. / *London* Printed for *F. Smith* at the Elephant and / Castle near the Royal Exchange in *Cornhill*, / At 1s. Bound. [fine rule round t.-p.]

Collation: 12mo. A⁴B⁸C¹²E¹²P–S¹²T⁶. 90 leaves. Title-page, A1ʳ; blank, A1ᵛ; A PREFACE, A2ʳ–B1ᵛ; text, pp. 1–170. Running title: 'Grace abounding / to the chief of sinners'. There is a change to smaller type on pp. 106–7 (Q10ᵛ and Q11ʳ).

In the unique copy of this edition in the Pierpont Morgan Library, C5 is signed D5, and as a consequence of this slip the signatures pass from C to E; in B only B1 is signed, and in T only T1, T2, and T3; the pagination passes from 110 to 113, and p. 94 is unnumbered; misprints: 'stait' for 'strait' (p. 27, l. 15), 'aganist' (p. 40, l. 20), 'New Tew Testament' (p. 137, catchword); the running headlines are reversed at C9ʳ (p. 31) and C10ᵛ (p. 34).

Copy collated: Pierpont Morgan Library.

THE FIFTH EDITION

Title-page: Grace Abounding. / To the Chief of / SINNERS: / OR, / A Brief and Faithful Relation of the ex-/ceeding Mercy of God in

Christ, / to His poor Servant / *JOHN BUNYAN. NAMELY* / *In his
taking of him out of the Dunghil, and Con-/verting of him to the Faith of his
Blessed Son,* / *Jesus Christ.* / HERE / *Is also particularly shewed what sight of,
and* / *what trouble he had for Sin; and also what va-/rious Temptations he hath
met with, and how* / *God hath carried him through them.* / [long fine rule]
Corrected and much enlarged now by the Au-/thor, for the benefit of
the Tempted and/ Dejected Christian. The Fifth Edition Corrected [long
fine rule] *Come and hear, all ye that fear God, and I will de-/clare what he hath
done for my Soul,* Psal. 66.16. [long fine rule] *London,* Printed for *Nath. Ponder,*
at the / *Peacock* in the *Poultrey,* over against the *Stocks-market.* 1680.

Collation: 12mo. A⁴, B–F¹², G⁸. 72 leaves. Title-page, A1ʳ; blank, A1ᵛ; A Preface,
A2ʳ–A4ᵛ; text, pp. 1–136. Portrait, 'I Sturt Sc:', with underneath '*John Bunyan*',
(twice). There is a change to smaller (italic) type at G8ᵛ (p. 136).

In the unique copy A3 is unsigned; p. 136 is unnumbered (the text is crowded
almost from the head to the foot of the page).

Copy collated: Bedford Public Library.

THE SIXTH EDITION

Title-page: Grace Abounding / TO THE / CHIEF / OF / SINNERS: /
OR, / A Brief and Faithful Relation of the / exceeding Mercy of God in
Christ, / to His poor Servant / *JOHN BUNYAN.* / NAMELY, / In his
taking of him out of the Dunghil, and / Converting of him to the Faith
of his / Blessed Son, Jesus Christ. / HERE / Is also particularly shewed,
what Sight of, and/ what Trouble he had for Sin; and also, what / various
Temptations he hath met with, and / how God hath carried him through
them. [long fine rule] Corrected, and much Enlarged now by / the
Author for the Benefit of the / Tempted and Dejected Christian. / [long
fine rule] The Sixth Edition, Corrected. [long fine rule] *Come and hear, all
ye that fear God, and I will declare what* / *he hath done by my soul,* Psal. 66.16.
[long fine rule] *LONDON,* Printed for *Nath. Ponder,* at / the *Pea-Cock* in
the *Poultry,* over against / the *Stocks-Market,* 1688.

Collation: 12mo. A–H¹². 96 leaves. Title-page, A2ʳ; blank, A2ᵛ; A PREFACE,
A3ʳ–A6ᵛ; text, pp. 1–173; '*Books Printed for* Nath. Ponder', pp. H9ᵛ–H12ᵛ (pages
unnumbered). Portrait. In the copies inspected p. 2 unnumbered, and the misprint
'sexered' occurs on p. 88, l. 9.

Copies collated: British Museum; Bedford Public Library; Bunyan Meeting, Bedford; Congregational Library, Memorial Hall, London; Rylands Library, Manchester.

Like Bunyan's other books, *Grace Abounding* was poorly produced
for the popular market; there is some improvement, however, in
the editions for which Francis Smith and Nathaniel Ponder were

responsible. George Larkin was a young man of about twenty-four when he issued the first edition; in 1666 he had only just begun publishing, and perhaps also printing, and the poor layout of the title-page shows his prentice hand. Francis Smith had previously published several works of Bunyan and other works by Noncon-formists and had himself suffered under the laws against Dissenters. When Nathaniel Ponder took the book over in 1680 he had already laid his claim to fame as 'Bunyan Ponder', the publisher of *The Pilgrim's Progress*, Larkin, like Smith, was soon to be involved in trouble with the authorities for printing unlicensed pamphlets.[1] In 1666 a large stock of unlicensed books, including Bunyan's, was seized by warrant from Smith's warehouse near Temple Bar and afterwards destroyed in the Great Fire.[2] This may help to explain the disappearance of all but three copies of the first edition;[3] early Bunyan editions are in any case notoriously rare: the earliest ones were read to pieces so that Charles Doe found it impossible to amass a complete set of the works for the Folio in 1692: only one copy of the first edition of *Christian Behaviour* (1663) survives, and only one fragment of *The Barren Fig-tree* (1673).

Larkin was prosecuted in 1668 for his connexion with the publica-tion of *Advice to a Painter* and other pamphlets, and examined before a committee of the House of Lords; since there is no record of a second edition in the Term Catalogue, it may be presumed that it had already appeared before 1668 when the Catalogues begin; it may thus again have been under Larkin's imprint, but soon after his prosecution it was transferred to other booksellers. The undated third edition is registered in the Catalogue for Trinity Term 1679 under the heading 'Reprinted'. In it the duration of Bunyan's im-prisonment is given as 'compleat twelve years' instead of 'above five year and a quarter'[4] (i.e. since his arrest in 1660). In another revised

---

[1] H. R. Plomer, *Dictionary of Printers and Booksellers 1668–1725* (1922), pp. 183–4; *The Life and Errors of John Dunton* (1705), p. 245.

[2] *Account of the Injurious Proceedings against Francis Smith* (1680).

[3] Some idea of the size of these editions can be gained from the figures given in the lawsuit brought by Nathaniel Ponder against his former confederate Thomas Braddyl. Editions of 10,000 and 5,000 copies are there mentioned (P.R.O. C24/1201/41), though *P.P.* was of course a much more popular book than *G.A.* See *P.P.*, pp. lxxiii–lxxiv.

[4] *G.A.* (1666), § 252.

passage he states that he has 'lain above as long again to confirm the Truth by way of Suffering, as I was before in testifying of it . . . in a way of Preaching.'[1] The revision must therefore have been carried out in or about 1672, the year of his release; it does not contain his rebuttal of the slanderous accusations made about his association with Agnes Beaumont in 1674;[2] the original third edition must have come out between 1672 and 1674: probably the book had already been transferred to Francis Smith, who was again in business in the earlier year when he published Bunyan's *A Confession of My Faith and a Reason of My Practice*. The 'reprinted' third of 1679 is likely to have been made up from the remaining sheets of this edition, and not to have been an entirely fresh issue.[3]

The fifth edition (1680), the first to bear Ponder's imprint, contains the sections relating to the Agnes Beaumont affair which complete the additions to the text. These may, of course, have first appeared in a lost fourth edition appearing between 1674 and 1680.

The third and fifth editions contain additional numbered paragraphs, thus altering the total numeration of the sections in the book; additional phrases and sentences are also inserted into the original paragraphs in these editions. Most of the additional matter is already present in the third. The sixth edition (1688) adds no new sections and differs from the fifth only in a few minor points. It is unlikely that Bunyan, in the last months of his life, was able to see the sixth edition through the press. In the last ten years of his career he was busy as preacher and pastor, and also published no less than seventeen treatises as well as *Mr. Badman*, *The Holy War*, and the Second Part of *The Pilgrim's Progress*.[4] Ponder makes a tidier job of the book, but introduces some errors into his reprint of the fifth. Possibly, as with *The Pilgrim's Progress*, it was necessary for him to employ more than one printing-house in order to meet an unexpected demand.[5] It is a mistake to conclude, as did John Brown in

---

[1] *G.A.*, § 279.

[2] *Narrative of Agnes Beaumont*, pp. 58 ff.

[3] The same is the case with the second edition of *The Holy City* (1669); cf. F. M. Harrison, *A Bibliography of the Works of John Bunyan* (Oxford, 1932), p. xv; F. M. Harrison, 'Notes on the Early Editions of *Grace Abounding*', *Baptist Quarterly*, xi (1943), 160–4.

[4] Cf. *P.P.*, p. cxi.

[5] See H. R. Plomer, *Dictionary of Printers and Booksellers 1668–1725* (1922), pp. 240–1.

his edition in the Cambridge Classics, that because the sixth edition presents an inclusive text it is therefore definitive and approved by the author (the same mistake led him to select for his edition of *The Pilgrim's Progress*, Part One, the eleventh edition with its many imperfections).

Bunyan is deeply concerned to defend the integrity of his own work: he says that he 'never endeavoured to, nor durst make use of other men's lines' (§ 285); in the prefatory verses to the Second Part of *The Pilgrim's Progress*, when he warns his readers against the counterfeits of his fiction that began to circulate, he shows some sense of his individuality as a writer, speaking of his allegory's

> *own native Language, which no man*
> *Now useth, nor with ease dissemble can.*[1]

But there is no evidence that he was interested in the exact preservation of the minutiae of his original copy; nor does it appear that he felt strongly about the attempts of editors and printing-house correctors to improve on his provincial English and loose grammar. The third and fifth editions, those which contain substantial additions and were undoubtedly overlooked by the author, are also those in which certain colloquialisms of the first editions are exchanged for less colourful words and phrases. A few examples will suffice:

§ 11 as it made my heart to ake 1   that it made 3 5 6

39 as mistrusting 1   and mistrust 3 5 6

51 I was a going 1   a *om.* 6

102 took up under her apron 1   in her arms 3 5 6

162 passed 1 3   led 5 6

193 in my studies how 1   in my studies considering how 1 5 6

196 was brought those sayings 1   were brought 3 5 6 *and cf. a similar correction of a singular verb with a plural subject at* § 243.

241 sleeping 1   sleep 3 5 6

248 beaten off 1   holden off 3 5 6 *where the earlier reading is congruous with the imagery of violent physical effort running through the temptation passages.*

[1] *P.P.*, p. 168.

330 tuition 1 3   care 5 6 *where it is a case of the unlettered writer's preference for a rather over-bookish word, as in the* 'terrene and domestick matters' *and* 'dolorous notes' *of* The Holy War.

334 scrabling shift 1   scrambling 3 5 6   'Scrabbling' *occurs again in* The Pilgrim's Progress (*p. 125*).

The same applies to readings in the new sections of the third edition which are altered in the fifth or sixth in a manner suggesting editorial interference. The third edition 'stounded' is retained in the fifth but becomes 'stunned' in the sixth (§ 12). The 'witch' of the third and fifth becomes 'Wizzard' in the sixth.

There are also sheer mistakes and corruptions in the third and fifth editions side by side with the fresh insertions in the text. 'Thou art my Love' becomes 'Thou art my Dove' (p. 29, l. 27), 'alas poor fool' is altered to 'alas poor Soul' (p. 35, l. 1), 'seriousness' is changed to 'fearfulness' at p. 77, l. 10, and 'life' to 'love' at p. 92, l. 11. These mistakes all occur in the third and are repeated in the fifth and sixth. The sixth has the significant substitution of 'tests' for 'rests' in the phrase 'false and unsound rests', though the word in this context is established sectarian usage denoting the unreliable grounds for trust in personal salvation provided by a religion not truly reborn. The omission by the sixth of two lines in the first edition in § 324 makes nonsense of a paragraph.

Bunyan, then, even when in the third edition he had to work through almost the whole of the copy in the process of expansion, did not supervise the reproduction of his text with any care; his attitude to the verbal detail of his confession was one of indifference except when the accuracy of his record of personal experience was involved. His imagination sees his effort to reach the blessed state of the elect 'poor women' of Bedford as a struggle to pass through a little door in a mountain to the sunlight beyond. In the first edition this revelation is described as 'a Dream or Vision', in the third as 'a kind of Vision'; the change makes clearer the impression that this was a special kind of hallucination, not an ordinary dream (p. 19, l. 18). In another passage he tells how his resistance to the inner voices of temptation would be accompanied by automatic physical reactions, 'by way of pushing or thrusting': in the fifth edition he amplified this by the addition of the phrase 'with my hands or elbows' in order to render the action more precisely (p. 42, l. 28). It is only in the additions and in small but purposive alterations like these that Bunyan is at work as a reviser (the time references, brought up to date in the third, are another example).

The history of the text is that of a simple, vertical descent; the same pattern is found in the twelve editions of *The Pilgrim's Progress* published in Bunyan's lifetime. Each successive edition provided the copy for the next. Both the sixth and the fifth pass from 72 to 74 in their numbering of sections; in § 104 the printer of the sixth is deceived by a broken 'f' in the fifth and reproduces 'for sin' as 'or sin'. All the mistakes and alterations of the third are carried on into the fifth (e.g. 'Thou art my Love, thou art my Dove', already mentioned, p. 29, l. 27). The printer of the third, after introducing the additional passage which is later numbered §§ 12–14, repeats the number of § 30 so as conveniently to return to the numbering of the first; and many readings of the third agree with the first against the later editions. The vertical descent is complicated only by the inserted sections and the consequent renumbering. Changes in spelling, punctuation, and capitalization are most frequent in the third, and are generally accepted in the fifth and sixth. There is no important instance in which the fifth or the sixth goes behind its immediate predecessor to the first or the third.

In view of these facts the present text is based on the first edition for the original body of the narrative, and on the third and fifth for the additional passages which first appear in those editions. The punctuation, capitalization, and italicization of a passage on its first appearance has likewise usually been preserved.

There are a few revised readings in the third and fifth editions which give a clearer meaning than the first or third, or provide a less clumsy sentence structure. Usually this is achieved by breaking up longer sentences into shorter or employing adverbs and adverbial phrases to underline the drift of the sentence. For example, a sentence in Bunyan's account of his first meeting with Luther's *Commentary on the Epistle to the Galatians* reads thus in the third edition in which it first appears:

. . . the God in whose hands are all our days and ways did cast into my hand, one day, a book of Martin Luther, his comment on the *Galathians*, so old that it was ready to fall piece from piece, if I did but turn it over.

and thus in the fifth:

... the God in whose hands are all our days and ways did cast into my hand one day, a book of *Martin Luther*; it was his Comment on the *Galatians*, it also was so old that it was ready to fall piece from piece if I did but turn it over (p. 40, ll. 29–32).

This and a few more small alterations which attempt to turn the violent and headlong flow of Bunyan's thought into smoother prose, and in some cases to clear up obscurity, form a different group of changes from the two already mentioned: the standardizing of eccentric forms, and the examples of pure misunderstanding or mis-copying. The third group makes an editor uneasily aware that Bunyan himself, though no literary improver, might have altered a sentence for greater clarity, or at any rate have endorsed the process of correction and clarification. Happily the number of such altera-tions is not large, and I have rarely introduced the revised readings into the text.

The punctuation has been silently corrected in one or two places where a full stop or a question mark have been wrongly used. Errors in the scriptural references have been corrected in the text. The apparatus notes all variants, additions, and omissions, but not those in spelling or punctuation except where they are of special interest. In the apparatus the first, third, fifth, and sixth editions are indicated by arabic numerals; the abbreviations *add.* and *om.* denote the addition and omission of words, sentences, and sections; where whole new sections have been added to the first edition, the point where they have been inserted in the third or fifth edition is in-dicated between the foot of the text and the apparatus of variants.

(vii) *Later Editions*

The reprints after Bunyan's death generally follow the text of 1688; there was no attempt until our own day to restore readings from the earliest editions. *Grace Abounding* was not included in Doe's folio edition of the *Works* in 1692 because of copyright difficulties;

like *The Pilgrim's Progress* and *Badman* the book was the property of
Nathaniel Ponder, and afterwards of his son Robert. Robert Ponder
brought out the seventh edition in 1692, taking advantage of
the advertisement provided by Doe's truncated edition of the
complete works in the same year. There was added to this edition
(which like the previous ones is in duodecimo) 'the remainder of his
life and character, by a friend since his death', to balance the bio-
graphical notice in Doe's *The Struggler*. It is attributed to George
Cokayne, pastor of the Meeting in Red Cross Street, after his ejection
from the Parish of St. Pancras, Soper Lane.

An undated eighth edition, probably issued soon after 1692, bears
the imprint of Nathaniel Ponder; it is the last edition to do so. The
numbering of the editions now becomes complicated through the
habit of repeating the number on the original title-page in reprints:
thus there are two more eighths, in 1701 and 1707, the latter published at Edinburgh; and later in the eighteenth century a twelfth
of 1749 is succeeded by a tenth (1759) and an eleventh (1761) all
published by W. Johnston.

The ninth edition appeared in 1716, issued by N. and M. Bod-
dington, who had acquired many of Ponder's other copyrights including *The Pilgrim's Progress*. The original tenth edition was published in 1726. A British Museum copy of a twelfth edition of 1771,
to which has been prefixed a facsimile title-page of the first edition,
is interleaved, and contains manuscript notes on the text by Bunyan's
Victorian editor George Offor. Editions numbered as the thirteenth
appeared in 1776 and 1778; the fourteenth in 1791.

An edition of both parts of *The Pilgrim's Progress* in 1775 'with the
life of the Author prefixed', was the first of many to combine *Grace
Abounding* and *The Pilgrim's Progress* in one volume. That of 1798
had added to it 'his dying sayings' (taken from 1692).

A feature of the eighteenth- and nineteenth-century editions, as
with other works of Bunyan, is the very large number which issued
from provincial presses: Belfast (?1731); Glasgow (1735, reprinted
in 1745, 1750, 1755, and 1758); Berwick (1760); Leeds (1792, reprinted in 1798) are a few of these. The first American edition was
published at Boston in 1717 and the thirteenth was reached in 1732.
A French translation appeared at Geneva in 1824: *La Grâce de*

Dieu abondamment sur les plus grandus pécheurs . . . Traduite en français par Jean-Frédéric Nardin.

So far the successive editions in England had been unremarkable cheap reprints. The Evangelical movement revived interest in Bunyan and his theology, and produced a number of divines, Anglican and Nonconformist, prepared to introduce his works with commentaries. *The Life of Mr. John Bunyan . . . In which is exemplified the power of evangelical principles,* by Joseph Ivimey, is one of the first of these annotated editions: it presents *Grace Abounding* and *A Relation of the Imprisonment* with interpolations by the editor. It reached a third edition in 1823. Ivimey, who edited *The Pilgrim's Progress* with a commentary, also compiled a volume of selections from Bunyan's two autobiographical works into which he introduced 'Extracts from the Records of the Congregation at Bedford' (i.e. the *Church Book*); the second edition of this book was published in 1825.

The first real attempt to compare editions and establish a more accurate text was made by George Offor in his complete *Works* of Bunyan (first edition, 1852–3; second, 1860–2). He presents a conflated text, and indicates later additions by the somewhat clumsy method of placing them between inverted commas. But he does make extensive use of the first edition and so avoids many pitfalls into which later editors have fallen. The greater part, however, of Offor's notes offer theological and moral exegesis, often with a controversial tone; and he brought all the quotations from Scripture into conformity with the Authorized Version.

The edition by Edmund Venables, Preceptor and Canon of Lincoln (Oxford 1879; revised by Mabel Peacock, 1900 and reprinted in 1925), closely followed that of Offor, but had a valuable introduction and notes. John Brown, pastor of Bunyan Meeting and author of the standard life of Bunyan, first edited the work with an Introduction and Notes in 1888; his edition for the Cambridge Classics (Cambridge, 1907, with *The Pilgrim's Progress*) relies exclusively on the sixth edition (1688) but has a brief appendix of textual variants.

GRACE
Abounding to the chief of Sinners:

OR,
A Brief and Faithful

RELATION

Of the Exceeding Mercy of God in Chrift,
to his poor Servant

JOHN BUNYAN.

Wherein is particularly fhewed, The manner of his Converfion, his fight and trouble for
Sin, his Dreadful Temptations, alfo how he
defpaired of Gods mercy, and how the Lord at
length thorow Chrift did deliver him from all
the guilt and terrour that lay upon him.

Whereunto is added,

A brief Relation of his Call to the Work
of the Miniftry, of his Temptations therein,
as alfo what he hath met with in Prifon.

All which was written by his own hand
there, and now publifhed for the fupport
of the weak and tempted People of God.

*Come and hear, all ye that fear God; and I will declare
what he hath done for my foul,* Pfal.66.16.

LONDON:
Printed by *George Larkin.* 1666.

A PREFACE:

Or brief Account of the publish-
ing of this Work:

Written by the Author thereof,
and dedicated to those whom
God hath counted him wor-
thy to beget to Faith, by his
Ministry in the Word.

Children, Grace be with you, Amen. *I being taken from you in presence,
and so tied up, that I cannot perform that duty that from God doth lie upon
me, to you-ward, for your further edifying and building up in Faith and
Holiness,* &c., *yet that you may see my Soul hath fatherly care and desire
after your spiritual and everlasting welfare; I now once again, as before from* 5
the top of Shenir *and* Hermon, *so now from* the Lions Dens, and from
the Mountains of the Leopards (*Song* 4. 8), *do look yet after you all,
greatly longing to see your safe arrival into* THE *desired haven.*

    *I thank God upon every Remembrance of you, and rejoyce even while I
stick between the Teeth of the Lions in the Wilderness, at the grace, and* 10
*mercy, and knowledge of Christ our Saviour, which God hath bestowed upon
you, with abundance of Faith and Love. Your hungerings and thirstings also
after further acquaintance with the Father, in his Son; your tenderness of
Heart, your trembling at sin, your sober and holy deportment also, before
both God and men, is great refreshment to me:* For you are my glory and 15
joy, (I *Thes.* 2. 20).

    *I have sent you here enclosed a drop of that honey, that I have taken out of
the Carcase of a* Lyon (Judg. 14. 5, 6, 7, 8). *I have eaten thereof my self
also, and am much refreshed thereby.* (*Temptations when we meet them at
first, are as the* Lyon *that roared upon* Sampson; *but if we overcome them,* 20
the next time we see them, we shall finde a Nest of Honey within them.) *The
Philistians understand me not. It is a Relation of the work of God upon my*

4 *yet*] *Yet* 1   5–6 *before . . . now*] om. 1   22 *Philistians*] *Philistines* 3 6
22 *is a*] *is something a* 3 5 6

own Soul, even from the very first, till now; wherein you may perceive my castings down, and raisings up; for he woundeth, and his hands make whole. It is written in the Scripture (Isai. 38. 19), The father to the children shall make known the truth of God. *Yea, it was for this reason I lay so*
5 *long at* Sinai (Deut. 4. 10, 11), *to see the fire, and the cloud, and the darkness,* that I might fear the Lord all the days of my life upon earth, and tell of his wondrous works to my children, *Psal.* 78. 3, 4, 5.

Moses (Numb. 33. 1, 2) *writ of the Journeyings of the children of*
10 Israel, *from* Egypt *to the Land of* Canaan; *and commanded also, that they did remember their forty years travel in the wilderness.* Thou shalt remember all the way which the Lord thy God led thee these forty years in the wilderness, to humble thee, and to prove thee, to know what was in thine heart, whether thou wouldst keep his commandments,
15 or no, *Deut.* 8. 2, 3. *Wherefore this I have endeavoured to do; and not onely so, but to publish it also; that, if God will, others may be put in remembrance of what he hath done for their Souls, by reading his work upon me.*

It is profitable for Christians to be often calling to mind the very beginnings of Grace with their Souls. It is a night to be much observed to the
20 Lord, for bringing them out from the land of *Egypt.* This is that night of the Lord to be observed of all the children of *Israel* in their generations, *Exod.* 12. 42. My God, *saith David,* Psal. 42. 6. my soul is cast down within me; but I will remember thee from the land of Jordan, and of the Hermonites, from the hill Mizar. *He remembred*
25 *also the Lyon and the Bear, when he went to fight with the Giant of* Gath, I Sam. 17. 36, 37.

It was Pauls *accustomed manner,* Acts 22. *and that when tried for his life,* Acts 24. *even to open before his Judges, the manner of his Conversion: He would think of that day and that hour, in the which he first did meet with*
30 *Grace: for he found it support unto him. When God had brought the children of* Israel *thorow the* Red Sea, *far into the wilderness; yet they must turn quite about thither again, to remember the drowning of their enemies there,* Num. 14. 25. *for though they sang his praise before, yet they soon forgat his works,* Psal. 106. 12, 13.

---

2 *raisings*] *risings* 3 5 6　　　　5 Deut.] Dev. 1 Lev. 3　　　　29 *in the which*] *in which* 3 5 6　　　　30 *support unto him*] *supported him* 3 5 6　　　　31 *thorow*] *into*
5 *out of* 6　　　　34 12, 13] 11, 12 1-6

In this Discourse of mine, you may see much; much, I say, of the Grace of God towards me: I thank God *I can count it much; for it was above my sins, and Satans temptations too. I can remember my fears, and doubts, and sad moneths, with comfort; they are as the head of* Goliah *in my hand. There was nothing to* David *like* Goliahs *sword, even that sword that should have* 5 *been sheathed in his bowels; for the very sight and remembrance of that, did preach forth* Gods *Deliverance to him. O the remembrance of my great sins, of my great temptations, and of my great fears of perishing for ever! They bring fresh into my mind the remembrance of my great help, my great support from Heaven, and the great grace that* God *extended to such a* 10 *Wretch as I.*

My dear Children, call to mind the former days, the years of ancient times; remember also your songs in the night, and commune with your own heart, Psal. 77. 5, 6, 7, 8, 9, 10, 11, 12. *Yea, look diligently, and leave no corner therein unsearched, for there is treasure hid, even the treasure of your* 15 *first and second experience of the grace of* God *toward you. Remember, I say, the Word that first laid hold upon you; remember your terrours of conscience, and fear of death and hell: remember also your tears and prayers to* God; *yea, how you sighed under every hedge for mercy. Have you never a Hill* Mizar *to remember? Have you forgot the Close, the Milk-house, the* 20 *Stable, the Barn, and the like, where* God *did visit your Soul? Remember also the Word, the Word, I say, upon which the Lord hath caused you to hope: If you have sinned against light, if you are tempted to blaspheme, if you are down in despair, if you think* God *fights against you, or if heaven is hid from your eyes; remember 'twas thus with your father,* but out of them 25 all the Lord delivered me.

I could have enlarged much in this my discourse of my temptations and troubles for sin, as also of the merciful kindness and working of God *with my Soul: I could also have stepped into a stile much higher then this in which I have here discoursed, and could have adorned all things more then here I* 30 *have seemed to do: but I dare not:* God *did not play in convincing of me; the* Devil *did not play in tempting of me; neither did I play when I sunk as into a bottomless pit, when* the pangs of hell caught hold upon me: *wherefore I may not play in my relating of them, but be plain and simple, and lay down*

---

12 *the years*] *and Years* 5 6   14 *heart*] *Hearts* 6   Psal. 77] Psal. 73 1–6
15 *there*] *that* 3 5 6   19 *for*] *of* 3 5 6   21 *Soul*] *Souls* 6   31 *convincing*]
tempting 5 6   31–32 *the* Devil *did not play in tempting of me;*] om. 5 6

the thing as it was: He that liketh it, let him receive it; *and he that does not, let him produce a better.* Farewel.

 My dear Children,

The Milk and Honey is beyond this Wilderness: God be merciful to
5 you, and grant that you be not slothful to go in to possess the Land.
Jo. Bunyan.

GRACE

Abounding to the chief of Sinners:

OR,

A Brief Relation
Of the exceeding mercy of God
in Christ, to his poor Servant
John Bunyan.

1. IN this my relation of the merciful working of God upon my
Soul, it will not be amiss, if in the first place, I do, in a few words,
give you a hint of my pedegree, and manner of bringing up; that
thereby the goodness and bounty of God towards me, may be the
more advanced and magnified before the sons of men.   5

2. For my descent then, it was, as is well known by many, of a
low and inconsiderable generation; my fathers house being of that
rank that is meanest, and most despised of all the families in the
Land. Wherefore I have not here, as others, to boast of Noble blood,
or of a High-born state according to the flesh; though all things 10
considered, I magnifie the Heavenly Majesty, for that by this door
he brought me into this world, to partake of the Grace and Life
that is in Christ by the Gospel.

3. But yet notwithstanding the meanness and inconsiderableness
of my Parents, it pleased God to put it into their heart, to put me 15
to School, to learn both to Read and Write; the which I also
attained, according to the rate of other poor mens children, though
to my shame I confess, I did soon loose that little I learned, even
almost utterly, and that long before the Lord did work his gracious
work of conversion upon my Soul.   20

4. As for my own natural life, for the time that I was without God
in the world, it was indeed according to the course of this world,
and the spirit that now worketh in the children of disobedience:

Eph. 2. 2, 3. it was my delight to be taken captive by the Devil *at his will,* 2 Tim. 2. 26. being filled with all unrighteousness; the which did also so strongly work, and put forth itself, both in my heart and life, and that from a childe, that I had but few
5 Equals, (especially considering my years, which were tender, being few) both for cursing, swearing, lying and blaspheming the holy Name of God.

5. Yea, so setled and rooted was I in these things, that they became as a second Nature to me; the which, as I also have with
10 soberness considered since, did so offend the Lord, that even in my childhood he did scare and affright me with fearful dreams, and did terrifie me with dreadful visions. For often, after I had spent this and the other day in sin, I have in my bed been greatly afflicted, while asleep, with the apprehensions of Devils, and wicked spirits,
15 who still, as I then thought, laboured to draw me away with them; of which I could never be rid.

6. Also I should at these years be greatly afflicted and troubled with the thoughts of the day of Judgment, and that both night and day, and should tremble at the thoughts of the fearful torments of
20 Hell-fire; still fearing that it would be my lot to be found at last amongst those Devils and Hellish Fiends, who are there bound down with the chains and bonds of eternal darkness.

7. These things, I say, when I was but a childe, about nine or ten years old, did so distress my Soul, that then in the midst of my
25 many sports and childish vanities, amidst my vain companions, I was often much cast down and afflicted in my mind therewith, yet could I not let go my sins: yea, I was so overcome with despair of Life and Heaven, that then I should often wish, either that there had been no Hell, or that I had been a Devil; supposing they were
30 onely tormentors; that if it must needs be, that I indeed went thither, I might be rather a tormentor, then tormented my self.

8. A while after, these terrible dreams did leave me, which also I soon forgot; for my pleasures did quickly cut off the remembrance

---

§§ 5 *and* 6 *form a single* § *in* 1 *and* 3

1 Eph. 2. 2, 3] *add.* 3   2 2 Tim. 2. 26] *add.* 3   18–19 day . . . thoughts of] *om.* 6   22 darkness, unto the judgment of the great Day.] *add.* 5 6   eternal] *om.* 5   23–24 about nine or ten years old,] *add.* 3   24 then] when 1 3 27 was so] was also then so 5 6   28 then] *om.* 5 6

of them, as if they had never been: wherefore, with more greediness, according to the strength of Nature, I did still let loose the reins to my lusts, and delighted in all transgression against the Law of God: so that until I came to the state of marriage, I was the very ring-leader of all the Youth that kept me company, into all manner of 5 vice and ungodliness.

9. Yea, such prevalency had the lusts and fruits of the flesh, in this poor Soul of mine, that had not a miracle of precious grace prevented, I had not onely perished by the stroke of eternal Justice, but had also laid my self open, even to the stroke of those Laws, 10 which bring some to disgrace and open shame before the face of the world.

10. In these days, the thoughts of Religion was very grievous to me; I could neither endure it my self, nor that any other should; so that when I have but seen some read in those books that con- 15 cerned Christian piety, it would be as it were a prison to me. *Then I said unto God, Depart from me, for I desire not the knowledge of thy ways,* Job. 21. 14, 15. I was now void of all good consideration; Heaven and Hell were both out of sight and minde; and as for Saving and Damning, they were least in my thoughts. *O Lord, thou knowest my* 20 *life, and my ways were not hid from thee.*

11. Yet this I well remember, that though I could my self sin with the greatest delight and ease, and also take pleasure in the vileness of my companions; yet even then, if I have at any time seen wicked things by those who professed goodness, it would 25 make my spirit tremble. As once above all the rest, when I was in my heighth of vanity, yet hearing one to swear that was reckoned for a religious man, it had so great a stroke upon my spirit, as it made my heart to ake.

12. But God did not utterly leave me, but followed me still, not 30 now with convictions, but Judgements, yet such as were mixed with mercy. For once I fell into a crick of the Sea, and hardly escaped drowning: another time I fell out of a Boat into *Bedford*-River, but mercy yet preserved me alive: Besides, another time being in the

§§ 12–14 *added in* 3 *and remain as a single* § *till* 6

3 lusts] lust 5 6   5 into] in 5 6   22 Yet] But 3 5 6   28–29 as it made my heart to ake] that it made my heart ake 3 5 6

field, with one of my companions, it chanced that an Adder passed over the High way, so I having a stick in mine hand, struck her over the back; and having stounded her, I forced open her mouth with my stick, and plucked her sting out with my fingers, by which
5 act had not God been mercifull to me, I might by my desperateness have brought myself to mine end.

13. This also have I taken notice of with thanksgiving; when I was a Souldier, I with others were drawn out to go to such a place to besiege it; but when I was just ready to go, one of the company
10 desired to go in my room, to which, when I had consented he took my place; and coming to the siege, as he stood Sentinel, he was shot into the head with a Musket bullet and died.

14. Here, as I said, were Judgements and Mercy, but neither of them did awaken my soul to Righteousness, wherefore I sinned
15 still, and grew more and more rebellious against God, and careless of mine own Salvation.

15. Presently after this, I changed my condition into a married state, and my mercy was, to light upon a Wife whose Father was counted godly: this Woman and I, though we came together as
20 poor as poor might be, (not having so much houshold-stuff as a Dish or Spoon betwixt us both), yet this she had for her part, *The Plain Mans Path-way to Heaven,* and *The Practice of Piety,* which her Father had left her when he died. In these two Books I should sometimes read with her, wherein I also found some things that
25 were somewhat pleasing to me: (but all this while I met with no conviction.) She also would be often telling of me what a godly man her Father was, and how he would reprove and correct Vice, both in his house, and amongst his neighbours; what a strict and holy life he lived in his day, both in word and deed.

30 16. Wherefore these books, with this relation, though they did not reach my heart to awaken it about my sad and sinful state, yet they did beget within me some desires to Religion: so that, because I knew no better, I fell in very eagerly with the Religion of the times, to wit, to go to Church twice a day, and that too with the
35 foremost, and there should very devoutly both say and sing as

---

3 stounded] stunned 6   5 desperateness] departures 3   20 houshold-
stuff] *add.* 3

others did; yet retaining my wicked life: but withal, I was so over-run with the spirit of superstition, that I adored, and that with great devotion, even all things, (both the High-place, Priest, Clerk, Vestments, Service, and what else) belonging to the Church; count-ing all things holy that were therein contained; and especially the Priest and Clerk most happy, and without doubt greatly blessed, because they were the Servants, as I then thought, of God, and were principal in the holy Temple, to do his work therein.

17. This conceit grew so strong in little time upon my spirit, that had I but seen a Priest, (though never so sordid and debauched in his life) I should find my spirit fall under him, reverence him, and knit unto him; yea, I thought for the love I did bear unto them, (supposing they were the Ministers of God) I could have layn down at their feet, and have been trampled upon by them; their Name, their Garb, and Work, did so intoxicate and bewitch me.

18. After I had been thus for some considerable time, another thought came into my mind, and that was, Whether we were of the *Israelites*, or no: for finding in the Scriptures that they were once the peculiar People of God, thought I, if I were one of this race, my Soul must needs be happy. Now again I found within me a great longing to be resolved about this question, but could not tell how I should: at last, I asked my father of it, who told me, *No, we were not*: wherefore then I fell in my spirit, as to the hopes of that, and so remained.

19. But all this while, I was not sensible of the danger and evil of sin; I was kept from considering that sin would damn me, what Religion soever I followed, unless I was found in Christ: nay, I never thought of him, nor whether there was one or no. Thus man, while blind, doth wander, but wearieth himself with vanity: for he knoweth not the way to the City of God, *Eccles.* 10. 15.

20. But one day, (amongst all the Sermons our Parson made) his subject was, to treat of the Sabbath day, and of the evil of breaking that, either with labour, sports, or otherwise: (now I was, not-withstanding my Religion, one that took much delight in all man-ner of vice, and especially that was the Day that I did solace my

1 so] *om.* 1   13 of God] of my God 1   28 one or no] such an one or
no 5 6   33–34 , notwithstanding my Religion,] *add.* 3

self therewith.) Wherefore I fell in my conscience under his Sermon, thinking and believing that he made that Sermon on purpose to shew me my evil-doing; and at that time I felt what guilt was, though never before, that I can remember; but then I was for the
5 present greatly loaden therewith, and so went home when the Sermon was ended, with a great burden upon my spirit.

21. This, for that instant, did benum the sinews of my best delights, and did imbitter my former pleasures to me: but behold, it lasted not; for before I had well dined, the trouble began to go off
10 my minde, and my heart returned to its old course: but Oh how glad was I, that this trouble was gone from me, and that the fire was put out, that I might sin again without controul! Wherefore, when I had satisfied nature with my food, I shook the Sermon out of my mind, and to my old custom of sports and gaming I returned
15 with great delight.

22. But the same day, as I was in the midst of a game at Cat, and having struck it one blow from the hole; just as I was about to strike it the second time, a voice did suddenly dart from Heaven into my Soul, which said, *Wilt thou leave thy sins, and go to Heaven? or*
20 *have thy sins, and go to Hell?* At this I was put to an exceeding maze; wherefore, leaving my Cat upon the ground, I looked up to Heaven, and was as if I had with the eyes of my understanding, seen the Lord Jesus looking down upon me, as being very hotly displeased with me, and as if he did severely threaten me with some grievous
25 punishment for these, and other my ungodly practices.

23. I had no sooner thus conceived in my mind, but suddenly this conclusion was fastned on my spirit (for the former hint did set my sins again before my face) *That I had been a great and grievous Sinner, and that it was now too late for me to look after Heaven; for Christ*
30 *would not forgive me, nor pardon my transgressions.* Then I fell to musing upon this also; and while I was thinking on it, and fearing lest it should be so, I felt my heart sink in despair, concluding it was too late; and therefore I resolved in my mind I would go on in sin: for thought I, if the case be thus, my state is surely miserable; miser-
35 able if I leave my sins; and but miserable if I follow them: I can but

7–8 did benum the sinews of my best delights] did cut the sinews of my delights 1   12 , that I might sin again without controul!] *add.* 3

be damned; and if I must be so, I had as good be damned for many sins, as be damned for few.

24. Thus I stood in the midst of my play, before all that then were present; but yet I told them nothing: but, I say, I having made this conclusion, I returned desperately to my sport again; and I well remember, that presently this kind of despair did so possess my Soul, that I was perswaded I could never attain to other comfort then what I should get in sin; for Heaven was gone already, so that on that I must not think: wherefore I found within me a great desire to take my fill of sin, still studdying what sin was set to be committed, that I might taste the sweetness of it; and I made as much haste as I could to fill my belly with its delicates, lest I should die before I had my desire; for that I feared greatly. In these things, I protest before *God*, I lye not, neither do I feign this sort of speech: these were really, strongly, and with all my heart, my desires; *the good Lord, whose mercy is unsearchable, forgive me my transgressions.*

25. (And I am very confident, that this temptation of the Devil is more than usual amongst poor creatures then many are aware of, even to over-run their spirits with a scurvie and seared frame of heart, and benumming of conscience: which frame, he stilly and slyly supplyeth with such despair, that though not much guilt attendeth the Soul, yet they continually have a secret conclusion within them, that there is no hopes for them; *for they have loved sins, therefor after them they will go,* Jer. 2. 25 & 18. 12.)

26. Now therefore I went on in sin with great greediness of mind, still grudging that I could not be so satisfied with it as I would: this did continue with me about a moneth, or more. But one day, as I was standing at a Neighbours Shop-window, and there cursing and swearing, and playing the Mad-man, after my wonted manner, there sate within the woman of the house, and heard me; who, though she was a very loose and ungodly Wretch, yet protested that I swore and cursed at that most fearful rate, that she was made to tremble to hear me; And told me further, *That I was the ungodliest Fellow for swearing that ever she heard in all her life; and*

that I, by thus doing, was able to spoile all the Youth in a whole Town, if
they came but in my company.

27. At this reproof I was silenced, and put to secret shame; and
that too, as I thought, before the God of Heaven: wherefore, while
5 I stood there, and hanging down my head, I wished with all my
heart that I might be a little childe again, that my Father might
learn me to speak without this wicked way of swearing: for, thought
I, I am so accustomed to it, that it is but in vain for me to think of
a reformation, for I thought it could never be.

10   28. But how it came to pass I know not, I did from this time
forward so leave my swearing, that it was a great wonder to my self
to observe it; and whereas before I knew not how to speak unless I
put an Oath before, and another behind, to make my words have
authority, now, I could, without it, speak better, and with more
15 pleasantness then ever I could before: all this while I knew not
Jesus Christ, neither did I leave my sports and play.

29. But quickly after this, I fell in company with one poor man
that made profession of Religion; who, as I then thought, did talk
pleasantly of the Scriptures, and of the matters of Religion: where-
20 fore falling into some love and liking to what he said, I betook me
to my Bible, and began to take great pleasure in reading, but
especially with the historical part thereof: for, as for *Pauls* Epistles,
and Scriptures of that nature, I could not away with them, being
as yet but ignorant either of the corruptions of my nature, or of the
25 want and worth of Jesus Christ to save me.

30. Wherefore I fell to some outward Reformation, both in my
words and life, and did set the Commandments before me for my
way to Heaven: which Commandments I also did strive to keep;
and, as I thought, did keep them pretty well sometimes, and then I
30 should have comfort; yet now and then should break one, and so
afflict my Conscience; but then I should repent, and say I was sorry
for it, and promise God to do better next time, and there get help
again, for then I thought I pleased God as well as any man in
England.

35   31. Thus I continued about a year, all which time our Neighbours

did take me to be a very godly man, a new and religious man, and did marvel much to see such a great and famous alteration in my life and manners; and indeed so it was, though yet I knew not Christ, nor Grace, nor Faith, nor Hope; and truly as I have well seen since, had I then died, my state had been most fearful: well, this I say, continued about a twelve-month, or more.

32. But, I say, my Neighbours were amazed at this my great Conversion, from prodigious profaneness, to something like a moral life; and, truly, so they well might; for this my Conversion was as great, as for *Tom* of *Bethlem* to become a sober man. Now, therefore, they began to praise, to commend, and to speak well of me, both to my face, and behind my back. Now, I was, as they said, become godly; now, I was become a right honest man. But Oh! when I understood that these were their words and opinions of me, it pleased me mighty well: For though, as yet, I was nothing but a poor painted Hypocrite, yet I loved to be talked of as one that was truly Godly. I was proud of my Godliness; and, I did all I did, either to be seen of, or to be well spoken of, by men: well, this I say, continued for about a twelve-month or more.

33. Now you must know, that before this I had taken much delight in ringing, but my Conscience beginning to be tender, I thought that such a practice was but vain, and therefore forced my self to leave it, yet my mind hanckered, wherefore I should go to the Steeple house, and look on: though I durst not ring. But I thought this did not become Religion neither, yet I forced my self and would look on still; but quickly after, I began to think, How, if one of the Bells should fall: then I chose to stand under a main Beam that lay over thwart the Steeple from side to side, thinking there I might stand sure: But then I should think again, Should the Bell fall with a swing, it might first hit the Wall, and then rebounding upon me, might kill me for all this Beam; this made me stand in the Steeple door, and now thought I, I am safe enough, for if a Bell should then fall, I can slip out behind these thick Walls, and so be preserved notwithstanding.

34. So after this, I would yet go to see them ring, but would not

go further than the Steeple door; but then it came into my head, how if the Steeple it self should fall, and this thought, (it may fall for ought I know) would when I stood and looked on, continually so shake my mind, that I durst not stand at the Steeple door any 5 longer, but was forced to fly, for fear it should fall upon my head.

35. Another thing was my dancing, I was a full year before I could quite leave it; but all this while, when I thought I kept this or that Commandment, or did by word or deed any thing that I thought were good, I had great peace in my Conscience, and 10 should think with my self, God cannot chuse but be now pleased with me, yea, to relate it in mine own way, I thought no man in *England* could please God better than I.

36. But poor Wretch as I was, I was all this while ignorant of Jesus Christ, and going about to establish my own righteousness, 15 had perished therein, had not God in mercy shewed me more of my state by nature.

37. But upon a day, the good providence of God did cast me to *Bedford*, to work on my calling; and in one of the streets of that town, I came where there was three or four poor women sitting at 20 a door in the Sun, and talking about the things of God; and being now willing to hear them discourse, I drew near to hear what they said; for I was now a brisk talker also my self in the matters of Religion: but now I may say, *I heard, but I understood not*; for they were far above out of my reach, for their talk was about a new 25 birth, the work of God on their hearts, also how they were convinced of their miserable state by nature: they talked how God had visited their souls with his love in the Lord Jesus, and with what words and promises they had been refreshed, comforted, and supported against the temptations of the Devil; moreover, they 30 reasoned of the suggestions and temptations of Satan in particular, and told to each other by which they had been afflicted, and how they were borne up under his assaults: they also discoursed of their own wretchedness of heart, of their unbelief, and did contemn, slight, and abhor their own righteousness, as filthy, and insufficient 35 to do them any good.

3 would] did 5 6   5 fly] flee 6   it] the Steeple 5 6   20 and¹] *om.* 5 6
24 for] *om.* 5 6

38. And me thought they spake as if joy did make them speak: they spake with such pleasantness of Scripture language, and with such appearance of grace in all they said, that they were to me as if they had found a new world, as if they were people that dwelt alone, and were not to be reckoned among their Neighbours, Num. 23. 9.   5

39. At this I felt my own heart began to shake, as mistrusting my condition to be naught; for I saw that in all my thoughts about Religion and Salvation, the New birth did never enter into my mind, neither knew I the comfort of the Word and Promise, nor the deceitfulness and treachery of my own wicked heart. As for secret 10 thoughts, I took no notice of them; neither did I understand what Satans temptations were, nor how they were to be withstood and resisted, &c.

40. Thus therefore when I had heard and considered what they said, I left them, and went about my employment again: but their 15 talk and discourse went with me, also my heart would tarry with them, for I was greatly affected with their words, both because by them I was convinced that I wanted the true tokens of a truly godly man, and also because by them I was convinced of the happy and blessed condition of him that was such a one.   20

41. Therefore I should often make it my business to be going again and again into the company of these poor people; for I could not stay away; and the more I went amongst them, the more I did question my condition; and as still I do remember, presently I found two things within me, at which I did sometimes marvel, (especially 25 considering what a blind, ignorant, sordid, and ungodly Wretch but just before I was) the one was, a very great softness and tenderness of heart, which caused me to fall under the conviction of what by Scripture they asserted; and the other was, a great bending in my mind to a continual meditating on them, and on all other good 30 things which at any time I heard or read of.

42. By these things my mind was now so turned, that it lay like a Horseleach at the vein, still crying out, *Give, give*, Prov. 30. 15. Yea, it was so fixed on Eternity, and on the things about the Kingdome of Heaven, that is, so far as I knew, though as yet God knows, 35

I knew but little, that neither pleasures nor profits, nor perswasions, nor threats, could loosen it, or make it let go its hold; and though I may speak it with shame, yet it is in very deed a certain truth, it would then have been as difficult for me to have taken my mind
5 from heaven to earth, as I have found it often since to get it again from earth to heaven.

43. One thing I may not omit, there was a young man in our Town, to whom my heart before was knit more than to any other, but he being a most wicked Creature for cursing and swearing,
10 and whoring, I shook him off and forsook his company; but about a quarter of a year after I had left him, I met him in a certain Lane, and asked him how he did; he after his old swearing and mad way, answered, he was well. *But* Harry, said I, *why do you swear and curse thus? what will become of you if you die in this condition?* He answered
15 me in a great chafe, *What would the Devil do for company if it were not for such as I am?*

44. About this time I met with some *Ranters* books, that were put forth by some of our Country men; which Books were also highly in esteem by several old Professors; some of these I read, but was
20 not able to make a Judgement about them; wherefore, as I read in them, and thought upon them, feeling myself unable to judge, I should betake myself to hearty prayer, in this manner; *O Lord, I am a fool, and not able to know the Truth from Errour; Lord leave me not to my own blindness, either to approve of, or condemn this Doctrine; If it be
25 of God, let me not despise it; if it be of the Devil, let me not embrace it. Lord, I lay my Soul, in this matter, only at thy foot, let me not be deceived, I humbly beseech thee.* I had one religious intimate Companion all this while, and that was the poor man that I spoke of before; but about this time he also turned a most devilish *Ranter*, and gave himself up
30 to all manner of filthiness, especially Uncleanness; he would also deny that there was a God, Angel, or Spirit, and would laugh at all exhortations to sobriety. When I laboured to rebuke his wickedness, he would laugh the more, and pretend that he had gone through all Religions, and could never light on the right till now,
35 he told me also that in little time I should see all Professors turn to

the ways of the Ranters: Wherefore abominating those cursed principles, I left his company forth with, and became to him as great a stranger as I had been before a familiar.

45. Neither was this man onely a temptation to me, but my Calling lying in the Countrey, I happened to light into several peoples company; who though strict in Religion formerly, yet were also swept away by these Ranters. These would also talk with me of their ways, and condemn me as legal and dark, pretending that they only had attained to perfection that could do what they would and not sin. O these temptations were suitable to my flesh, I being but a young man and my nature in its prime; but God, who had as I hope designed me for better things, kept me in the fear of his name, and did not suffer me to accept of such cursed principles. And blessed be God, who put it into my heart to cry to him to be kept and directed, still distrusting mine own Wisdom; for I have since seen even the effect of that prayer in his preserving me, not onely from *Ranting* Errors, but from those also that have sprung up since. The Bible was precious to me in those days.

46. And now, me thought, I began to look into the Bible with new eyes, and read as I never did before; and especially the Epistles of the Apostle S. *Paul* were sweet and pleasant to me: and indeed, I was then never out of the Bible, either by reading or meditation, still crying out to *God*, that I might know the truth, and way to Heaven and Glory.

47. And as I went on and read, I lighted on that passage, *To one is given by the Spirit the word of wisdom; to another the word of knowledge by the same Spirit, and to another Faith*, &c. I Cor. 12. And though, as I have since seen, that by this Scripture the holy Ghost intends, in special, things extraordinary, yet on me it did then fasten with conviction, that I did want things ordinary, even that understanding and wisdome that other Christians had. On this word I mused, and could not tell what to do, especially this word Faith put me to it, for I could not help it, but sometimes must question, whether I had any Faith or no; for I feared that it shut me out of all the blessings that other good people had given them of *God*: but I was

loath to conclude I had no Faith in my soul: for if I do so, thought I, then I shall count my self a very Cast-away indeed.

48. No, said I with myself, though I am convinced that I am an ignorant Sot, and that I want those blessed gifts of knowledge and understanding that other good people have, yet at a venture I will conclude I am not altogether faithless, though I know not what Faith is. For it was shewed me, and that too (as I have since seen) by Satan, That those who conclude themselves in a faithless state, have neither rest nor quiet in their Souls; and I was loath to fall quite into despair.

49. Wherefore by this suggestion, I was for a while made afraid to see my want of Faith; but God would not suffer me thus to undo and destroy my *Soul*, but did continually, against 'this my blinde and sad conclusion, create still within me such suppositions, insomuch that I could not rest content until I did now come to some certain knowledge whether I had Faith or no; this always running in my minde, *But how if you want Faith indeed? But how can you tell you have Faith?* And besides, I saw for certain, if I had not, I was sure to perish for ever.

50. So that though I endeavoured at the first to look over the business of Faith, yet in a little time, I better considering the matter, was willing to put myself upon the tryal, whether I had Faith or no. But alas, poor Wretch! so ignorant and brutish was I, that I knew to this day no more how to do it, than I know how to begin and accomplish that rare and curious piece of Art, which I never yet saw nor considered.

51. Wherefore while I was thus considering, and being put to my plunge about it, (for you must know that as yet I had in this matter broken my mind to no man, onely did hear and consider) the Tempter came in with this delusion, That there was no way for me to know I had Faith, but by trying to work some miracle, urging those *Scriptures* that seem to look that way, for the inforcing and strengthening his Temptation. Nay, one day as I was betwixt *Elstow* and *Bedford*, the Temptation was hot upon me to try if I had

---

1 in my soul] *om.* 3   7 since seen] seen since 6   14–15 suppositions, insomuch that] suppositions. That I might in this deceive myself; that 1
18–19 And . . . ever.] *add.* 3   30 this] his 6

Faith by doing of some miracle; which miracle at that time was this, I must say to the puddles that were in the horse pads, *Be dry*; and to the dry places, *Be you the puddles*: and truly, one time I was a going to say so indeed; but just as I was about to speak, this thought came into my minde, *But go under yonder Hedge, and pray first, that* 5 *God would make you able*: but when I had concluded to pray, this came hot upon me, That if I prayed and came again and tried to do it, and yet did nothing notwithstanding, then besure I had no Faith, but was a Cast-away and lost: Nay, thought I, if it be so, I will never try yet, but will stay a little longer.   10

52. So I continued at a great loss; for I thought, if they onely had Faith, which could do such wonderful things, then I concluded that for the present I neither had it, nor yet for time to come were ever like to have it. Thus I was tossed betwixt the Devil and my own ignorance, and so perplexed, especially at some times, that I could 15 not tell what to doe.

53. About this time, the state and happiness of these poor people at *Bedford* was thus, in a kind of Vision, presented to me: I saw as if they were set on the Sunny side of some high Mountain, there refreshing themselves with the pleasant beams of the Sun, while I 20 was shivering and shrinking in the cold, afflicted with frost, snow, and dark clouds; methought also betwixt me and them I saw a wall that did compass about this Mountain; now, thorow this wall my Soul did greatly desire to pass, concluding that if I could, I would goe even into the very midst of them, and there also comfort myself 25 with the heat of their Sun.

54. About this wall I thought myself to goe again and again, still prying as I went, to see if I could find some way or passage, by which I might enter therein, but none could I find for some time: at the last I saw as it were, a narrow gap, like a little door-way in 30 the wall, thorow which I attempted to pass: but the passage being very straight, and narrow, I made many offers to get in, but all in vain, even untill I was well nigh quite beat out by striving to get in: at last, with great striving, me thought I at first did get in my head, and after that, by a side-ling striving, my shoulders, and my 35

1 of] *om.* 3   3 a] *om.* 6   10 never] not 5 6   18 kind of Vision, presented] Dream or Vision represented 1   31 but] Now 5 6

E

whole body; then I was exceeding glad, and went and sat down in the midst of them, and so was comforted with the light and heat of their Sun.

55. Now, this Mountain and Wall, &c., was thus made out to
5 me; the Mountain signified the Church of the living God; the Sun that shone thereon, the comfortable shining of his mercifull face on them that were therein: the wall I thought was the Word that did make separation between the Christians and the world: and the gap which was in this wall, I thought was Jesus Christ, who is the way
10 to God the Father, *Joh.* 14. 6. *Mat.* 7. 14. But for as much as the passage was wonderful narrow, even so narrow, that I could not but with great difficulty, enter in thereat; it shewed me, that none could enter into life but those that were in down-right earnest, and unless they left this wicked world behind them; for here was only
15 roome for Body and Soul, but not for Body and Soul, and Sin.

56. This resemblance abode upon my spirit many dayes, all which time I saw myself in a forlorn and sad condition, but yet was provoked to a vehement hunger and desire to be one of that number that did sit in this Sun-shine: now also I should pray where ever I
20 was, whether at home or abroad, in house or field, and should also often with lifting up of heart, sing that of the fifty first Psalm, *O Lord, consider my distress*: for as yet I knew not where I was.

57. Neither as yet could I attain to any comfortable perswasion that I had Faith in Christ, but instead of having satisfaction, here
25 I began to find my Soul to be assaulted with fresh doubts about my future happiness, especially with such as these, Whether I was elected; but how if the day of grace should now be past and gone?

58. By these two temptations I was very much afflicted and dis-
30 quieted; sometimes by one, and sometimes by the other of them. And first, to speak of that about my questioning my election, I found at this time that though I was in a flame to find the way to Heaven and Glory, and though nothing could beat me off from this, yet this question did so offend and discourage me, that I was,
35 especially at sometimes, as if the very strength of my body also had been taken away by the force and power thereof. This Scripture

also did seem to me to trample upon all my desires, *It is neither in him that willeth, nor in him that runneth, but in God that sheweth mercy,* Rom. 9. 16.

59. With this Scripture I could not tell what to do; for I evidently saw that unless the great God of his infinite grace and bounty, had voluntarily chosen me to be a vessel of mercy, though I should desire, and long, and labour untill my heart did break, no good could come of it. Therefore, this would still stick with me, How can you tell you are Elected? and what if you should not? how then?

60. O Lord, thought I, what if I should not indeed? It may be you are not, said the Tempter: it may be so indeed, thought I. Why then, said Satan, you had as good leave off, and strive no further; for if indeed you should not be Elected and chosen of God, there is no talke of your being saved: *For it is neither in him that willeth, nor in him that runneth, but in God that sheweth mercy.*

61. By these things I was driven to my wits end, not knowing what to say, or how to answer these temptations, (indeed, I little thought that Satan had thus assaulted me, but that rather it was my own prudence thus to start the question) for that the Elect only attained eternal life, that I without scruple did heartily close with-all: but that my self was one of them, there lay all the question.

62. Thus therefore for several dayes I was greatly assaulted and perplexed, and was often, when I have been walking, ready to sink where I went with faintness in my mind: but one day, after I had been so many weeks oppressed and cast down therewith, as I was now quite giving up the Ghost of all my hopes of ever attaining life, that sentence fell with weight upon my spirit, *Look at the generations of old, and see, did ever any trust in God and were confounded?*

63. At which I was greatly lightened and encouraged in my Soul; for thus at that very instant it was expounded to me: *Begin at the beginning of Genesis, and read to the end of the Revelations, and see if you can find that there was any that ever trusted in the Lord, and was Confounded.* So coming home, I presently went to my Bible to see if I could find that saying, not doubting but to find it presently, for it was so fresh, and with such strength and comfort on my spirit, that I was as if it talked with me.

64. Well, I looked, but I found it not; only it abode upon me: then I did aske first this good man, and then another, if they knew where it was, but they knew no such place: at this I wondered that such a sentence should so suddenly and with such comfort, and 5 strength seize and abide upon my heart, and yet that none could find it, (for I doubted not but it was in holy Scripture.)

65. Thus I continued above a year, and could not find the place, but at last, casting my eye into the Apocrypha-Books, I found it in *Ecclesiasticus* 2. 10; this, at the first, did somewhat daunt me; but 10 because by this time I had got more experience of the love and kindness of God, it troubled me the less; especially when I considered, that though it was not in those Texts that we call holy and Canonical, yet forasmuch as this sentence was the sum and substance of many of the promises, it was my duty to take the 15 comfort of it, and I bless God for that word, for it was of God to me: that word doth still, at times, shine before my face.

66. After this, that other doubt did come with strength upon me, *But how if the day of grace should be past and gone?* how if you have over-stood the time of mercy? Now I remember that one day as I 20 was walking into the Country, I was much in the thoughts of this, But how if the day of grace be past? and to aggravate my trouble, the Tempter presented to my mind those good people of *Bedford,* and suggested thus unto me, That these being converted already, they were all that God would save in those parts, and that I came 25 too late, for these had got the blessing before I came.

67. Now was I in great distress, thinking in very deed that this might well be so: wherefore I went up and down bemoaning my sad condition, counting myself far worse then a thousand fools, for standing off thus long, and spending so many years in sin as I have 30 done; still crying out, Oh that I had turned sooner! Oh that I had turned seven years agoe; it made me also angry with my self, to think that I should have no more wit but to trifle away my time till my Soul and Heaven were lost.

68. But when I had been long vexed with this fear, and was 35 scarce able to take one step more, just about the same place where I received my other encouragement, these words broke in upon my

·9 2. 10] *add.* 3

mind, *Compell them to come in, that my house may be filled, and yet there is roome,* Luke 14. 22, 23. These words, but especially them, *And yet there is roome,* were sweet words to me; for, truly, I thought that by them I saw there was place enough in Heaven for me, and, moreover, that when the Lord Jesus did speak these words, he then did ₅ think of me, and that he knowing that the time would come that I should be afflicted with fear, that there was no place left for me in his bosome, did before speak this word, and leave it upon record, that I might find help thereby against this vile temptation. This, I then verily believed.   10

69. In the light and encouragement of this word, I went a pretty while, and the comfort was the more, when I thought that the Lord Jesus should think on me so long agoe, and that he should speak them words on purpose for my sake, for I did then think verily, that he did on purpose speak them to encourage me withall. ₁₅

70. But I was not without my temptations to go back again; temptations, I say, both from Satan, mine own heart, and carnal acquaintance; but I thank God, these were outweighed by that sound sense of death and of the Day of Judgment, which abode, as it were continually in my view. I should often also think on ₂₀ *Nebuchadnezzar,* of whom it is said, *He had given him all the kingdoms of the earth,* Dan. 5. 18, 19. Yet, I thought, if this great man had all his Portion in this World, one hour in Hell Fire would make him forget all. Which consideration was a great help to me.

71. I was also made about this time to see something concerning ₂₅ the Beasts that *Moses* counted clean, and unclean. I thought those Beasts were types of men; the *clean* types of them that were the People of God; but the *unclean* types of such as were the children of the wicked One. Now I read, that the clean beasts chewed the Cud; that is, thought I, they shew us we must feed upon the Word of ₃₀ God: They also parted the hoof, I thought that signified, we must part, if we would be saved, with the ways of ungodly men. And also, in further reading about them, I found that though we did chew the Cud as the *Hare,* yet if we walked with Claws like a *Dog,* or if we did part the Hoof like the *Swine,* yet if we did not chew the ₃₅

§§ 70 *and* 71 *add.* 3, *joining* §§ 69 *and* 70, *which are divided again in* 5
9–10 This, I then verily believed.] *add.* 3

Cud as the *Sheep,* we were still for all that, but unclean: for I thought the *Hare* to be a type of those that talk of the Word, yet walk in ways of sin; and that the *Swine* was like him that parteth with his outward Pollutions, but still wanteth the Word of Faith,
5 without which there could be no way of Salvation, let a man be never so devout, *Deut.* 14.

After this, I found by reading the word, that those that must be glorified with Christ in another world *Must be called by him here.* Called to the partaking of a share in his word and righteousness,
10 and to the comforts & first-fruits of his Spirit, and to a peculiar interest in all those Heavenly things, which do indeed fore-fit the Soul for that rest and house of glory which is in Heaven above.

72. Here again I was at a very great stand, not knowing what to doe, fearing I was not called; for thought I, if I be not called, what
15 then can doe me good? None but those who are effectually called, inherit the Kingdom of Heaven. But oh how I now loved those words that spake of a *Christians calling!* as when the Lord said to one, *Follow me*; and to another, *Come after me,* and oh thought I, that he would say so to me too! how gladly would I run after him.

20 73. I cannot now express with what longings and breakings in my Soul, I cryed to Christ to call me. Thus I continued for a time all on a flame to be converted to Jesus Christ, and did also see at that day such glory in a converted state, that I could not be contented without a share therein. Gold! could it have been gotten
25 for Gold, what could I have given for it! had I had a whole world, it had all gone ten thousand times over, for this, that my Soul might have been in a converted state.

74. How lovely now was every one in my eyes, that I thought to be converted men and women! they shone, they walked like a
30 people that carried the broad Seal of Heaven about them. Oh I saw the lot was fallen to them in pleasant places, and they had a goodly heritage. *Psal.* 16. But that which made me sick, was that of Christ, in Mark, *He went up into a Mountain, and called to him whom he would, and they came unto him,* Mark 3. 13.

§ 73 *numbered* 74 *in* 6

15–16 None but those who are effectually called, inherit the Kingdom of Heaven.]
add. 3   32. *Psal.* 16.] *add.* 3

75. This Scripture made me faint and fear, yet it kindled fire in my Soul. That which made me fear, was this, lest Christ should have no liking to me, for he called *whom he would*. But oh the glory that I saw in that condition, did still so engage my heart, that I could seldome read of any that Christ did call, but I presently 5 wished, Would I had been in their cloaths, would I had been born *Peter*, would I had been born *John*, or would I had been by, and heard him when he called them, how would I have cryed, O Lord, call me also! but oh I feared he would not call me.

76. And truly the Lord let me goe thus many months together, 10 and shewed me nothing, either that I was already, or should be called hereafter. But at last, after much time spent, and many groans to God, that I might be made partaker of the holy and heavenly calling, that Word came in upon me, *I will cleanse their blood that I have not cleansed: for the Lord dwelleth in Zion.* Joel 3. 21. These words 15 I thought were sent to encourage me to wait still upon God, and signified unto me, that if I were not already, yet time might come I might be in truth converted to Christ.

77. About this time I began to break my mind to those poor people in *Bedford*, and to tell them my condition: which, when they 20 had heard, they told *Mr. Gifford* of me, who himself also took occasion to talke with me, and was willing to be well perswaded of me, though I think but from little grounds; but he invited me to his house, where I should hear him confer with others about the dealings of God with the Soul: from all which I still received more 25 conviction, and from that time began to see something of the vanity and inward wretchedness of my wicked heart, for as yet I knew no great matter therein, but now it began to be discovered unto me, and also to worke at that rate for wickedness as it never did before. Now I evidently found, that lusts and corruptions would 30 strongly put forth themselves within me, in wicked thoughts and desires, which I did not regard before: my desires also for heaven and life began to fail; I found also, that whereas before my Soul was full of longings after God, now my heart began to hanker after every foolish vanity; yea, my heart would not be moved to mind 35 that that was good, it began to be careless, both of my Soul and

29 for wickedness] *om.* 3   34 my heart] it 3 5 6

Heaven; it would now continually hang back both to, and in every duty, and was as a clog on the leg of a Bird to hinder her from flying.

78. Nay, thought I, now I grow worse and worse, now am I farther from conversion than ever I was before; wherefore, I began to sink greatly in my soul, and began to entertain such discouragement in my heart, as laid me as low as Hell. If now I should have burned at a stake, I could not believe that Christ had love for me. Alas, I could neither hear him, nor see him, nor feel him, nor savor any of his things; I was driven as with a Tempest, my heart would be unclean, the *Cananites* would dwell in the Land.

79. Sometimes I would tell my condition to the people of God; which when they heard, they would pity me, and would tell me of the Promises; but they had as good have told me that I must reach the Sun with my finger, as have bidden me receive or relie upon the Promise, and as soon as I should have done it, all my sence and feeling was against me, and I saw I had a heart that would sin, and lay under a Law that would condemn.

80. (These things have often made me think of that Child which the Father brought to Christ, *Who while he was yet a coming to him, was thrown down by the Devil, and also so rent and torn by him, that he lay and wallowed foaming:*) Luke 9. 42, Mark 9. 20.

81. Further, in these days I should find my heart to shut itself up against the Lord, and against his holy Word; I have found my unbelief to set as it were the shoulder to the door to keep him out, and that too, even then when I have with many a bitter sigh cried, Good Lord, break it open; *Lord, break these gates of brass, and cut these bars of iron asunder*, Psa. 107. 16. Yet that Word would sometime create in my heart a peaceable pause, *I girded thee, though thou hast not known me*, Isa. 45. 5.

82. But all this while, as to the act of sinning, I never was more tender then now; my hinder parts was inward: I durst not take a pin or a stick, though but so big as a straw; for my conscience now was sore, and would smart at every touch: I could not now tell how

2 her] me 3 5 6   9 savor] favour 6   16 as²] *om.* 1   18 lay] that lay 5 6   27-28 *these bars*] *the bars* 3 5 6   28 , Psa. 107. 16] *add.* 3   30 Isa. 45. 5] *add.* 3   32 my hinder parts was inward:] *add.* 5   was] were 6

to speak my words, for fear I should mis-place them: O how gingerly did I then go, in all I did or said! I found myself as on a miry bog, that shook if I did but stir, and as there left both of God and Christ, and the Spirit, and all good things.

83. But I observe, though I was such a great sinner before con- 5
version, yet God never much charged the guilt of the sins of my Ignorance upon me, only he shewed me I was lost if I had not Christ because I had been a sinner. I saw that I wanted a perfect righteousness to present me without fault before God and that this righteousness was nowhere to be found but in the person of Jesus Christ.   10

84. But my Original and inward pollution, that, that was my plague and my affliction; that I saw at a dreadful rate always putting forth it selfe within me, that I had the guilt of to amazement; by reason of that, I was more loathsom in mine own eyes then was a toad, and I thought I was so in Gods eyes too: Sin and corruption, 15 I said, would as naturally bubble out of my heart, as water would bubble out of a fountain. I thought now that every one had a better heart then I had; I could have changed heart with any body, I thought none but the Devil himself could equalize me for inward wickednes and pollution of minde. I fell therfore at the sight of 20 mine own vileness, deeply into dispair, for I concluded that this condition that I was in, Could not stand with a state of Grace, sure, thought I, I am forsaken of God, sure I am given up, to the Devil, and to a reprobate mind: and thus I continued a long while, even for some years together.   25

85. While I was thus afflicted with the fears of my own damna-tion, there were two things would make me wonder; the one was, when I saw old people hunting after the things of this life, as if they should live here alwayes; the other was, when I found Pro-fessors much distressed and cast down when they met with out- 30 ward losses, as of Husband, Wife, Child, &c. Lord, thought I, what a doe is here about such little things as these? what seeking after carnal things by some, and what grief in others for the loss of them! if they so much labour after, and spend so many tears for the things of this present life; how am I to be bemoaned, pitied, and prayed 35

§§ 83–85 *add.* 3

3 as there] was, as there left 3 5

for! my Soul is dying, my soul is damning. Were my Soul but in a good condition, and were I but sure of it, ah! how rich should I esteem myself, though blest but with Bread and Water: I should count those but small afflictions, and should bear them as little 5 burdens. *A wounded Spirit who can bear?*

86. And though I was thus troubled and tossed and afflicted with the sight and sence and terrour of my own wickedness, yet I was afraid to let this sence and sight go quite off my minde: for I found that unless guilt of conscience was taken off the right way, that is, 10 by the Blood of Christ, a man grew rather worse for the loss of his trouble of minde, than better. Wherefore if my guilt lay hard upon me, then I should cry that the Blood of Christ might take it off: and if it was going off without it (for the sence of sin would be sometimes as if it would die, and go quite away), then I would also 15 strive to fetch it upon my heart again, by bringing the punishment for sin in Hell-fire upon my Spirit; and should cry, *Lord, let it not go off my heart but the right way, but by the Blood of Christ, and by the application of thy mercy thorow him to my Soul*; for that Scripture lay much upon me, *Without shedding of Blood there is no Remission*, 20 Heb. 9. 22. And that which made me the more afraid of this, was, Because I had seen some, who though when they were under Wounds of Conscience, then they would cry and pray, but they seeking rather present Ease from their Trouble, then Pardon for their Sin, cared not how they lost their guilt, so they got it out of 25 their minde; and, therefore having got it off the wrong way, it was not sanctified unto them, but they grew harder and blinder, and more wicked after their trouble. This made me afraid, and made me cry to God the more, that it might not be so with me.

87. And now was I sorry that God had made me a man, for I 30 feared I was a reprobate: I counted man, as unconverted, the most doleful of all the Creatures: Thus being afflicted and tossed about by my sad condition, I counted my self alone, and above the most of men unblest.

88. Yea, I thought it impossible that ever I should attain to so

§ 88 *add.* 3
22 then] *om.* 3   25 and, therefore] Now 3 5 6   28 the more] *add.* 3
32 by] *om.* 1–6.

much goodness of heart, as to thank God that he had made me a man. Man Indeed is the most noble, by creation, of all the creatures in the visible World; but by sin he has made himself the most ignoble. The beasts, birds, fishes, &c., I blessed their condition, for they had not a sinful nature, they were not obnoxious in the sight of God; they were not to go to Hell fire after death; I could therefore a rejoyced had my condition been as any of theirs.

89. In this condition I went a great while, but when comforting time was come, I heard one preach a sermon upon those words in the *Song* (*Song* 4. 1), *Behold thou art fair, my Love; behold, thou art fair;* but at that time he made these two words, *My Love,* his chief and subject matter; from which after he had a little opened the text, he observed these several conclusions: 1. *That the Church, and so every saved Soul, is Christs Love, when loveless: 2. Christs Love without a cause: 3. Christs Love when hated of the world: 4. Christs Love when under temptation, and under dissertion: 5. Christs Love from first to last.*

90. But I got nothing by what he said at present, only when he came to the application of the fourth particular, this was the word he said, *If it be so, that the saved soul is Christs love when under temptation and dissertion; then poor tempted Soul, when thou art assaulted and afflicted with temptation, and the hidings of Gods Face, yet think on these two words, MY LOVE, still.*

91. So as I was a going home, these words came again into my thoughts, and I well remember as they came in, I said thus in my heart, What shall I get by thinking on these two words? this thought had no sooner passed thorow my heart, but the words began thus to kindle in my Spirit, *Thou art my Love, thou art my Love,* twenty times together; and still as they ran thus in my minde, they waxed stronger and warmer, and began to make me look up; but being as yet between hope and fear, I still replied in my heart, *But is it true too? but is it true?* at which, that sentence fell in upon me, *He wist not that it was true which was done unto him of the angel,* Act. 12. 9.

92. Then I began to give place to the Word, which with power, did over and over make this joyful sound within my Soul, *Thou art my Love, thou art my Love; and nothing shall separate thee from my love;*

7 a] have 6   21 *temptation*] *temptations* 3 5 6   27 *Love²*] *Dove* 3 5 6
31 *too*] om. 3 5 6

and with that *Rom.* 8. 39 came into my minde. Now was my heart filled full of comfort and hope, and now I could believe that my sins should be forgiven me; yea, I was now so taken with the love and mercy of God, that I remember I could not tell how to contain till 5 I got home; I thought I could have spoken of his Love, and of his mercy to me, even to the very Crows that sat upon the plow'd lands before me, had they been capable to have understood me, wherefore I said in my Soul with much gladness, Well, I would I had a pen and ink here, I would write this down before I go any 10 further, for surely I will not forget *this* forty years hence; but alas! within less then forty days I began to question all again.

93. Yet still at times, I was helped to believe that it was a true manifestation of Grace unto my Soul, though I had lost much of the life and savour of it. Now about a week or fortnight after this, I was 15 much followed by this scripture, *Simon, Simon, behold, Satan hath desire to have you,* Luk. 22. 31. And sometimes it would sound so loud within me, yea, and as it were call so strongly after me, that once above all the rest, I turned my head over my shoulder, thinking verily that some man had behind me called to me, being at a great 20 distance, methought he called so loud, it came as I have thought since to have stirred me up to prayer and to watchfulness. It came to acquaint me that a cloud and a storm was coming down upon me, but I understood it not.

94. Also as I remember, that time as it called to me so loud, it 25 was the last time that it sounded in mine ears, but methinks I hear still with what a loud voice these words, *Simon, Simon,* sounded in my ears. I thought verily, as I have told you, that somebody had called after me that was half a mile behind me; and although that was not my name, yet it made me suddenly look behind me, 30 believing that he that called so loud meant me.

95. But so foolish was I, and ignorant, that I knew not the reason for this sound, (which as I did both see and feel soon after, was sent from heaven as an alarm to awaken me to provide for

---

§ 93 methought he . . . understood it not. *and* § 94 *add.* 3   §§ 93 *and* 94 *form a single* § *in* 3

3–7 yea, I was . . . understood me,] *add.* 5   11 again.] again, and by times, fell to my old courses again which made me begin to question all still *add.* 3

what was coming;) onely it would make me muse, and wonder in my minde to think what should be the reason that this Scripture, and that at this rate, so often and so loud, should still be sounding and ratling in mine ears. But, as I said before, I soon after perceived the end of God therein. 5

96. For about the space of a month after, a very great storm came down upon me, which handled me twenty times worse then all I had met with before: it came stealing upon me, now by one piece, then by another; first all my comfort was taken from me, then darkness seized upon me; after which whole flouds of Blas- 10 phemies, both against God, Christ, and the Scriptures, was poured upon my spirit, to my great confusion and astonishment. These blasphemous thoughts were such as also stirred up questions in me, against the very *being* of God, and of his onely beloved Son; as whether there were in truth a God or Christ, or no? and whether 15 the holy Scriptures were not rather a Fable and cunning Story, then the holy and pure Word of God?

97. The Tempter would also much assault me with this: How can you tell but that the Turks had as good Scriptures to prove their *Mahomet* the Saviour, as we have to prove our *Jesus* is; and 20 could I think that so many ten thousands in so many Countreys and Kingdoms, should be without the knowledge of the right way to Heaven (if there were indeed a Heaven) and that we onely, who live but in a corner of the Earth, should alone be blessed therewith? Everyone doth think his own Religion rightest, both *Jews*, and 25 *Moors*, and *Pagans*; and how if all our Faith, and Christ, and Scriptures, should be but a think-so too?

98. Sometime I have endeavoured to argue against these sugges- tions, and to set some of the Sentences of blessed *Paul* against them; but, alas! I quickly felt when I thus did, such arguings as these 30 would return again upon me; Though we made so great a matter of *Paul*, and of his words, yet how could I tell but that in very deed, he, being a subtle and cunning man, might give himself up to deceive with strong delusions, and also take both that pains and travel to undo and destroy his fellows? 35

99. These suggestions (with many other which at this time I

24 but] *om.* 3   34 that] the 5 6

may not, nor dare not utter, neither by word nor pen) did make
such a seizure upon my spirit, and did so over-weigh my heart,
both with their number, continuance, and fiery force, that I felt as
if there were nothing else but these from morning to night within
5 me, and as though, indeed, there could be room for nothing else;
and also concluded that God had in very wrath to my Soul given
me up unto them, to be carried away with them, as with a mighty
whirlwind.

100. Onely by the distaste that they gave unto my spirit, I felt
10 there was something in me that refused to embrace them: but this
consideration I then onely had, when God gave me leave to swallow
my spittle, otherwise the noise, and strength, and force of these
temptations would drown and overflow, and as it were bury all
such thoughts or the remembrance of any such thing. While I was
15 in this temptation, I should often find my mind suddenly put
upon it, to curse and swear, or to speak some grievous thing of *God*,
or *Christ* his *Son*, and of the *Scriptures*.

101. Now I thought surely I am possessed of the Devil; at other
times again I thought I should be bereft of my wits, for instead of
20 lauding and magnifying of *God* the *Lord* with others, if I have but
heard him spoken of, presently some most horrible blasphemous
thought or other would bolt out of my heart against him. So that
whether I did think that God was, or again did think there were
no such thing; no love, nor peace, nor gracious disposition could I
25 feel within me.

102. These things did sink me into very deep despair, for I
concluded, that such things could not possibly be found amongst
them that loved God. I often, when these temptations have been
with force upon me, did compare my self in the case of such a
30 Child, whom some Gypsie hath by force took up under her apron,
and is carrying from Friend and Country; kick sometimes I did,
and also scream and cry; but yet I was as bound in the wings of
the temptation, and the wind would carry me away. I thought also
of *Saul*, and of the evil spirit that did possess him; and did greatly
35 fear that my condition was the same with that of his, 1 Sam. 16. 14.

    29 in] to 5 6   30 under her apron] in her arms 3 5 6   32 scream]
shriek 3   35 , 1 Sam. 16. 14] *add.* 3

103. In these days, when I have heard others talk of what was the sin against the Holy *Ghost*, then would the Tempter so provoke me to desire to sin that sin, that I was as if I could not, must not, neither should be quiet until I had committed that; now no sin would serve but that: if it were to be committed by speaking of such a word, then I have been as if my mouth would have spoken that word whether I would or no; and in so strong a measure was this temptation upon me, that often I have been ready to clap my hand under my chin, to hold my mouth from opening; and to that end also I have had thoughts at other times to leap with my head downward, into some Muckhil-hole or other, to keep my mouth from speaking.

104. Now again I blessed the condition of the Dogge and Toad, and counted the estate of everything that *God* had made far better then this dreadfull state of mine, and such as my companions was: yea, gladly would I have been in the condition of Dog or Horse, for I knew they had no Soul to perish under the everlasting weights of Hell for sin, as mine was like to do: Nay, and though I saw this, felt this, and was broken to pieces with it, yet that which added to my sorrow, was, that I could not finde that with all my Soul I did desire deliverance. That Scripture did also tear and rend my soul in the midst of these distractions. *The wicked are like the troubled Sea which cannot rest, whose waters cast up mire and dirt: There is no peace to the wicked, saith my God*, Isa. 57. 20, 21.

105. And now my heart was, at times, exceeding hard; if I would have given a thousand pounds for a tear, I could not shed one; no, nor sometimes scarce desire to shed one. I was much dejected to think that this should be my lot. I saw some could mourn and lament their sin; and others, again, could rejoyce, and bless God for Christ; and others, again, could quietly talk of, and with gladness remember, the Word of God; while I only was in the storm or tempest. This much sunk me; I thought my condition was alone. I should, therefore, much bewail my hard hap; but get out of, or get rid of, these things, I could not.

106. While this temptation lasted, which was about a year, I

§ 105 *add.* 3
13 again] *add.* 3

could attend upon none of the Ordinances of *God*, but with sore and great affliction; yea, then was I most distressed with blasphemies: if I have been hearing the Word, then uncleanness, blasphemies, and despair, would hold me as Captive there; if I have been reading,
5 then sometimes I had sudden thoughts to question all I read; sometimes again my mind would be so strangely snatched away, and possessed with other things, that I have neither known, nor regarded, nor remembred so much as the sentence that but now I have read.

10 107. In prayer also, I have been greatly troubled at this time: sometimes I have thought I should see the Devil, nay, thought I have felt him behind me pull my cloaths: he would be also continually at me in the time of prayer, to have done, break off, make haste, you have prayed enough, and stay no longer: still drawing
15 my minde away. Sometimes also he would cast in such wicked thoughts as these, that I must pray to him, or for him: I have thought sometimes of that, *Fall down*, or, *If thou wilt fall down and worship me*, Mat. 4. 9.

108. Also when because I have had wandering thoughts in the
20 time of this duty, I have laboured to compose my mind and fix it upon God; then, with great force, hath the Tempter laboured to distract me and confound me, and to turn away my mind, by presenting to my heart and fancy the form of a Bush, a Bull, a Besom, or the like, as if I should pray to those; to these he would
25 also at some times (especially) so hold my mind, that I was as if I could think of nothing else, or pray to nothing else but to these, or such as they.

109. Yet at times I should have some strong and heart-affecting apprehensions of God, and the reality of the truth of his Gospel:
30 but oh how would my heart at such times put forth itself with unexpressable groanings! my whole Soul was then in every word; I should cry with pangs after *God*, that he would be merciful to me; but then I should be daunted again with such conceits as these, I should think that *God* did mock at these my prayers, saying,
35 and that in the audience of the holy Angels, This poor simple Wretch doth hanker after me, as if I had nothing to do with my

18, Mat. 4. 9] *add.* 3

mercy, but to bestow it on such as he: alas poor fool! how art thou deceived, it is not for such as thee to have favour with the Highest.

110. Then hath the Tempter come upon me also with such discouragements as these: You are very hot for mercy, but I will cool you; this frame shall not last alwayes; many have been as hot as you for a spirt, but I have quench'd their Zeal (and with this such and such who were fallen off, would be set before mine eyes) then I should be afraid that I should do so too: but, thought I, I am glad this comes into my minde; well, I will watch and take what heed I can: Though you do, said Satan, I shall be too hard for you, I will cool you insensibly, by degrees, by little and little: what care I, saith he, though I be seven years in chilling your heart, if I can do it at last; continual rocking will lull a crying Child asleep: I will ply it close, but I will have my end accomplished: though you be burning hot at present, yet, if I can pull you from this fire, I shall have you cold before it be long.

111. These things brought me into great straights; for as I at present could not find myself fit for present death, so I thought to live long would make me yet more unfit; for time would make me forget all, and wear even the remembrance of the evil of sin, the worth of Heaven, and the need I had of the Blood of Christ to wash me, both out of mind and thought: but I thank Christ Jesus, these things did not at present make me slack my crying, but rather did put me more upon it (*like her who met with the Adulterer*, Deut. 22. 25); in which dayes that was a good word to me, after I had suffered these things a while, *I am perswaded that neither Height, nor Depth, nor death nor life, &c. shall separate us from the love of God, which is in Christ Jesus*, Rom. 8. 38. And now I hoped long life should not destroy me, nor make me miss of Heaven.

112. Yet I had some supports in this temptation, though they were then all questioned by me: That in the third of *Jeremiah*, at the first, was something to me, and so was the consideration of the fifth verse of that Chapter; that though we have spoken and done

§§ 110 *and* 111 *form a single* § *in* 1 *and* 3

1 fool] Soul 3 5 6   27 *Height   nor Depth, nor*] add. 3

F

as evil things as we could, yet we should cry unto *God, My Father, thou art the Guide of my youth,* and should return unto him.

113. I had, also, once a sweet glance from that in 2 Cor. 5. 21. *For he hath made him to be sin for us, who knew no sin, that we might be made the righteousness of God in him.* I remember also that one day, as I was sitting in a Neighbours House, and there very sad at the consideration of my many blasphemies, and as I was saying in my mind, What ground have I to think that I, who have been so vile and abominable, should ever inherit eternal life; that word came suddenly upon me, *What shall we say to these things? If God be for us, who can be against us?* Rom. 8. 31. That also was an help unto me, *Because I live, you shall live also,* Joh. 14. 19. But these were but hints, touches, and short visits, though very sweet when present, onely they lasted not; *but, like to Peters Sheet, of a sudden were caught up from me to Heaven again,* Act. 10. 16.

114. But afterwards the Lord did more fully and graciously discover himself unto me; and indeed did quite not onely deliver me from the guilt that by these things was laid upon my Conscience, but also from the very filth thereof, for the temptation was removed, and I was put into my right mind again, as other Christians were.

115. I remember that one day, as I was travelling into the Countrey and musing on the wickedness and blasphemy of my heart, and considering of the enmity that was in me to *God,* that Scripture came in my mind, *He hath made peace by the blood of his Cross,* Col. 1. 20. by which I was made to see both again, and again, and again, that day, that *God* and my Soul were friends by this blood; yea, I saw that the *justice* of *God* and my *sinful* Soul, could imbrace and kiss each other through this blood: this was a good day to me, I hope I shall not forget it.

116. At another time, as I sat by the fire in my house, and musing on my wretchedness, the Lord made that also a precious word unto me, *For as much then as the children are partakers of flesh and blood, he also himself likewise took part of the same, that through death he might destroy him that had the power of death, that is the Devil: and deliver those who through the fear of death were all their life time subject to bondage,*

1 as¹] *add.* 3	24 *God*] rom. 1	27 and again,] *om.* 5

Heb. 2. 14, 15. I thought that the glory of these words was then so weighty on me, that I was both once and twice ready to swoon as I sat, yet not with grief and trouble, but with sollid joy and peace.

117. At this time also I sat under the Ministry of holy Mr. *Gifford*, whose Doctrine, by Gods grace, was much for my stability. This man made it much his business to deliver the People of God from all those false and unsound rests that by Nature we are prone to take and make to our Souls; he pressed us to take special heed, that we took not up any truth upon trust, as from this or that or another man or men, but to cry mightily to God, that he would convince us of the reality thereof, and set us down therein, by his own Spirit in the holy Word; for, said he, if you do otherwise, when temptations come, if strongly, you not having received them with evidence from Heaven, will find you want that help and strength now to resist, as once you thought you had.

118. This was as seasonable to my Soul, as the former and latter rain in their season; for I had found, and that by sad experience, the truth of these his words. (For I had felt, *no man can say*, especially when tempted of the Devil, *that Jesus Christ is Lord, but by the holy Ghost.*) Wherefore I found my Soul thorow Grace very apt to drink in this Doctrine, and to incline to pray to God that in nothing that pertained to Gods glory and my own eternal happiness, he would suffer me to be without the confirmation thereof from Heaven; for now I saw clearly there was an exceeding difference betwixt the notions of flesh and blood, and the Revelations of God in Heaven; also a great difference between that faith that is fained, and according to man's wisdom, and that which comes by a man being born thereto of God, *Mat.* 16. 15, 16, 1 *John* 5. 1.

119. But, oh! now, how was my Soul led from truth to truth by God! even from the birth and cradle of the Son of God, to his ascention and second coming from Heaven to judge the World.

120. Truly, I then found upon this account the great God was very Good unto me, for to my remembrance there was not any thing that I then cried unto God to make known and reveal unto me but he was pleased to do it for me, I mean not one part of the Gospel of the Lord Jesus, but I was orderly led into it; me thought

7 rests] tests 5 6   25 notions] notion 3 5 6   27 that] of that 1 3 5 6.

I saw with great evidence, from the relation of the four Evangelists, the wonderful work of God in giving Jesus Christ to save us, from his conception and birth, even to his second coming to judgement: me thought I was as if I had seen him born, as if I had seen him
5 grow up, as if I had seen him walk thorow this world, from the Cradle to his Cross; to which, also, when he came, I saw how gently he gave himself to be hanged and nailed on it for my sins and wicked doings; also as I was musing on this his progress, that droped on my Spirit, *He was ordained for the slaughter*, 1 Pet. 1. 19, 20.
10   121. When I have considered also the truth of his resurrection, and have remembred that word, *Touch me not Mary*, &c., I have seen, as if he leaped at the Graves mouth for joy that he was risen again, and had got the conquest over our dreadful foes, *John* 20. 17. I have also in the spirit seen him a man on the right hand of God the
15 Father for me, and have seen the manner of his comming from Heaven to judge the world with glory, and have been confirmed in these things by these Scriptures following, *Acts* 1. 9, 10; *Acts*. 7. 56; *Acts*. 10. 42; *Heb*. 7. 24; *Heb*. 8. 38; *Rev*. 1. 18; 1 *Thes*. 4. 17, 18.
     122. Once I was much troubled to know whether the Lord Jesus
20 was both Man as well as God, and God as well as Man; and truly in those dayes, let men say what they would, unless I had it with evidence from Heaven, all was as nothing to me, I counted not myself set down in any truth of God; well, I was much troubled about this point, and could not tell how to be resolved: at last, that
25 in the fift of the *Revelations* came into my mind, *And I beheld, and lo, in the midst of the Throne and of the four Beasts, and in the midst of the Elders stood a Lamb*; In the midst of the Throne, thought I, there is his Godhead, in the midst of the Elders, there is his man hood; but O methought this did glister, it was a goodly touch and gave me
30 sweet satisfaction; that other Scripture also did help me much in this, *To us a Child is born, to us a Son is given; and the government shall be upon his shoulder: and his Name shall be called Wonderful, Counsellor, the Mighty God, the Everlasting Father, the Prince of Peace*, &c. Isa. 9. 6.
     123. Also besides these teachings of God in his Word, the Lord
35 made use of two things to confirm me in these things, the one was

§§ 121 *and* 122 *form a single* § *in* 1 *and* 3
6 his] the 6   27 thought I,] *add.* 5

the errors of the *Quakers*, and the other was the guilt of sin; for as the *Quakers* did oppose his Truth, so God did the more confirm me in it, by leading me into the Scriptures that did wonderfully maintain it.

124. The errors that this people then maintained were: 1. That the holy Scriptures were not the Word of God. 2. That every man in the world had the spirit of Christ, grace, faith, &c. 3. That Christ Jesus, as crucified, and dying 1600 years ago, did not satisfy divine justice for the sins of the people. 4. That Christ's flesh and blood was within the saints. 5. That the bodies of the good and bad that are buried in the churchyard shall not arise again. 6. That the resurrection is past with good men already. 7. That that man Jesus, that was crucified between two thieves on Mount Calvary, in the land of Canaan, by Jerusalem, was not ascended up above the starry heavens. 8. That he should not, even the same Jesus that died by the hands of the Jews, come again at the last day, and as man judge all nations, &c.

125. Many more vile and abominable things were in those days fomented by them, by which I was driven to a more narrow search of the Scriptures, and was, through their light and testimony, not only enlightened, but greatly confirmed and comforted in the truth; and as I said, the guilt of sin did help me much, for still as that would come upon me, the blood of Christ did take it off again, and again, and again, and that too, sweetly, according to the Scriptures; O Friends, cry to God to reveal Jesus Christ unto you, *there is none teacheth like him.*

126. It would be too long for me here to stay, to tell you in particular how God did set me down in all the things of Christ, and how he did, that he might so do, lead me into his words, yea and also how he did open them unto me, make them shine before me, and cause them to dwell with me and comfort me over and over, both of his own being, and the being of his Son, and Spirit, and Word, and Gospel.

127. Onely this, as I said before I will say unto you again, that in general he was pleased to take this course with me, first, to suffer

§§ 124 *and* 125 *to* . . . comforted in the truth *add.* 5
27 for me] *om.* 5

me to be afflicted with temptation concerning them, and then reveal them to me; as sometimes I should lie under great guilt for sin, even crushed to the ground therewith, and then the Lord would shew me the death of Christ, yea and so sprinkle my Con-
5 science with his Blood, that I should find, and that before I was aware, that in that Conscience where but just now did reign and rage the Law, even there would rest and abide the Peace and Love of *God* thorow Christ.

128. Now had I an evidence, as I thought, of my salvation from
10 Heaven, with many golden Seals thereon, all hanging in my sight; now could I remember this manifestation, and the other discovery of grace with comfort; and should often long and desire that the last day were come, that I might for ever be inflamed with the sight, and joy, and communion of him, whose Head was crowned
15 with Thorns, whose Face was spit on, and Body broken, and Soul made an offering for my sins: for whereas before I lay continually trembling at the mouth of Hell; now me thought I was got so far therefrom, that I could not, when I looked back, scarce discern it; and O thought I, that I were fourscore years old now, that I might
20 die quickly, that my soul might be gone to rest.

129. But before I had got thus far out of these my temptations, I did greatly long to see some ancient Godly man's Experience, who had writ some hundred of years before I was born; for, for those who had writ in our days, I thought (but I desire them now to
25 pardon me) that they had Writ only that which others felt, or else had, thorow the strength of their Wits and Parts, studied to answer such Objections as they perceived others were perplexed with, without going down themselves into the deep. Well, after many such longings in my mind, the God in whose hands are all our days
30 and ways, did cast into my hand, one day, a book of *Martin Luther*, his comment on the *Galathians*, so old that it was ready to fall piece from piece, if I did but turn it over. Now I was pleased much that such an old book had fallen into my hand; the which, when I had

§§ 129–31 *add.* 3

9–10 Now had I . . . from Heaven] Now had I an evidence for Heaven 1 3
28–29 many such longings] many longings 3   30 and ways] *add.* 5
31 his comment on the *Galathians*, so old] ; it was his Comment on the *Galatians*; it also was so old 5

but a little way perused, I found my condition in his experience, so largely and profoundly handled, as if his Book had been written out of my heart; this made me marvel: for thus thought I, this man could not know anything of the state of Christians now, but must needs write and speak of the Experience of former days.   5

130. Besides, he doth most gravely also, in that book debate of the rise of these temptations, namely, Blasphemy, Desperation, and the like, shewing that the law of *Moses*, as well as the Devil, Death, and Hell, hath a very great hand therein; the which at first was very strange to me, but considering and watching, I found it so 10 indeed. But of Particulars here I intend nothing, only this methinks I must let fall before all men, I do prefer this book of Mr. *Luther* upon the *Galathians*, (excepting the Holy Bible) before all the books that ever I have seen, as most fit for a wounded Conscience.

131. And now I found, as I thought, that I loved Christ dearly. 15 O me thought my Soul cleaved unto him, my affections cleaved unto him. I felt love to him as hot as fire, and now, as Job said, I thought I should die in my nest; but I did quickly find, that my great love was but little, and that I, who had, as I thought, such burning love to Jesus Christ, could let him go again for a very trifle. God can 20 tell how to abase us; and can hide pride from Man. Quickly after this my love was tried to purpose.

132. For after the Lord had in this manner thus graciously delivered me from this great and sore temptation, and had set me down so sweetly in the Faith of his holy gospel, and had given me 25 such strong consolation and blessed evidence from heaven touching my interest in his love through Christ; the Tempter came upon me again, and that with a more grievous and dreadful temptation then before.

133. And that was to sell and part with this most blessed Christ, 30 to exchange him for the things of this life; for any thing: the temptation lay upon me for the space of a year, and did follow me so continually, that I was not rid of it one day in a month, no not sometimes one hour in many dayes together, unless I was asleep.

134. And though, in my judgement, I was perswaded, that those 35

12 Mr. *Luther*] *Martin Luther* 6   16 cleaved²] cleave 3 5 6   23 For] But 1
34 unless] unless when 5 6

who were once effectually in Christ (as I hoped, through his grace,
I had seen my self) could never lose him for ever, *For the land shall
not be sold for ever, for the Land is mine,* saith *God,* Levit. 25. 23, yet it
was a continual vexation to me, to think that I should have so
5 much as one such thought within me against a Christ, a Jesus, that
had done for me as he had done; and yet then I had almost none
others, but such blasphemous ones.

135. But it was neither my dislike of the thought, nor yet any
desire and endeavour to resist it, that in the least did shake or
10 abate the continuation or force and strength thereof; for it did
alwayes in almost whatever I thought, intermix itself therewith,
in such sort that I could neither eat my food, stoop for a pin, chop a
stick, or cast mine eye to look on this or that, but still the temptation would come, *Sell Christ for this, or sell Christ for that; sell him, sell*
15 *him.*

136. Sometimes it would run in my thoughts not so little as
a hundred times together, Sell him, sell him, sell him; against
which, I may say, for whole hours together I have been forced to
stand as continually leaning and forcing my spirit against it, lest
20 haply before I were aware, some wicked thought might arise in my
heart that might consent thereto; and sometimes also the Tempter
would make me believe I had consented to it, then should I be as
tortured on a Rack for whole dayes together.

137. This temptation did put me to such scares lest I should at
25 sometimes, I say, consent thereto, and be overcome therewith, that
by the very force of my mind in labouring to gainsay and resist this
wickedness my very Body also would be put into action or motion,
by way of pushing or thrusting with my hands or elbows; still
answering, as fast as the destroyer said, *Sell him;* I will not, I will not,
30 I will not, I will not, no not for thousands, thousands, thousands of
worlds; thus reckoning lest I should in the midst of these assaults,
set too low a vallue of him, even until I scarce well knew where I
was, or how to be composed again.

138. At these seasons he would not let me eat my food at quiet,

§ 138 *add.* 3

6–7 and yet . . . blasphemous ones] *add.* 5   14–15 ; sell him, sell him] *add.* 3
28 with my hands or elbows] *add.* 5   34 eat] *om.* 3

but forsooth, when I was set at the Table at my meat, I must go hence to pray, I must leave my food now, just now, so counterfeit holy would this Divel be. When I was thus tempted, I should say in myself, *Now I am at my meat, let me make an end. No*, said he, *you must do it now, or you will displease God, and despise Christ.* Wherefore I was much 5 afflicted with these things; and because of the sinfulness of my nature, (imagining that these things were impulses from God) I should deny to do it as if I denyed God; and then should I be as guilty because I did not obey a temptation of the Devil, as if I had broken the Law of God indeed. 10

139. But to be brief, one morning, as I did lie in my Bed, I was, as at other times, most fiercely assaulted with this temptation, to *sell and part with Christ*; the wicked suggestion still running in my mind, *Sell him, sell him, sell him, sell him*, as fast as a man could speak; against which also in my mind, as at other times, I answered, No, 15 no, not for thousands, thousands, thousands, at least twenty times together; but at last, after much striving, even until I was almost out of breath, I felt this thought pass through my heart, *Let him go if he will!* and I thought also that I felt my heart freely consent thereto. Oh, the diligence of Satan! Oh, the desperateness of man's 20 heart!

140. Now was the battel won, and down I fell, as a Bird that is shot from the top of a Tree, into great guilt and fearful despair; thus getting out of my Bed, I went moping into the field; but God knows with as heavy a heart as mortal man, I think, could bear; 25 where for the space of two hours, I was like a man bereft of life, and as now past all recovery, and bound over to eternal punishment.

141. And withal, that Scripture did seize upon my Soul, *Or profane person, as Esau, who for one morsel of meat sold his Birth-right; for you know how that afterwards when he would have inherited the blessing, he* 30 *was rejected, for he found no place of repentance, though he sought it carefully with tears*, Heb. 12. 16, 17.

142. Now was I as one bound, I felt myself shut up unto the Judgment to come; nothing now for two years together would

§ 142 *add.* 5
4–5 *Now . . . Christ*] rom. 3   5 *you will*] I should 3   19 freely] *add.* 5
20–21 thereto. . . . heart!] *add.* 5   thereto,] thereto, and where was my love to
Christ now. 3

abide with me, but damnation, and an expectation of damnation: I say, nothing now would abide with me but this, save some few moments for relief, as in the sequel you will see.

143. These words were to my Soul like Fetters of Brass to my 5 Legs, in the continual sound of which I went for several months together. But about ten or eleven a Clock one day, as I was walking under a Hedge, full of sorrow and guilt God knows, and bemoaning my self for this hard hap, that such a thought should arise within me, suddenly this sentence bolted in upon me, *The Blood of Christ remits* 10 *all guilt*; at this I made a stand in my Spirit: with that, this word took hold upon me, *The blood of Jesus Christ his Son cleanseth us from all sin*, 1 John 1. 7.

144. Now I began to conceive peace in my Soul, and methought I saw as if the Tempter did lear and steal away from me, as being 15 ashamed of what he had done. At the same time also I had my sin, and the Blood of Christ thus represented to me, That my sin when compared to the Blood of Christ, was no more to it, than this little clot or stone before me, is to this vast and wide field that here I see: This gave me good encouragement for the space of two or three 20 hours; in which time also, me thought I saw by faith the Son of God as suffering for my sins. But because it tarried not, I therefore sunk in my spirit under exceeding guilt again.

145. But chiefly by the aforementioned Scripture, concerning *Esaus* selling of his Birth-right; for that Scripture would lie all day 25 long, all the week long; yea, all the year long in my mind, and hold me down, so that I could by no means lift up my self; for when I would strive to turn me to this Scripture, or that for relief, still that Sentence would be sounding in me, *For ye know, how that afterward, when he would have inherited the blessing he found no place of repentance,* 30 *though he sought it carefully with tears.*

146. Sometimes, indeed, I should have a touch from that in *Luk.* 22. 31, *I have prayed for thee, that thy Faith fail not*; but it would not abide upon me: neither could I indeed, when I consider'd my state, find ground to conceive in the least, that there should be the root

of that Grace within me, having sinned as I had done. Now was I tore and rent in heavy case, for many days together.

147. Then began I with sad and careful heart, to consider of the nature and largeness of my sin, and to search in the word of God, if I could in any place espy a word of Promise, or any encouraging Sentence by which I might take relief. Wherefore I began to consider that third of *Mark, All manner of sins and blasphemies shall be forgiven unto the sons of men, wherewith soever they shall blaspheme*: Which place, me thought, at a blush, did contain a large and glorious Promise for the pardon of high offences; but considering the place more fully, I thought it was rather to be understood, as relating more chiefly to those who had, while in a natural state, committed such things as there are mentioned, but not to me, who had not onely received light and mercie but that had both after and also contrary to that, so slighted Christ as I had done.

148. I feared therefore that this wicked sin of mine might be that sin unpardonable, of which he there thus speaketh, *But he that shall blaspheme against the Holy Ghost, hath never forgiveness, but is in danger of eternal damnation*, Mar. 3: And I did the rather give credit to this, because of that sentence in the *Hebrews, For you know how that afterwards, when he would have inherited the blessing, he was rejected; for he found no place of repentance, though he sought it carefully with tears.* For this stuck always with me.

149. And *now* was I both a burthen and a terror to myself, nor did I ever so know, as *now*, what it was to be weary of my life, and yet afraid to die. Oh, how gladly now would I have been anybody but myself! Any thing but a man! and in any condition but mine own! for there was nothing did pass more frequently over my mind, than that it was impossible for me to be forgiven my transgression, and to be saved from wrath to come.

150. And now began I to labour to call again time that was past; wishing a thousand times twice told, that the day was yet to come, when I should be tempted to such a sin; concluding with great indignation, both against my heart and all assaults, how I would

§ 149 *add*. 5

2 in heavy] in a heavy 3 5 6   19 Mar. 3.] *add*. 3   22–23 For this stuck always with me.] *add*. 3   For] And 5 6

rather have been torn in pieces, than found a consenter thereto: but alas! these thoughts and wishings, and resolvings, were now too late to help me; the thought had passed my heart, God hath let me go, and I am fallen: *O,* thought I, *that it was with me as in months past,* 5 *as in the days when God preserved me!* Job 29. 2.

151. Then again, being loath and unwilling to perish, I began to compare my sin with others, to see if I could find that any of those that are saved had done as I had done. So I considered *David's* Adultery and Murder, and found them most hainous crimes, and 10 those too committed after light and grace received: but yet by considering, I perceived that his transgressions were onely such as were against the Law of *Moses,* from which the Lord Christ could, with the consent of his Word deliver him: but mine was against the *Gospel,* yea, against the Mediator thereof; I had sold my Saviour.

15 152. Now again should I be as if racked upon the Wheel; when I considered, that, besides the guilt that possessed me, I should be *so* void of grace, *so* bewitched: What, thought I, must it be no sin but this? Must it needs be the *great transgression,* Psal. 19. 13? Must *that* wicked one touch my Soul, 1 *Joh.* 5. 18? O what stings did I find 20 in all these Sentences!

153. What? thought I, is there but one sin that is unpardonable? But one sin that layeth the Soul without the reach of Gods Mercy, and must I be guilty of that? Must it needs be that? Is there but one sin among so many millions of sins, for which there is no forgiveness, 25 and must I commit this? Oh! unhappy sin! Oh unhappy Man! These things would so break and confound my Spirit, that I could not tell what to do, I thought at times they would have broke my wits, and still to aggravate my misery, that would run in my mind, *You know how that afterwards when he would have inherited the blessing, he* 30 *was rejected.* Oh! none knows the terrors of those days but my self.

154. After this I came to consider of *Peters* sin which he committed in denying his Master; and indeed this came nighest to mine, of any that I could find; for he had denied his Saviour as I, and that after Light and Mercy received; yea, and that too, after warning

§ 153 *add.* 3

5 *preserved*] *persecuted* 3   14 I had sold my Saviour.] *add.* 3   23 Must it needs be that?] *add.* 5   30 Oh! . . . my self.] *ital.* 3 6

given him: I also considered that he did it both once and twice; and that, after time to consider betwixt. But though I put all these circumstances together, that if possible I might find help, yet I considered again, that his was but *a denial of his Master*, but mine was *a selling of my Saviour*. Wherefore I thought with my self, that I came nearer to *Judas*, than either to *David* or *Peter*.

155. Here again, my torment would flame out and afflict me; yea, it would grind me as it were to powder, to discern the preservation of God towards others, while I fell into the snare: For in my thus considering of other mens sins, and comparing of them with my own, I could evidently see how God preserved them notwithstanding their wickedness, and would not let them, as he had let me, to become a son of perdition.

156. But O how did my Soul at this time prize the preservation that God did set about his People! Ah how safely did I see them walk, whom God had hedged in! they were within his care, protection, and special providence: though they were full as bad as I by nature, yet because he loved them, he would not suffer them to fall without the range of Mercy: but as for me, I was gone, I had done it; he would not preserve me, nor keep me, but suffered me, because I was a Reprobate, to fall as I had done. Now did those blessed places, that spake of *Gods keeping his people*, shine like the Sun before me, though not to comfort me, but to shew me the blessed state and heritage of those whom the Lord had blessed.

157. Now I saw, that as God had his hand in all providences and dispensations that overtook his Elect, so he had his hand in all the temptations that they had to sin against him, not to animate them unto wickedness, but to chuse their temptations and troubles for them; and also to leave them, for a time, to such sins only as might not destroy, but humble them; as might not put them beyond, but lay them in the way of the renewing of his mercie. But Oh, what love, what care, what kindness and mercy did I now see, mixing itself with the most severe and dreadful of all God's ways to his people! He would let *David, Hezekiah, Solomon, Peter,* and others fall, but he would not let them fall into sin unpardonable, nor into hell

§ 157 *add.* 5
13 to] *om.* 3 5 6   26 dispensations] dispensation 5 6.

for sin. Oh! thought I, these be the men that God hath loved; these be the men that God, though he chastizes them, keeps them in safety by him, and them whom he makes to abide under the shaddow of the Almighty. But all these thoughts added sorrow, 5 grief, and horrour to me, as whatever I now thought on, it was killing to me. If I thought how God kept his own, that was killing to me; If I thought of how I was falling myself, that was killing to me. As all things wrought together for the best, and to do good to them that were the called, according to his purpose; so I thought 10 that all things wrought for my dammage, and for my eternal overthrow.

158. Then again, I began to compare my sin with the sin of *Judas*, that if possible I might find that mine differed from that which in truth is unpardonable; and, O thought I, if it should differ 15 from it, though but the breadth of an hair, what a happy condition is my Soul in! And, by considering, I found that *Judas* did his intentionally, but mine was against my prayer and strivings; besides, his was committed with much deliberation, but mine in a fearful hurry, on a sudden; all this while I was tossed to and fro, 20 like the Locusts, and driven from trouble to sorrow; hearing always the sound of *Esau's* fall in mine ears, and of the dreadful consequences thereof.

159. Yet this consideration about *Judas*, his sin, was for a while some little relief unto me: for I saw I had not, as to the circum- 25 stances, transgressed so foully as he: but this was quickly gone again, for, I thought with my self, there might be more ways then one to commit the unpardonable sin; and that too, there might be degrees of that, as well as of other transgressions: wherefore, for ought I yet could perceive, this iniquity of mine might be such as 30 might never be passed by.

160. I was often now ashamed, that I should be like such an ugly man as *Judas*: I thought also how loathsome I should be unto all the Saints at the Day of Judgment, insomuch that now I could scarce see a good Man, that I believed had a good Conscience, but I should

§§ 160-3 to . . . *was rejected.* add. 3   About this time . . . *with tears.* add. 5

14-15 if . . . hair] if it should be but the breadth of an hair 1 3   19 all this while] Thus I was 1   27 and that too,] also I thought that 1

feel my heart tremble at him, while I was in his presence. Oh! now I saw a glory in walking with God, and what a mercy it was to have a good Conscience before him.

161. I was much about this time tempted to content myself, by receiving some false Opinion; as that there should be no such thing 5 as a Day of Judgment, that we should not rise again, and that sin was no such grievous thing. The Tempter suggesting thus, *For if these things should indeed be true, yet to believe otherwise, would yield you ease for the present. If you must perish, never torment yourself so much beforehand, drive the thoughts of damning out of your mind, by possessing* 10 *your mind with some such conclusions that* Atheists *and* Ranters *use to help themselves withal.*

162. But Oh! when such thoughts have passed thorow my heart, how, as it were within a step hath Death and Judgement been in my view! Methought the Judge stood at the door, I was as if 'twas 15 come already: so that such things could have no entertainment; but methinks I see by this, that Satan will use any means to keep the Soul from Christ. He loveth not an awakened frame of spirit, security, blindness, darkness, and error is the very kingdom and habitation of the Wicked one.   20

163. I found it hard work now to pray to God, because despair was swallowing me up. I thought I was as with a Tempest driven away from God, for always when I cried to God for mercy, this would come in, *'Tis too late; I am lost, God hath let me fall, not to my correction, but condemnation: My sin is unpardonable, and I know, concern-* 25 *ing* Esau, *how that, after he had sold his Birth-right, he would have received the Blessing, but was rejected.* About this time, I did light on that dreadful story of that miserable mortal, *Francis Spira*; A book that was to my troubled spirit as salt, when rubbed into a fresh wound; every sentence in that book, every groan of that man, with 30 all the rest of his actions in his dolors, as his tears, his prayers, his gnashing of teeth, his wringing of hands, his twining and twisting, languishing and pining away under that mighty hand of God that was upon him, was as knives and daggers in my Soul; especially that sentence of his was frightful to me, *Man knows the beginning of* 35

sin, but who bounds the issues thereof? Then would the former sentence, as the conclusion of all, fall like a hot thunder-bolt again upon my Conscience; *for you know how that afterwards, when he would have inherited the blessing, he was rejected; for he found no place of repentance,* 5 *though he sought it carefully with tears.*

164. Then was I struck into a very great trembling, insomuch that at sometimes I could for whole days together feel my very body as well as my minde to shake and totter under the sence of the dreadful Judgement of God, that should fall on those that have 10 sinned that most fearful and unpardonable sin. I felt also such a clogging and heat at my stomach by reason of this my terrour, that I was, especially at some times, as if my breast-bone would have split in sunder. Then I thought of that concerning *Judas, Who, by his falling headlong, burst asunder, and all his bowels gushed out,* Act. 1.

15 165. I feared also that this was the mark that the Lord did set on *Cain,* even continued fear and trembling under the heavy load of guilt that he had charged on him for the blood of his Brother *Abel.* Thus did I wind, and twine, and shrink under the burden that was upon me; which burden also did so oppress me, that I could neither 20 stand nor go, nor lie either at rest or quiet.

166. Yet that saying would sometimes come to my mind, *He hath received gifts for the rebellious,* Psal. 68. 18. *The rebellious?* thought I; Why surely they are such as once were under subjection to their Prince, even those who after they have sworn subjection to his 25 Government, have taken up arms against him; and this, thought I, is my very condition; once I loved him, feared him, served him; but now I am a rebel; I have sold him, I have said, Let him go if he will; but yet he has gifts for rebels, and then why not for me?

167. This sometimes I thought on, and should labour to take 30 hold thereof; that some, though small, refreshment might have been conceived by me: but in this also I missed of my desire, I was driven with force beyond it, like a man that is going to the place of execution, even by that place where he would fain creep in, and hide himself, but may not.

35 168. Again, After I had thus considered the sins of the Saints in

§ 166 and this . . . not for me? *add.* 5
21 my] *om.* 1   32 like] I was like 5 6

particular, and found mine went beyond them; then I began to think thus with myself: Set case I should put all theirs together, and mine alone against them, might I not then finde some encouragement? for if mine, though bigger than any one, yet should but be equal to all, then there is hopes: for that Blood that hath 5 vertue enough to wash away all theirs, hath also vertue enough to do away mine, though this one be full as big, if no bigger, then all theirs. Here again, I should consider the sin of *David*, of *Solomon*, of *Manasseh*, of *Peter*, and the rest of the great offenders, and should also labour what I might, with fairness, to aggravate and heighten 10 their sins by several circumstances: but, alas! 'twas all in vain.

169. I should think with myself that *David* shed blood to cover his Adultery, and that by the Sword of the Children of *Ammon*, a work that could not be done but by continuance and deliberate contrivance, which was a great aggravation to his sin. But then this 15 would turn upon me: Ah, but these were but sins against the Law, from which there was a Jesus sent to save them, but yours is a sin against the Saviour, and who shall save you from that?

170. Then I thought on *Solomon*, and how he sinned, in loving strange women, in falling away to their Idols, in building them 20 Temples, in doing this after light, in his old age, after great mercy received: but the same Conclusion that cut me off in the former consideration, cut me off as to this; namely, that all those were but sins against the Law, for which God had provided a remedy, *but I had sold my Saviour*, and there now remained no more Sacrifice for sin. 25

171. I would then add to those mens sins the sins of *Manasseh*, how that he built Altars for Idols in the house of the Lord, he also observed times, used Inchantments, had to do with Wizzards, was a Witch, had his familiar Spirits, burned his Children in the fire in Sacrifice to Devils, and made the Streets of *Jerusalem* run down with the blood 30 of Innocents. These thought I are great sins, sins of a bloudy colour, yea, it would turn again upon me, *they are none of them of the nature of yours, you have parted with Jesus! you have sold your Saviour!*

§§ 169, 170, *and* 171 add. 3

6–8 vertue enough . . . all theirs] virtue enough in it to wash away all theirs, hath virtue enough in it to do away mine 3 5 6   11 but, alas! 'twas all in vain.] *om.* 5 6   17 a sin] *add.* 5   24–25 *but . . . Saviour*] rom. 3   28 Witch] Wizzard 6   32–33 *they . . . Saviour!*] rom. 3

G

172. This one consideration would always kill my Heart, *My sin was point-blank against my Saviour*, and that too, at that height, that I had in my heart said of him, *Let him go if he will*. Oh! me thoughts, this sin was bigger than the sins of a Countrey, of a Kingdom, or
5 of the whole World, no one pardonable, nor all of them together, was able to equal mine, mine out-went them every one.

173. Now I should find my minde to flee from God, as from the face of a dreadful Judge; yet this was my torment, I could not escape his hand. (*It is a fearful thing to fall into the hands of the living*
10 *God*, Heb. 10.). But blessed be his grace, that scripture, in these flying fits would call as running after me, *I have blotted out as a thick cloud thy transgressions, and, as a cloud thy sins: Return unto me, for I have redeemed thee*, Isa. 44. 22. This, I say, would come in upon my mind, when I was fleeing from the face of God; for I did flee from his face,
15 that is, my mind and spirit fled before him; by reason of his highness, I could not endure; then would the text cry, *Return unto me, for I have redeemed thee*. Indeed, this would make me make a little stop, and, as it were, look over my shoulder behind me, to see if I could discern that the God of grace did follow me with a pardon in
20 his hand, but I could no sooner do that, but all would be clouded and darkened again by that sentence, *For you know how that afterward, when he would have inherited the blessing, he found no place of repentance, though he sought it carefully with tears*. Wherefore I could not return, but fled, though at some times it cried *Return, return*, as if it did
25 hollow after me: But I feared to close in therewith, lest it should not come from God, for that other, as I said was still sounding in my conscience, *For you know how that afterwards, when he would have inherited the Blessing, he was rejected*, &c.

174. Once as I was walking to and fro in a good mans Shop,
30 bemoaning to myself in my sad and doleful state, afflicting myself with self abhorrence for this wicked and ungodly thought; lamenting also this hard hap of mine, for that I should commit so great a sin, greatly fearing I should not be pardoned; praying also in my heart, That if this sin of mine did differ from that against the Holy

§ 174 *add.* 3

13–23 This, I say . . . *tears.*] add. 5   23 Wherefore] But 1 3   24 *return²*] add. 3
26 as I said] *add.* 5

Ghost, the Lord would shew it me: and being now ready to sink
with fear, suddenly there was as if there had rushed in at the Window, the noise of Wind upon me, but very pleasant, and as if I had
heard a Voice speaking, *Didst ever refuse to be justified by the Blood of
Christ?* and withal my whole life of profession past, was in a moment 5
opened to me, wherein I was made to see, that designedly I had
not; so my heart answered groaningly *No.* Then fell with power
that Word of God upon me, *See that ye refuse not him that speaketh,*
Heb. 12. 25. This made a strange seisure upon my spirit; it brought
light with it, and commanded a silence in my heart of all those 10
tumultuous thoughts that before did use, like masterless hell-
hounds, to roar and bellow, and make a hideous noise within me.
It showed me, also, that Jesus Christ had yet a work of Grace and
Mercy for me, that he had not, as I had feared, quite forsaken and
cast off my Soul; yea, this was a kind of chide for my proneness to 15
desparation; a kind of a threatning me if I did not, notwithstanding
my sins and the hainousness of them, venture my Salvation upon
the Son of God. But as to my determining about this strange dispensation, what it was, I knew not; from whence it came, I knew
not. I have not yet in twenty years time been able to make a Judg- 20
ment of it. *I thought then what here I should be loath to speak.* But verily
that sudden rushing Wind, was as if an Angel had come upon me;
but both it and the Salutation I will leave until the Day of Judgement, only this I say, it commanded a great calm in my Soul, it
perswaded me there might be hope; it shewed me, as I thought, 25
what the sin unpardonable was, and that my Soul had yet the blessed
priviledge to flie to Jesus Christ for Mercy. But, I say, concerning
this dispensation, I know not what yet to say unto it; which was
also in truth the cause that at first I did not speak of it in the Book.
I do now, also, leave it to be thought on by men of sound Judgment. 30
I lay not the stress of my Salvation thereupon, but upon the Lord
Jesus, in the Promise; yet, seeing I am here unfolding of my secret
things, I thought it might not be altogether inexpedient to let
this also shew itself, though I cannot now relate the matter as
there I did experience it. This lasted in the savour of it, for about 35

7 *No*] rom. 3   9–19 This ... dispensation,] *add.* 5   19 it¹] this 3   knew]
know 3   from] or from 3

three or four dayes, and then I began to mistrust, and to despair again.

175. Wherefore still my life hung in doubt before me, *not knowing which way I should tip*; only this I found my Soul desire, even to cast it self at the foot of Grace by Prayer and Supplication. But, O 'twas hard for me now to bear the face to pray to this Christ for mercie, against whom I had thus most vilely sinned! it was hard work, I say, to offer to look him in the face against whom I had so vilely sinned; and, indeed, I have found it as difficult to come to God by prayer, after backsliding from him, as to do any other thing. O the shame that did *now* attend me! especially when I thought I am *now* a-going to pray to him for mercy that I had so lightly esteemed but a while before! I was ashamed; yea, even confounded, because this villainy had been committed by me; but I saw there was but one way with me, I must go to him and humble myself unto him, and beg that he, of his wonderful mercy, would show pity to me, and have mercy upon my wretched sinful Soul.

176. Which when the Tempter perceived, he strongly suggested to me, That I ought not to pray to God, for Prayer was not for any in my case, neither could it do me good, because I had rejected the Mediator, by whom all Prayers came with acceptance to God the Father, and without whom no Prayer could come into his presence; wherefore now to pray, is but to adde sin to sin: yea, now to pray, seeing God hath cast you off, is the next way to anger and offend him more then ever you did before.

177. For God (said he) hath been weary of you for these several years already, because you are none of his; your bauling in his ears hath been no pleasant voice to him; and, therefore he let you sin this sin, that you might be quite cut off, and will you pray still? This the Devil urged, and set forth by that in *Numbers*, which *Moses* said to the children of *Israel*, *That because they would not go up to possess the Land when God would have them, therefore for ever after he did bar them out from thence, though they prayed they might with tears*, Num. 14. 36, 37, &c.

---

3 Wherefore still] All this while 1   4 Soul desire] Soul's desire 6   6 now] *add.* 5   7–17 it was hard . . . sinful Soul.] yet I knew this must be the way, for mercy was no where else. 1 3   25 ever you] you ever 6   30 by that . . . which] that . . . when 3

178. As 'tis said in another place, *Exod.* 21. 14: *The man that sins presumptuously, shall be taken from Gods Altar, that he may die*: even as *Joab* was by King *Solomon*, when he thought to find shelter there, 1 Kings 2. 28, &c. These places did pinch me very sore; yet my case being desperate, I thought with myself, I can but die; and if it must be so, it shall once be said, That such a one died at the foot of Christ in Prayer: this I did, but with great difficulty, God doth know; and that because, together with this, still that saying about *Esau* would be set at my heart, even like a flaming sword, to keep the way of the tree of Life, lest I should take thereof, and live. O who knows how hard a thing I found it to come to God in prayer?

179. I did also desire the Prayers of the people of God for me, but I feared that God would give them no heart to do it; yea, I trembled in my Soul to think that some or other of them shortly would tell me, that God had said those words to them that he once did say to the Prophet concerning the Children of Israel, *Pray not for this People, for I have rejected them,* Jer. 11. 14. So, *pray not for him, for I have rejected him*: Yea, I thought that he had whispered this to some of them already, onely they durst not tell me so, neither durst I ask them of it, for fear if it should be so, it would make me quite besides my self: *Man knows the beginning of sin,* (said *Spira*) *but who bounds the issues thereof?*

180. About this time I took an opportunity to break my Mind to an Antient Christian; and told him all my case. I told him also that I was afraid that I had sinned the sin against the Holy Ghost; and he told me, *He thought so too.* Here therefore I had but cold comfort, but, talking a little more with him, I found him, though a good man, a stranger to much Combate with the Devil. Wherefore I went to God again as well as I could, for Mercie still.

181. Now also did the Tempter begin to mock me in my misery, saying, That seeing I had thus parted with the Lord Jesus, and provoked him to displeasure who should have stood between my Soul and the flame of devouring fire, there was now but one way; and that was, to pray that God the Father would be the Mediator

§ 180 *add.* 3

8 and . . . this] for 1   16 *not*] *not thou* 6   33 there was now but one way] the way was now but one 3

betwixt his Son and me, that we might be reconciled again, and
that I might have that blessed benefit in him that his blessed Saints
enjoyed.

182. Then did that Scripture seize upon my soul, *He is of one*
5 *mind, and who can turn him?* Oh I saw 'twas as easie to perswade him
to make a new World, a new Covenant, or new Bible besides that
we have already, as to pray for such a thing: this was to perswade
him that what he had done already was meer folly, and perswade
with him to alter, yea, to disanul the whole way of Salvation; and
10 then would that saying rent my Soul asunder, *Neither is there salvation*
in any other, for there is none other Name under heaven, given amongst men,
whereby we must be saved, Act. 4. 12.

183. Now the most free, and full, and gracious words of the
Gospel were the greatest torment to me; yea, nothing so afflicted
15 me as the thoughts of Jesus Christ: for the remembrance of a
Saviour, because I had cast him off, brought both the villainy of my
sin, and my loss by it to mind. Nothing did twinge my Conscience
like this. Every time that I thought of the Lord Jesus, of his Grace,
Love, Goodness, Kindness, Gentleness, Meekness, Death, Blood,
20 Promises and blessed Exhortations, Comforts and Consolations, it
went to my Soul like a Sword; for still, unto these my considerations
of the Lord Jesus, these thoughts would make place for themselves
in my heart; *Ay, This is the Jesus, the loving Saviour, the Son of God,*
whom thou hast parted with, whom you slighted, despised, and abused. This
25 *is the only Saviour, the only Redeemer, the only one that could so love*
sinners as to wash them from their sins in his own most precious Blood: but
you have no part nor lot in this Jesus, you have put him away from you, you
have said in your heart, Let him go if he will. *Now, therefore, you are*
severed from him; you have severed yourself from him. Behold, then, his
30 *Goodness, but you yourself be no partaker of it.* O thought I, what have I
lost! What have I parted with! What have I dis-inherited my poor
Soul of! Oh! 'tis sad to be destroyed by the grace and mercy of
God; to have the Lamb, the Saviour, turn Lyon and Destroyer,
Rev. 6. I also trembled, as I have said, at the sight of the Saints of
35 God, especially at those that greatly loved him, and that made it

16 both] forth 5 6   17–32 Nothing did ... poor Soul of!] *add.* 5   34 as
I have said,] *add.* 3

their business to walk continually with him in this world: for they did both in their words, their carriages, and all their expressions of tenderness and fear to sin against their precious Saviour, condemn, lay guilt upon, and also add continual affliction and shame unto my soul. *The dread of them was upon me, and I trembled at God's* Samuels, 5 1 *Sam.* 16. 4.

184. Now, also, the Tempter began afresh to mock my soul another way, saying, That Christ, indeed, did pity my case, and was sorry for my loss, but forasmuch as I had sinned, and transgressed as I had done, he could by no means help me, nor save me 10 from what I feared; for my sin was not of the nature of theirs, for whom he bled and died, neither was it counted with those that were laid to his charge when he hanged on the tree; therefore unless he should come down from Heaven, and die anew for this sin, though indeed he did greatly pity me, yet I could have no benefit 15 of him. These things may seem ridiculous to others, even as ridiculous as they were in themselves, but to me they were most tormenting cogitations; every of them augmented my misery, that Jesus Christ should have so much love as to pity me when he could not help me; nor did I think that the reason why he could not help 20 me was because his Merits were weak, or his Grace and Salvation spent on them already, but because his faithfulness to his threatning would not let him extend his mercy to me. Besides, I thought, as I have already hinted, that my sin was not within the bounds of that pardon that was wrapped up in a promise; and if not, then I knew 25 assuredly, that it was more easie for Heaven and Earth to pass away than for me to have Eternal Life. So that the ground of all these fears of mine did arise from a stedfast belief that I had of the stability of the holy Word of God, and, also, from my being misinformed of the nature of my sin. 30

185. But O how this would add to my affliction, to conceit that I should be guilty of such a sin, for which he did not die! These thoughts would so confound me, and imprison me, and tie me up from Faith, that I knew not what to do: but Oh thought I, that he would come down again, O that the work of Mans Redemption 35

5–6 *The dread . . .* 1 *Sam.* 16. 4.] *add.* 3   8 another way] *add.* 5
16–30 These things . . . of my sin.] *add.* 5

was yet to be done by Christ; how would I pray him, and intreat him to count and reckon this sin amongst the rest for which he died! But this Scripture would strike me down, as dead, *Christ being raised from the dead, dieth no more: Death hath no more dominion over him,* 5 Rom. 6. 9.

186. Thus, by the strange and unusual assaults of the tempter, was my Soul, like a broken Vessel, driven, as with the Winds, and tossed sometimes head-long into dispair; sometimes upon the Covenant of works, and sometimes to wish that the new Covenant, 10 and the conditions thereof, might, so far forth as I thought myself concerned, be turned another way, and changed. But in all these, I was but as those that jostle against the Rocks; more broken, scattered, and rent. Oh, the unthought of imaginations, frights, fears, and terrors that are affected by a thorow application of guilt, 15 yielding to desparation! This is the man that hath his dwelling among the Tombs with the dead; that is alwayes crying out, and cutting himself with stones, Mark 5. 2–5. But I say, all in vain; desparation will not comfort him, the old Covenant will not save him. Nay, Heaven and Earth shall pass away before one jot or tittle 20 of the Word and Law of Grace shall fall or be removed: this I saw, this I felt, and under this I groaned. Yet this advantage I got thereby, namely, a further confirmation of the certainty of the way of Salvation, and that the Scriptures were the Word of God. Oh! I cannot now express what then I saw and felt of the steadiness of 25 Jesus Christ, the Rock of Man's Salvation, what was done could not be undone, added to, nor altered; I saw, indeed, that sin might drive the Soul beyond Christ, even the sin which is unpardonable; but woe to him that was so driven, for the word would shut him out.

187. Thus was I always sinking, whatever I did think or do. So 30 one day I walked to a neighbouring Town, and sate down upon a Settle in the Street, and fell into a very deep pause about the most fearful state my sin had brought me to; and, after long musing, I lifted up my head, but methought I saw as if the Sun that shineth in the Heavens did grudge to give me light, and as if the very stones

§ 186 *add.* 3

3 as dead] *add.* 3   15 yielding] and yielding 3 5   26 I saw, indeed, that] indeed 3

in the street, and tiles upon the houses, did bend themselves against me, me-thought that they all combined together to banish me out of the World; I was abhorred of them, and unfit to dwell among them, or be partaker of their benefits, because I had sinned against the Saviour. O how happy now was every creature over I was! For they stood fast and kept their station, but I was gone and lost.

188. Then breaking out in the bitterness of my Soul, I said to my self, with a grievous sigh, *How can God comfort such a wretch as I?* I had no sooner said it but this returned upon me, as an eccho doth answer a voice, *This sin is not unto death.* At which I was as if I had been raised out of a grave, and cryed out again, *Lord, how couldst thou find out such a word as this?* For I was filled with admiration at the fitness, and also at the unexpectedness of the sentence. The fitness of the word, the rightness of the timing of it: the power, and sweetness, and light, and glory that came with it also, was marvelous to me to find. I was now, for the time, out of doubt, as to that about which I so much was in doubt before, my fears before were, that my sin was not pardonable, and so that I had no right to pray, to repent, &c., or that if I did, it would be of no advantage or profit to me, but now, thought I, if this sin is not unto death, then it is pardonable, therefore from this I have encouragement to come to God by Christ for mercie, to consider the promise of forgiveness, as that which stands with open arms to receive me as well as others; this, therefore, was a great easment to my mind, to wit, that my sin was pardonable, that it was not the sin unto death, 1 *Jo.* 5. 16, 17. None but those that know what my trouble, (by their own experience,) was, can tell what relief came to my soul by this consideration; it was a release to me, from my former bonds, and a shelter from my former storm, I seemed now to stand upon the same ground with other sinners and to have as good right to the word and prayer as any of they.

189. Now, I say, I was in hopes that my sin was not unpardonable, but that there might be hopes for me to obtain forgiveness. But O how Satan now did lay about him, for to bring me down again! But he could by no means do it, neither this day nor the

2–5 me-thought . . . Saviour] *add.* 5   7–8 to my self] *add.* 3   13–31 The fitness of the word . . . as any of they.] *add.* 5   32 , I say,] *add.* 6

most part of the next: for this sentence stood like a Mill-post at my
back. Yet towards the evening of the next day, I felt this word
begin to leave me, and to withdraw its supportation from me, and
so I returned to my old fears again, but with a great deal of grudg-
5 ing and peevishness, for I feared the sorrow of despair; nor could
my faith now longer retain this word.

190. But the next day at evening, being under many fears, I
went to seek the Lord; and as I prayed, I cryed, and my Soul cried
to him in these words, with strong cries: *O Lord, I beseech thee show*
10 *me that thou hast loved me with an everlasting love*, Jer. 31. 3. I had no
sooner said it, but with sweetness it returned upon me, as an ecco
or sounding again, *I have loved thee with an everlasting love*. Now I went
to bed at quiet, also when I awaked the next morning, it was fresh
upon my Soul and I believed it.

15 191. But yet the Tempter left me not, for it could not be so little
as an hundred times that he that day did labour to break my peace.
O the combats and conflicts that I did then meet with! as I strove to
hold by this word, that of *Esau* would flie in my face, like to
Lightning: I should be sometimes up and down twenty times in an
20 hour. Yet God did bear me up, and keep my heart upon this word,
from which I had also for several days together very much sweetness and comfortable hopes of pardon. For thus it was made out to
me, *I loved thee whilst thou wast committing this sin, I loved thee before, I*
love thee still, and I will love thee for ever.

25 192. Yet I saw my sin most barbarous, and a filthy crime, and
could not but conclude, and that with great shame and astonishment, that I had horribly abused the holy *Son* of *God*: wherefore I
felt my soul greatly to love and pity him, and my bowels to yearn
towards him: for I saw he was still my friend, and did reward me
30 good for evil: yea, the love and affection that then did burn within
to my Lord and Saviour Jesus Christ, did work at this time such a
strong and hot desire of revengement upon my self for the abuse
I had done unto him, that, to speak as then I thought, had I
had a thousand gallons of blood within my veins, I could freely

5–6 despair . . . word] it 1 3   8–9 I . . . cries] I cryed to him in these
words 1   11 it]this 5   11–12 as an ecco or sounding again,] *add.* 5
14 and I believed it] *add.* 5

then have spilt it all at the command and feet of this my Lord and Saviour.

193. And as I was thus in musing and in my studies, how to love the Lord and to express my love to him, that saying came in upon me, *If thou, Lord, shouldst mark iniquity, O Lord, who should stand? but there is forgiveness with thee, that thou mayst be feared,* Psal. 130. 3, 4. These were good words to me, especially the latter part thereof, to wit, that there is forgiveness with the Lord, that he might be feared; that is, as then I understood it, that he might be loved, and had in reverence: for it was thus made out to me, *That the great God did set so high an esteem upon the love of his poor Creatures, that rather then he would go without their love he would pardon their transgressions.*

194. And now was that word fulfilled on me, and I was also refreshed by it, *Then shall they be ashamed and confounded, and never open their mouth any more because of their shame, when I am pacified towards thee for all that thou hast done, saith the Lord God,* Ezek. 16. 36. Thus was my Soul at this time, (and as I then did think for ever) set at liberty from being again afflicted with my former guilt and amazement.

195. But before many weeks were over I began to dispond again, fearing lest notwithstanding all that I had injoyed, that yet I might be deceived and destroyed at the last: for this consideration came strong into my mind, That whatever comfort and peace I thought I might have from the word of the Promise of Life, yet unless there could be found in my refreshment a concurrance and agreement in the Scriptures, let me think what I will thereof, and hold it never so fast, I should finde no such thing at the end: *For the Scriptures cannot be broken,* John 10. 35.

196. Now began my heart again to ake, and fear I might meet with disappointment at the last. Wherefore I began with all seriousness to examine my former comfort, and to consider whether one that had sinned as I had done, might with confidence trust upon the faithfulness of God laid down in those words by which I had been comforted, and on which I had leaned myself; but now was brought those sayings to my minde, *For it is impossible for those*

who were once enlightned and have tasted of the heavenly gift, and were made partakers of the holy Ghost, and have tasted the good word of God, and the Powers of the World to come; if they shall fall away, to renew them again unto repentance Heb. 6. *For if we sin wilfully after we have received*
5 *the knowledge of the truth, there remains no more sacrifice for sin, but a certain fearful looking for of Judgement and fiery Indignation, which shall devour the adversaries,* Heb. 10. *Even as Esau, who for one morsel of meat sold his Birthright; for ye know how that afterwards, when he would have inherited the Blessing, he was rejected; for he found no place of repentance,*
10 *though he sought it carefully with tears,* Heb. 12.

197. Now was the word of the Gospel forced from my Soul, so that no Promise or Encouragement was to be found in the Bible for me: and now would that saying work upon my spirit to afflict me, *Rejoyce not, O Israel, for joy, as other People,* Hos. 9. 1. For I saw indeed
15 there was cause of rejoycing for those that held to Jesus; but as for me, I had cut myself off by my transgressions, and left myself neither foot-hold, nor hand-hold amongst all the stayes and props in the precious Word of Life.

198. And truly I did now feel myself to sink into a gulf, as an
20 house whose foundation is destroyed. I did liken myself in this condition unto the case of some Child that was fallen into a Mill-pit, who though it could make some shift to scrable and spraul in the water, yet because it could find neither hold for hand nor foot, therefore at last it must die in that condition. So soon as this fresh
25 assault had fastened on my Soul, that Scripture came into my heart, *This is for many days,* Dan. 10. 14. and indeed I found it was so: for I could not be delivered nor brought to peace again until well-nigh two years and an half were compleatly finished. Wherefore these words, though in themselves they tended to discouragement, yet to
30 me, who feared this condition would be eternal, they were at some times as an help and refreshment to me.

199. For, thought I, *many days* are not for ever; *many days* will have an end; therefore seeing I was to be afflicted, not a few, but *many days,* yet I was glad it was but *for many days.* Thus, I say, I could
35 recal myself sometimes, and give myself a help: for as soon as ever the word came in, at first I knew my trouble would be long, yet this

would be but sometimes, for I could not always think on this, nor ever be helped by it though I did.

200. Now while these Scriptures lay before me, and laid sin anew at my door, that saying in the 18 of *Luke*, with others, did encourage me to prayer: then the Tempter again laid at me very sore, suggest- 5 ing, That neither the mercy of God, nor yet the blood of Christ, did at all concern me, nor could they help me, for my sin; therefore it was but in vain to pray. Yet, thought I, I will pray. But, said the Tempter, Your sin is unpardonable. Well, said I, I will pray. 'Tis no boot, said he. Yet, said I, I will pray. So I went to prayer to 10 God; and while I was at prayer, I uttered words to this effect: *Lord, Satan tells me, That neither thy mercy, nor Christs blood is sufficient to save my soul: Lord, shall I honour thee most by believing thou wilt and canst, or him, by believing thou neither wilt nor canst? Lord, I would fain honour thee by believing thou wilt and canst.* 15

201. And as I was thus before the Lord, that Scripture fastned on my heart, *O man, great is thy Faith*, Matt. 15. 28. even as if one had clapt me on the back, as I lay on my knees before *God*; yet I was not able to believe this, that this was a prayer of Faith, till almost six months after; for I could not think that I had Faith, or that there 20 should be a word for me to act Faith on; therefore I should still be as sticking in the jaws of desparation, and went mourning up and down in a sad condition, crying, *Is his mercy clean gone? is his mercy clean gone for ever?* And I thought sometimes, even while I was groaning in these expressions, they did seem to make a question 25 whether it was or no; yet I greatly feared it was.

202. There was nothing now that I longed for more then to be put out of doubt as to this thing in question, and as I was vehemently desiring to know if there was hope, these words came rowling into my mind, *will the Lord cast off forever? and will he be favourable no* 30 *more? Is his mercie clean gone for ever? doth his promise fail for evermore? Hath God forgotten to be gracious? hath he in anger shut up his tender*

---

§ 202 *add.* 3

2 by it] *add.* 5   3 anew] *add.* 3   7–8 therefore it was but in vain to pray.] *add.* 5   9–10 'Tis no boot, said he. Yet, said I, I will pray.] *add.* 5   14 *him*] add. 5   17 Matt. 15. 28.] *add.* 3   18 lay] was 3 5 6   19 that this was a prayer of Faith] *add.* 5   23–26 crying . . . feared it was.] *add.* 5   27 now] *add.* 5   28 in question] *add.* 5   29 hope] indeed hopes for me 5

mercies? Psal. 77. 7, 8, 9. and all the while they run in my minde, methought I had this still as the answer, 'Tis a question whether he hath or no; It may be he hath not: yea, the interrogatory seemed to me to carry in it a sure affirmation that indeed he had not, nor
5 would so cast off, but would be favourable, that his promise doth not fail, and that he had not forgotten to be gracious, nor would in anger shut up tender mercie; Something also there was upon my heart at the same time which I now cannot call to minde, which with this Text did sweeten my heart, and made me conclude that
10 his mercie might not be quite gone, not clean gone for ever.

203. At another time I remember I was again much under the Question, Whether the blood of Christ was sufficient to save my Soul? In which doubt I continued from morning till about seven or eight at night; and at last, when I was, as it were, quite worn out
15 with fear lest it should not lay hold on me, those words did sound suddenly within me, *He is able*: but me thought this word *able*, was spoke so loud unto me, it shewed such a *great* word, it seemed to be writ in *great* letters, and gave such a justle to my fear and doubt, (I mean for the time it tarried with me, which was about a day) as I
20 never had from that, all my life either before or after that, *Heb.* 7. 25.

204. But one morning when I was again at prayer and trembling under the fear of this, that no word of God could help me, that piece of a sentence darted in upon me, *My Grace is sufficient.* At this me thought I felt some stay, as if there might be hopes. But O how
25 good a thing is it for God to send his Word! for about a fortnight before, I was looking on this very place, and then I thought it could not come near my Soul with comfort, and threw down my Book in a pet; then I thought it was not large enough for me; no, not large enough; but now it was as if it had arms of grace so wide,
30 that it could not onely inclose me, but many more besides.

205. By these words I was sustained, yet not without exceeding conflicts, for the space of seven or eight weeks: for my peace would be in and out sometimes twenty times a day: Comfort now, and

3–7 yea . . . mercie;] *add.* 5   15 those] these 3 5 6   16 me] my
heart 5 6   17–18 it seemed to be writ in *great* letters,] *add.* 3   20 that]
om. 5   27 and]; therefore I 5 6   26–28 then I . . . large enough] *add.* 5
30 besides] such as I besides 5 6   33 in] in it 3 5 6

Trouble presently; Peace now, and before I could go a furlong, as full of Fear and Guilt as ever heart could hold; and this was not onely now and then, but my whole seven weeks experience; for this about the sufficiency of grace, and that of *Esau*'s parting with his Birth-right, would be like a pair of scales within my mind, some- 5 times one end would be uppermost, and sometimes again the other, according to which would be my peace or trouble.

206. Therefore I still did pray to God, that he would come in with this Scripture more fully on my heart, to wit, that he would help me to apply the whole sentence, for as yet I could not: that he 10 gave, I gathered; but farther I could not go, for as yet it only helped me to hope there might be mercy for me, *My grace is sufficient*; and tho it came no farther, it answered my former question; to wit, that there was hope; yet, because *for thee* was left out, I was not con- tented, but prayed to God for that also: Wherefore, one day as I 15 was in a Meeting of Gods People, full of sadness and terrour, for my fears again were strong upon me, and as I was now thinking, my soul was never the better, but my case most sad and fearful, these words did with great power suddainly break in upon me, *My grace is sufficient for thee, my grace is sufficient for thee, my grace is sufficient for* 20 *thee*; three times together; and, O me-thought that every word was a mighty word unto me; as *my*, and *grace*, and *sufficient*, and *for thee*; they were then, and sometimes are still, far bigger than others be.

207. At which time, my Understanding was so enlightned, that I was as though I had seen the Lord Jesus look down from Heaven 25 through the Tiles upon me, and direct these words unto me; this sent me mourning home, it broke my heart, and filled me full of joy, and laid me as low as the dust, only it stayed not long with me, I mean in this glory and refreshing comfort, yet it continued with me for several weeks, and did encourage me to hope. But so soon 30 as that powerful operation of it was taken off my heart, that other about *Esau* returned upon me as before; so my soul did hang as in a pair of Scales again, sometimes up, and sometimes down, now in peace, and anon again in terror.

208. Thus I went on for many weeks, sometimes comforted, and 35

10–11 for as yet . . . could not go] *add.* 5   12 to hope . . . for me] thus far 1 3
31 off] of 3

sometimes tormented, and, especially at some times my torment would be very sore, for all those Scriptures forenam'd in the *Hebrews* would be set before me, as the only sentences that would keep me out of Heaven. Then, again, I should begin to repent, that ever that thought went thorow me; I should also think thus with myself, why, How many Scriptures are there against me? there is but three or four, and cannot God miss them, and save me for all of them? Sometimes again I should think, O if it were not for these three or four words, now how might I be comforted! and I could hardly forbear at some times, but to wish them out of the Book.

209. Then methought I should see as if both *Peter,* and *Paul,* and *John,* and all the Writers did look with scorn upon me, and hold me in derision; and as if they said unto me, All our words are truth, one of as much force as another; it is not we that 'have cut you off, but you have cast away yourself; there is none of our sentences that you must take hold upon but these, and such as these; *It is impossible; there remains no more sacrifice for sin,* Heb. 6. *And it had been better for them not to have known the will of God, than after they have known it, to turn from the holy commandment delivered unto them,* Heb. 10. *For the Scriptures cannot be broken,* 2 Pet. 2. 21.

210. These, as the Elders of the City of Refuge, I saw were to be the Judges both of my Case and me, while I stood with the avenger of blood at my heels, trembling at their Gate for deliverance; also with a thousand fears and mistrusts, that they would shut me out for ever, *Josh.* 20. 3, 4.

211. Thus was I confounded, not knowing what to do nor how to be satisfied in this question, whether the Scriptures could agree in the salvation of my Soul? I quaked at the Apostles; I knew their words were true, and that they must stand for ever.

212. And I remember one day, as I was in diverse frames of Spirit, and considering that these frames were still according to the nature of the several Scriptures that came in upon my mind; if this of Grace, then I was quiet; but if that of *Esau,* then tormented. Lord, thought I, if both these Scriptures would meet in my heart at once, I wonder which of them would get the better of me. So

§ 210 *add.* 3

6 is] are 5 6   24 that] I doubted that 5 6

me thought I had a longing mind that they might come both together upon me; yea, I desired of God they might.

213. Well, about two or three dayes after, so they did indeed;
they boulted both upon me at a time, and did work and struggle
strangly in me for a while; at last, that about *Esaus* birthright began 5
to wax weak, and withdraw, and vanish; and this about the
sufficiency of Grace prevailed, with peace and joy. And as I was in a
muse about this thing, that Scripture came home upon me, *Mercy
rejoyceth against Judgment*, Jas. 2. 13.

214. This was a wonderment to me, yet truly I am apt to think 10
it was of God, for the Word of the Law and Wrath must give place
to the Word of Life and Grace; because, though the Word of Condemnation be glorious, yet the Word of Life and Salvation, doth far
exceed in glory, 2 *Cor.* 3. 8, 9, 10, 11. *Mar.* 9. 5, 6, 7. *John.* 6. 37.
Also, that *Moses* and *Elias* must both vanish, and leave Christ and 15
his Saints alone.

215. This Scripture also did now most sweetly visit my soul,
And him that cometh to me I will in no wise cast out, John 6. 37. O the
comfort that I have had from this word, *in no wise*! as who should
say, by no means, for no thing, what-ever he hath done. But Satan 20
would greatly labour to pull this promise from me, telling of me,
that Christ did not mean me, and such as I, but sinners of a lower
rank, that had not done as I had done. But I should answer him
again, Satan, here is in this word no such exception; but *him that
comes, him,* any *him; him that cometh to me, I will in no wise cast out.* And 25
this I well remember still, that of all the slights that Satan used to
take this Scripture from me, yet he never did so much as put this
Question, But do you come aright? And I have thought the reason
was, because he thought I knew full well what coming a-right was;
for I saw that to come aright was to come as I was, a vile and 30
ungodly sinner, and to cast myself at the feet of Mercy, condemning
myself for sin: If ever Satan and I did strive for any word of God in
all my life, it was for this good word of Christ; he at one end and I
at the other. Oh, what work did we make! It was for this in *John,*

9 Jas. 2. 13.] *add.* 3   24 this word] these words 6   29 a-right] *add.* 5
32—p. 68, line 3 If ever Satan . . . sweetness from it.] If ever Satan and I did strive
for any word, it was for this in *John*; he pull'd, and I pull'd, but God be praised, I got
some sweetness from it. 1 3

H

I say, that we did so tug and strive: he pull'd and I pull'd; but, God be praised, I got the better of him, I got some sweetness from it.

216. But, notwithstanding all these helps and blessed words of grace, yet that of *Esaus* selling of his birthright would still at times distress my Conscience; for though I had been most sweetly comforted, and that but just before, yet when that came into my mind, 'twould make me fear again. I could not be quite rid thereof, 'twould every day be with me: wherefore now I went another way to work, even to consider the nature of this blasphemous thought; I mean if I should take the words at the largest, and give them their own natural force and scope, even every word therein: So when I had thus considered, I found, that if they were fairly taken, they would amount to this, That I had freely left the Lord Jesus Christ to his choice, whether he would be my Saviour or no, for the wicked words were these, *Let him go if he will.* Then that Scripture gave me hope, *I will never leave thee nor forsake thee,* Heb. 13. 5. O Lord, said I, but I have left thee; then it answered again, *but I will not leave thee.* For this I thank God also.

217. Yet I was grievous afraid he should, and found it exceedingly hard to trust him, seeing I had so offended him: I could have been exceeding glad that this thought had never befallen, for then I thought I could, with more ease, freedom and abundance, have leaned upon his grace: I see it was with me, as it was with *Josephs* Brethren; the guilt of their own wickedness did often fill them with fears, that their Brother would at last despise them, *Gen.* 50. 15, 16, 17, 18.

218. But above all the Scriptures that yet I did meet with, that in the twentieth of *Joshua* was the greatest comfort to me, which speaks of the slayer that was to flee for refuge. *And if the avenger of blood pursue the slayer, then,* saith Moses, *they that are the Elders of the City of Refuge, shall not deliver him into his hand; because he smote his Neighbour unwittingly, and hated him not afore-time.* O blessed be God for this word! I was convinced that I was the slayer; and that the avenger of blood pursued me, that I felt with great terrour; only now it remained that I enquire whether I have right to enter the

23 freedom and] and freedom *all edd.*

City of Refuge. So I found, That he must not, *who lay in wait to shed blood*: it was not the wilful murderer, but he who *unwittingly* did it, he who did *unawares shed blood*; not out of spight, or grudge, or malice, he that shed it unwittingly, even he who did not *hate his Neighbour before*. Wherefore,   5

219. I thought verily I was the man that must enter, for because I had smitten my Neighbour *unwittingly, and hated him not afore-time*. I hated Him not afore-time, no, I prayed unto him, was tender of sinning against him; yea, and against this wicked Temptation I had strove for a twelve-moneth before; yea, and also when it did pass 10 thorow my heart, it did it in spite of my teeth: Wherefore I thought I had right to enter this City, and the Elders, which are the Apostles, were not to deliver me up. This, therefore, was great comfort to me, and did give me much ground of hope.

220. Yet being very critical, for my smart had made me that I 15 knew not what ground was sure enough to bear me, I had one question that my Soul did much desire to be resolved about; and that was, *Whether it be possible for any Soul that hath indeed sinned the unpardonable sin, yet after that to receive, though but the least true spiritual comfort from God thorow Christ?* the which, after I had much con- 20 sidered, I found the answer was, No, they could not: and that for these reasons:

221. First, Because those that have sinned that sin, they are debarred a share in the Blood of Christ, and being shut out of that, they must needs be void of the least ground of hope, and so of 25 spiritual comfort; *for to such there remains no more sacrifice for sins*, Heb. 10. 26, 27. Secondly, Because they are denied a share in the promise of Life: they shall never be forgiven, neither in this world, nor in that which is to come, *Mat.* 12. 32. Thirdly, The Son of God excludes them also from a share in his blessed intercession, being for ever 30 shamed to own them both before his holy Father, and the blessed Angels in heaven, *Mark* 8.

222. When I had with much deliberation considered of this matter, and could not but conclude that the Lord had comforted me, and that too after this my wicked sin: then methought I durst 35

2–4 it was not . . . shed it unwittingly,] but he who *unwittingly*, or that did un-awares shed blood. 1 3

venture to come nigh unto those most fearful and terrible Scriptures, with which all this while I had been so greatly affrighted, and on which indeed before I durst scarce cast mine eye, (yea, had much ado an hundred times to forbear wishing of them out of the Bible, 5 for I thought they would destroy me) but now, I say, I began to take some measure of incouragement, to come close to them, to read them, and consider them, and to weigh their scope and tendence.

223. The which when I began to do, I found their visage changed; for they looked not so grimly on me as before I thought they did: 10 And first, I came to the sixth of the *Hebrews*, yet trembling for fear it should strike me; which, when I had considered, I found that the falling there intended was a falling *quite away*; that is, as I conceived, a falling from, and an absolute denial of, the Gospel of Remission of sins by Christ: for from them the Apostle begins his argument, *ver.* 15 1, 2, 3. Secondly, I found that this falling away must be openly, even in the view of the World, even so as *to put Christ to an open shame*. Thirdly, I found that those he there intendeth were for ever shut up of God both in blindness, hardness, and impenitency: *It is impossible they should be renewed again unto repentance.* By all these 20 particulars, I found, to Gods everlasting praise, my sin was not the sin in this place intended.

First, I confessed I was fallen, but not fallen away, that is, from the profession of Faith in Jesus unto eternal Life.

Secondly, I confessed that I had put Jesus Christ to *shame* by my 25 sin, but not to open *shame*. I did not deny him before men, nor condemn him as a fruitless one before the World.

Thirdly, nor did I find that God had shut me up, or denied me to come, though I found it hard work indeed to come to him by sorrow and repentance; blessed be God for unsearchable Grace.

30 224. Then I considered that in the tenth of the *Hebrews*; and found that the *wilful Sin* there mentioned is not every wilful sin, but that which doth throw off Christ, and then his Commandments too. Secondly, That must also be done openly, before two or three witnesses, to answer that of the law, *ver.* 28. Thirdly, This sin cannot 35 be committed but with great despite done to the Spirit of Grace;

despising both the disswasions from that sin, and the perswasions to the contrary: But the Lord knows, though this my sin was devilish, yet it did not amount to these.

225. And as touching that in the twelfth of the *Hebrews*, about *Esau's* selling his Birth-right, though this was that which kill'd 5 me, and stood like a Spear against me; yet now I did consider, First, That his was not a hasty thought against the continual labour of his mind; but a thought consented to and put in practice likewise, and that too after some deliberation, *Gen.* 25. Secondly, it was a publick and open action, even before his Brother, if not 10 before many more; this made his sin of a far more hainous nature than otherwise it would have been. Thirdly, He continued to slight his Birth-right: *He did eat and drink, and went his way; thus Esau* DESPISED *his birthright:* Yea, twenty year after, he was found to despise it still. *And Esau said, I have enough, my Brother, keep that thou* 15 *hast to thyself, Gen.* 33. 9.

226. Now as touching this, That *Esau sought a place of repentance;* thus I thought: First, This was not for the *Birth-right,* but for the *Blessing;* this is clear from the Apostle, and is distinguished by *Esau* himself, *He hath taken away my birthright* (that is, formerly); *and now* 20 *he hath taken away my Blessing also,* Gen. 27. 36. Secondly, Now, this being thus considered, I came again to the Apostle, to see what might be the mind of God in a New-Testament stile and sence concerning *Esau's* sin; and so far as I could conceive, this was the mind of God, that the *Birth-right* signified *Regeneration,* and the 25 *Blessing* the *Eternal Inheritance;* for so the Apostle seems to hint, *Lest there be any profane person, as Esau, who for one morsel of meat sold his Birth-right:* as if he should say, Lest there be any person amongst you that shall cast off all those blessed beginnings of God that at present are upon him, in order to a new Birth, lest they become as 30 *Esau,* even be rejected afterwards, when they would inherit the Blessing.

227. For many there are who, in the day of Grace and Mercy despise those things which are indeed the Birth-right to Heaven, who yet, when the deciding-day appears, will cry as loud as *Esau,* 35 *Lord, Lord, open to us;* but then, as *Isaac* would not repent, no more will God the Father, but will say, *I have blessed these, yea, and they*

shall be blessed; but as for you, *Depart you are workers of iniquity*, Gen. 27. 32. Luk. 13. 25, 26, 7.

228. When I had thus considered these Scriptures, and found that thus to understand them was not against but according to other Scriptures; this still added further to my encouragement and comfort, and also gave a great blow to that objection, to wit, *That the Scriptures could not agree in the salvation of my Soul*. And now remained only the hinder part of the Tempest, for the thunder was gone beyond me, onely some drops did still remain, that now and then would fall upon me: but because my former frights and anguish were very sore and deep, therefore it did oft befal me still as it befalleth those that have been scared with fire, I thought every voice was fire, fire; every little touch would hurt my tender Conscience.

229. But one day, as I was passing in the field, and that too with some dashes on my Conscience, fearing lest yet all was not right, suddenly this sentence fell upon my Soul, *Thy righteousness is in Heaven*; and methought withall, I saw with the eyes of my Soul Jesus Christ at Gods right hand, there, I say, as my Righteousness; so that wherever I was, or whatever I was a doing, God could not say of me, *He wants my Righteousness*, for that was just before him. I also saw moreover, that it was not my good frame of Heart that made my Righteousness better, nor yet my bad frame that made my Righteousness worse: for my Righteousness was Jesus Christ himself, *the same yesterday, and to-day, and for ever*, Heb. 13. 8.

230. Now did my chains fall off my Legs indeed, I was loosed from my affliction and irons, my temptations also fled away: so that from that time those dreadful Scriptures of God left off to trouble me; now went I also home rejoycing, for the grace and love of God: So when I came home, I looked to see if I could find that Sentence, *Thy Righteousness is in Heaven*, but could not find such a Saying, wherefore my Heart began to sink again, onely that was brought to my remembrance, *He of God is made unto us Wisdom, Righteousness, Sanctification, and Redemption*; by this word I saw the other Sentence true, 1 Cor. 1. 30.

231. For by this Scripture, I saw that the Man Christ Jesus, as

19 as] was 3 5 6   35 1 Cor. 1. 30] 1 Cor. 1. 33 3–6

he is·distinct from us, as touching his bodily presence, so he is our Righteousness and Sanctification before God: here therefore I lived, for some time, very sweetly at peace with God thorow Christ; O methought Christ! Christ! there was nothing but Christ that was before my eyes: I was not onely for looking upon this and the other 5 benefit of Christ apart, as of his Blood, Burial, or Resurrection, but considered him as a whole Christ! As he in whom all these, and all his other Vertues, Relations, Offices, and Operations met together, and that as he sat on the right hand of God in Heaven.

232. 'Twas glorious to me to see his exaltation, and the worth 10 and prevalencie of all his benefits, and that because of this; Now I could look from my self to him, and should reckon that all those Graces of God that now were green in me, were yet but like those crack'd-Groats and Four-pence-half-pennies that rich men carry in their Purses, when their Gold is in their Trunks at home: O I saw 15 my Gold was in my Trunk at home! In Christ my Lord and Saviour! Now Christ was all; all my Wisdom, all my Righteousness, all my Sanctification, and all my Redemption.

233. Further, The Lord did also lead me into the mystery of Union with this Son of God, that I was joyned to him, that I was 20 flesh of his flesh, and bone of his bone, and now was that a sweet word to me in *Ephes.* 5. 3. By this also was my faith in him, as my Righteousness, the more confirmed to me; for if he and I were one, then his Righteousness was mine, his Merits mine, his Victory also mine. Now could I see myself in Heaven and Earth at once; in 25 heaven by my Christ, by my Head, by my Righteousness and Life, though on Earth by my Body or Person.

234. Now I saw Christ Jesus was looked on of God, and should also be looked on by us as that common or publick person, in whom all the whole Body of his Elect are always to be considered and 30 reckoned, that we fulfilled the Law by him, rose from the dead by him, got the Victory over sin, death, the devil, and hell, by him: when he died we died; and so of his Resurrection: *Thy dead men shall live, together with my dead body shall they arise,* saith he, *Isa.* 26. and again, *After two dayes he will revive us: and the third day we shall live in* 35 *his sight,* Hos. 6. 2. which is now fulfilled by the sitting down of the

7 a] *om.* 1   9 as he sat] *add.* 5   23 to me] in me 5 6

Son of Man on the right hand of the Majesty in the Heavens; according to that to the *Ephesians, He hath raised us up together, and made us sit together in heavenly places in Christ Jesus,* Ephes. 2. 6.

235. Ah these blessed considerations and Scriptures, with many
5 others of a like nature, were in those days made to spangle in mine eyes, so that I have cause to say, *Praise ye the Lord God in his Sanctuary, praise him in the firmament of his power, praise him for his mighty acts, praise him according to his excellent greatness,* Psal. 150. 1, 2.

236. Having thus in few words given you a taste of the sorrow
10 and affliction that my Soul went under, by the guilt and terror that this my wicked thought did lay me under; and having given you also a touch of my deliverance therefrom, and of the sweet and blessed comfort that I met with afterwards, (which comfort dwelt about a twelve-month with my heart, to my unspeakable admira-
15 tion) I will now (God willing) before I proceed any further, give you in a word or two, what, as I conceive, was the cause of this Temptation; and also after that, what advantage at the last it became unto my Soul.

237. For the causes, I conceived they were principally two, of
20 which two I also was deeply convinced all the time this trouble lay upon me. The first was, For that I did not, when I was delivered from the Temptation that went before, still pray to God to keep me from Temptations that were to come: for though, as I can say in truth, my Soul was much in prayer before this tryal seized me,
25 yet then I prayed onely, or at the most principally, for the removal of present troubles, and for fresh discoveries of love in Christ: which I saw afterwards was not enough to do; I also should have prayed that the great God would keep me from the evil that was to come.

238. Of this I was made deeply sensible by the prayer of holy
30 *David,* who when he was under present mercy, yet prayed that God would hold him back from sin and temptation to come: *For then,* saith he, *shall I be upright, I shall be innocent from the* GREAT *transgression,* Psal. 19. 13. By this very word was I gauled and condemned, quite thorow this long temptation.

35 239. That also was another word that did much condemn me for my folly, in the neglect of this duty, *Heb.* 4. 16, *Let us therefore*

6 so that . . . say,] *add.* 5

come boldly unto the Throne of grace, that we may obtain mercy, and find grace to help in time of need: this I had not done, and therefore was suffered thus to sin and fall, according to what is written, *Pray, that ye enter not into temptation*: and truly this very thing is to this day of such weight and awe upon me, that I dare not, when I come before 5 the Lord, go off my knees, until I intreat him for help and mercy against the temptations that are to come: and I do beseech thee, Reader, that thou learn to beware of my negligence, by the affliction that for this thing I did for days, and months, and years, with sorrow undergo. 10

240. Another cause of this temptation was, That I had tempted God; and on this manner did I do it: Upon a time my Wife was great with Child, and before her full time was come, her pangs, as of a woman in travel, were fierce and strong upon her, even as if she would have immediately fallen in labour, and been delivered 15 of an untimely birth: now, at this very time it was, that I had been so strongly tempted to question the being of God; wherefore, as my Wife lay crying by me, I said, but with all secresie imaginable, even thinking in my heart, *Lord, if thou wilt now remove this sad affliction from my Wife, and cause that she be troubled no more therewith this* 20 *night* (and now were her pangs just upon her) *then I shall know that thou canst discern the most secret thoughts of the heart.*

241. I had no sooner said it in my heart, but her pangs were taken from her, and she was cast into a deep sleep, and so she continued till morning; at this I greatly marvelled, not knowing 25 what to think; but after I had been awake a good while, and heard her cry no more, I fell to sleeping also: So when I waked in the morning, it came upon me again, even what I had said in my heart the last night, and how the Lord had shewed me that he knew my secret thoughts, which was a great astonishment unto me for 30 several weeks after.

242. Well, about a year and a half afterwards, that wicked sinful thought, of which I have spoken before, went thorow my wicked heart, even this thought, *Let Christ go if he will*; so when I was fallen under guilt for this, the remembrance of my other thought, and of 35 the effect thereof, would also come upon me with this retort, which

27 sleeping] sleep 3 5 6

also carried rebuke along with it, *Now you may see that God doth know the most secret thoughts of the heart!*

243. And with this, that of the passages that was betwixt the Lord, and his servant *Gideon* fell upon my spirit; how because that *Gideon* tempted God with his Fleece, both wet and dry, when he should have believed and ventured upon his Word, therefore the Lord did afterwards so try him, as to send him against an innumerable company of Enemies, and that too, as to outward appearance, without any strength or help, *Judg. Chap.* 6, 7. Thus he served me, and that justly, for I should have believed his Word, and not have put an *if* upon the all-seeingness of God.

244. And now to show you something of the advantages that I also gained by this Temptation: And first, By this I was made continually to possess in my Soul a very wonderful sence both of the being and glory of God, and of his beloved Son; in the temptation before, my Soul was perplexed with unbelief, blasphemy, hardness of heart, questions about the being of God, Christ, the truth of the Word, and certainty of the World to come: I say, then I was greatly assaulted and tormented with Atheism; but now the case was otherwise, now was God and Christ continually before my face, though not in a way of comfort, but in a way of exceeding dread and terrour. The glory of the Holiness of God did at this time break me to pieces, and the Bowels and Compassion of Christ did break me as on the Wheel; for I could not consider him but as a lost and rejected Christ, the remembrance of which was as the continual breaking of my bones.

245. The Scriptures now also were wonderful things unto me; I saw that the truth and verity of them were the Keys of the Kingdom of Heaven; those that the Scriptures favour they must inherit bliss; but those that they oppose and condemn, must perish for evermore. O this word, *For the Scriptures cannot be broken,* would rend the caul of my heart, and so would that other, *Whose sins ye remit, they are remitted, but whose sins ye retain, they are retained*: Now I saw the Apostles to be the Elders of the City of Refuge, *Josh.* 20. 4, those they were to receive in, were received to Life, but those that they shut out were to be slain by the avenger of blood.

246. O! one sentence of the Scripture did more afflict and terrify my mind, I mean those sentences that stood against me, (as sometimes I thought they every one did) more, I say, than an Army of forty thousand men that might have come against me. Wo be to him against whom the Scriptures bend themselves. 5

247. By this Temptation I was made to see more into the nature of the Promise, then ever I was before: for I lying now trembling under the mighty hand of God, continually torn and rent by the thunderings of his Justice; this made me, with careful heart and watchful eye, with great seriousness to turn over every leaf, and 10 with much diligence mixed with trembling, to consider every sentence, together with its natural force and latitude.

248. By this Temptation also, I was greatly beaten off my former foolish practice, of putting by the Word of Promise when it came into my mind: for now, though I could not suck that sweetness 15 and comfort from the Promise, as I had done at other times, yet, like to a man asinking, I should catch at all I saw: formerly I thought I might not meddle with the Promise, unless I felt its comfort; but now 'twas no time thus to do, the Avenger of blood too hardly did pursue me. 20

249. Now therefore I was glad to catch at that word, which yet I feared I had no ground or right to own; and even to leap into the Bosom of that Promise, that yet I feared did shut its heart against me. Now also I should labour to take the word as God had laid it down, without restraining the natural force of one syllable thereof: 25 O what did I now see in that blessed sixth of *John, And him that comes to me, I will in no wise cast out, John.* 6. 37. Now I began to consider with myself, that God had a bigger mouth to speak with, than I had heart to conceive with; I thought also with myself, that he spake not his words in haste, or in an unadvised heat, but with 30 infinite wisdom and judgement, and in very truth and faithfulness, 2 *Sam.* 7. 28.

250. I should in these dayes, often in my greatest agonies, even flounce towards the Promise, (as the horses do towards sound ground, that yet stick in the mire) concluding, (though as one 35

10 seriousness] fearfulness 3 5 6   12 latitude] fortitude 3   13 beaten] holden 3 5 6   27 *John.* 6. 37.] *add.* 3

almost bereft of his wits through fear) on this I will rest and stay, and leave the fulfilling of it to the God of heaven that made it. O! many a pull hath my heart had with Satan for that blessed sixth of *John*: I did not now, as at other times, look principally for comfort, (though O how welcome would it have been unto me!) but now a Word, a Word to lean a weary Soul upon, that I might not sink for ever! 'twas that I hunted for.

251. Yea, often when I have been making to the Promise, I have seen as if the Lord would refuse my Soul for ever; I was often as if I had run upon the pikes, and as if the Lord had thrust at me, to keep me from him, as with a flaming sword. Then I should think of *Esther*, who went to petition the King contrary to the Law, *Esth.* 4. 16. I thought also of *Benhadad*'s servants, who went with ropes upon their heads to their Enemies for mercy, 1 Kin. 20. 31 &c. the woman of *Canaan* also, that would not be daunted, though called dog by Christ, Mat. 15. 22 &c. and the man that went to borrow bread at midnight, Luk. 11. 5, 6, 7, 8 &c., were great encouragements unto me.

252. I never saw those heights and depths in grace, and love, and mercy, as I saw after this temptation: great sins do draw out great grace; and where guilt is most terrible and fierce, there the mercy of God in Christ, when shewed to the Soul, appears most high and mighty. When *Job* had passed thorow his captivity, *he had twice as much as he had before,* Job 42. 10. Blessed be God for Jesus Christ our Lord. Many other things I might here make observation of, but I would be brief, and therefore shall at this time omit them; and do pray God that my harms may make others fear to offend, lest they also be made to bear the iron yoak as I did.

I had two or three times, at or about my deliverance from this temptation, such strange apprehensions of the Grace of God, that I could hardly bear up under it; it was so out of measure amazing, when I thought it could reach me, that I do think, if that sense of it had abode long upon me, it would have made me uncapable for business.

253. Now I shall go forward to give you a relation of other of the

Lord's leadings with me, of his dealings with me at sundry other seasons, and of the temptations I then did meet withall. I shall begin with what I met when I first did joyn in fellowship with the people of God in *Bedford*. After I had propounded to the Church, that my desire was to walk in the Order and Ordinances of Christ with them, and was also admitted by them; while I thought of that blessed Ordinance of Christ, which was his last Supper with his Disciples before his death, that Scripture, *Do this in remembrance of me*, Luk. 22. 19, was made a very precious word unto me; for by it the Lord did come down upon my conscience with the discovery of his death for my sins, and as I then felt, did as if he plunged me in the vertue of the same. But, behold, I had not been long a partaker at that Ordinance, but such fierce and sad temptations did attend me at all times therein, both to blaspheme the Ordinance, and to wish some deadly thing to those that then did eat thereof; that lest I should at any time be guilty of consenting to these wicked and fearful thoughts, I was forced to bend myself all the while to pray to God to keep me from such blasphemies; and also to cry to God to bless the Bread and Cup to them as it went from mouth to mouth: The reason of this temptation I have thought since was, because I did not, with that reverence as became me, at first approach to partake thereof.

254. Thus I continued for three quarters of a year, and could never have rest nor ease; but at last the Lord came in upon my Soul with that same Scripture by which my Soul was visited before; and after that, I have been usually very well and comfortable in the partaking of that blessed Ordinance, and have, I trust, therein discerned the *Lords Body* as broken for my sins, and that his precious Blood had been shed for my transgressions.

255. Upon a time I was somewhat inclining to a Consumption, wherefore, about the spring, I was suddenly and violently seized with much weakness in my outward man; insomuch that I thought I could not live. Now began I afresh to give myself up to a serious examination after my state and condition for the future, and of my Evidences for that blessed world to come; for it hath, I bless the name of God, been my usual course, as alwayes, so especially in the

21 as became me] *add.* 3   31 wherefore] wherewith 3

day of affliction, to endeavour to keep my interest in Life to come, clear before my eye.

256. But I had no sooner began to recall to mind my former experience of the goodness of God to my Soul, but there came 5 flocking into my mind an innumerable company of my sins and transgressions, amongst which these were at this time most to my affliction, namely, my deadness, dulness, and coldness in holy Duties; my wandrings of heart, my wearisomness in all good things, my want of love to God, his wayes, and people, with this at the end 10 of all, *Are these the fruits of Christianity? are these the tokens of a blessed man?*

257. At the apprehension of these things, my sickness was doubled upon me, for now was I sick in my inward man, my Soul was clog'd with guilt, now also was my former experience of Gods 15 goodness to me quite taken out of my mind, and hid as if it had never been, nor seen: Now was my Soul greatly pinched between these two considerations. *Live I must not, Die I dare not*: now I sunk and fell in my Spirit, and was giving up all for lost; but as I was walking up and down in the house, as a man in a most woful state, 20 that word of God took hold of my heart, *Ye are justified freely by his grace, through the redemption that is in Christ Jesus*, Rom. 3. 24. But oh what a turn it made upon me!

258. Now was I as one awakened out of some troublesome sleep and dream, and listening to this heavenly sentence, I was as if I 25 had heard it thus expounded to me; Sinner, thou thinkest that because of thy sins and infirmities I cannot save thy Soul; but behold my Son is by me, and upon him I look, and not on thee, and will deal with thee according as I am pleased with him: at this I was greatly lightened in my mind, and made to understand that God 30 could justifie a sinner at any time; it was but looking upon Christ, and imputing of his benefits to us, and the work was forthwith done.

259. And as I was thus in a muse, that Scripture also came with great power upon my Spirit, *Not by works of righteousness that we have* 35 *done, but according to his mercy he hath saved us,* &c. 2 Tim. 1. 9, Tit. 3. 5. Now was I got on high; I saw myself within the arms of Grace

21-22 But . . . me!] *add.* 3   30 looking] his looking 5 6   33 also] *add.* 5

and Mercy; and though I was before afraid to think of a dying hour, yet now I cried, Let me die; now death was lovely and beautiful in my sight; for I saw we shall never live indeed till we be gone to the other World: O methought this life is but a slumber in comparison of that above: at this time also I saw more in those words, *Heirs of* 5 *God*, Rom. 8. 17. than ever I shall be able to express while I live in this world: *Heirs of God!* God himself is the portion of the Saints: this I saw and wondered at, but cannot tell you what I saw.

260. Again, as I was at another time very ill and weak, all that time also the Tempter did beset me strongly (for I find he is much 10 for assaulting the Soul, when it begins to approach towards the Grave, then is his Opportunity) labouring to hide from me my former experience of Gods goodness: Also setting before me the terrours of Death and the Judgment of God; insomuch, that at this time, through my fear of miscarrying for ever, (should I now die) 15 I was as one dead before Death came, and was as if I had felt my self already descending into the Pit; methought, I said, there was no way but to Hell I must; but behold, just as I was in the midst of those fears, these words of the Angels carrying *Lazarus* into *Abrahams* bosom darted in upon me, as who should say, *So it shall be with* 20 *thee when thou dost leave this World.* This did sweetly revive my Spirit, and help me to hope in God; which when I had with comfort mused on awhile, that word fell with great weight upon my mind, *O Death, where is thy sting? O Grave, where is thy victory?* 1 Cor. 15. 55. At this I became both well in body and mind at once, for my sickness 25 did presently vanish, and I walked comfortably in my Work for God again.

261. At another time, though just before I was pretty well and savoury in my spirit, yet suddenly there fell upon me a great cloud of darkness, which did so hide from me the things of God and 30 Christ, that I was as if I had never seen or known them in my life; I was also so over-run in my Soul, with a senceless heartless frame of spirit, that I could not feel my soul to move or stir after grace and life by Christ; I was as if my loyns were broken, or as if my hands and feet had been tied or bound with chains. At this time 35

also I felt some weakness to seiz my outward man, which made still the other affliction the more heavy and uncomfortable.

262. After I had been in this condition some three or four days, as I was sitting by the fire, I suddenly felt this word to sound in my heart, *I must go to Jesus*; at this my former darkness and atheism fled away, and the blessed things of heaven were set within my view; while I was on this sudden thus overtaken with surprize, Wife, said I, is there ever such a Scripture, *I must go to Jesus?* She said she could not tell; therefore I sat musing still to see if I could remember such a place, I had not sat above two or three minutes but that came bolting in upon me, *And to an innumerable company of Angels,* and withal, *Hebrews* the twelfth, about the mount *Zion,* was set before mine eyes. *Heb.* 12. 22, 23, 24.

263. Then with joy I told my Wife, O now I know, I know! but that night was a good night to me, I never had but few better; I longed for the company of some of Gods people, that I might have imparted unto them what God had showed me: Christ was a precious Christ to my Soul that night; I could scarce lie in my Bed for joy, and peace, and triumph, thorow Christ; this great glory did not continue upon me until morning, yet that twelfth of the Author to the *Hebrews,* Heb. 12. 21, 22, 23. was a blessed Scripture to me for many days together after this.

264. The words are these, *Ye are come to mount Zion, to the City of the living God, to the heavenly Jerusalem, and to an innumerable company of Angels, to the general assembly and Church of the first-born, which are written in heaven, and to God the Judge of all, and to the spirits of just men made perfect, and to Jesus the Mediator of the New Testament, and to the blood of sprinkling, that speaketh better things than that of Abel*: Thorow this blessed Sentence the Lord led me over and over, first to this word, and then to that, and shewed me wonderful glory in every one of them. These words also have oft since this time been great refreshment to my Spirit. Blessed be God for having mercy on me.

A brief Account of the Author's Call to the Work of the Ministry

265. And now I am speaking my Experience, I will in this place

thrust in a word or two concerning my preaching the Word, and of Gods dealing with me in that particular also: For after I had been about five or six years awakened, and helped my self to see both the want and worth of Jesus Christ our Lord, and also inabled to venture my Soul upon him, some of the most able among the Saints with us, 5 I say the most able for Judgment, and holiness of Life, as they conceived, did perceive that God had counted me worthy to understand something of his Will in his holy and blessed word, and had given me utterance in some measure to express, what I saw, to others for edification; therefore they desired me, and that with much 10 earnestness, that I would be willing, at sometime, to take in hand in one of the Meetings to speak a word of Exhortation unto them.

266. The which, though at the first it did much dash and abash my spirit, yet being still by them desired and intreated, I consented to their request, and did twice at two several Assemblies, (but in 15 private) though with much weakness and infirmity, discover my Gift amongst them; at which they not onely seemed to be, but did solemnly protest, as in the sight of the great God, they were both affected and comforted, and gave thanks to the Father of Mercies for the grace bestowed on me. 20

267. After this, sometimes when some of them did go into the Countrey to teach, they would also that I should go with them; where, though as yet I did not, nor durst not make use of my Gift in an open way, yet more privately still, as I came amongst the good People in those places, I did sometimes speak a word of Admonition unto them 25 also; the which they, as the other, received with rejoycing at the mercy of God to me-ward, professing their Souls were edified thereby.

268. Wherefore, to be brief, at last, being still desired by the Church, after some solemn prayer to the Lord, with fasting, I was more particularly called forth, and appointed to a more ordinary 30 and publick preaching the Word, not onely to and amongst them that believed, but also to offer the Gospel to those who had not yet received the faith thereof: about which time I did evidently find in my mind a secret pricking forward thereto: (tho I bless God not for desire of vain glory, for at that time I was most sorely afflicted 35 with the firy darts of the devil concerning my eternal state.)

3 my self] *add.* 5   4 also] *add.* 5   10 therefore] *add.* 5

I

269. But yet I could not be content unless I was found in the exercise of my Gift, unto which also I was greatly animated, not only by the continual desires of the Godly, but also by that saying of *Paul* to the *Corinthians, I beseech you, Brethren (ye know the household of Stephanas, that it is the first fruits of Achaia, and that they have addicted themselves to the ministery of the Saints) that you submit your selves unto such, and to every one that helpeth with us and laboureth,* 1 Cor. 16. 15, 16.

270. By this Text I was made to see that the holy Ghost never intended that men who have Gifts and Abilities should bury them in the earth, but rather did command and stir up such to the exercise of their gift, and also did commend those that were apt and ready so to do, *they have addicted themselves to the ministery of the Saints*: this Scripture in these days did continually run in my mind, to incourage me, and strengthen me in this my work for God: I have also been incouraged from several other Scriptures and examples of the Godly, both specified in the Word and other ancient Histories. *Act.* 8. 4; & 18. 24, 25 &c. 1 *Pet.* 4. 10; *Rom.* 12. 6; Fox. *Acts and Mon.*

271. Wherefore, though of my self, of all the Saints the most unworthy, yet I, but with great fear and trembling at the sight of my own weakness, did set upon the work, and did according to my Gift, and the proportion of my Faith, preach that blessed Gospel that God had shewed me in the holy Word of truth: which when the Countrey understood, they came in to hear the Word by hundreds, and that from all parts, though upon sundry and divers accounts.

272. And I thank God he gave unto me some measure of bowels and pity for their Souls, which also did put me forward to labour with great diligence and earnestness, to find out such a Word as might, if God would bless it, lay hold of and awaken the Conscience; in which also the good Lord had respect to the desire of his Servant: for I had not preached long before some began to be touched by the Word, and to be greatly afflicted in their minds at the apprehension of the greatness of their sin, and of their need of Jesus Christ.

273. But I at first could not believe that God should speak by

33 by the Word] *om.* 3 5 6

me to the heart of any man, still counting my self unworthy; yet those who were thus touched would love me, and have a peculiar respect for me; and though I did put it from me that they should be awakened by me, still they would confess it and affirm it before the Saints of God, they would also bless God for me, (unworthy Wretch that I am!) and count me Gods Instrument that shewed to them the Way of Salvation.

274. Wherefore seeing them in both their words and deeds to be so constant, & also in their hearts so earnestly pressing after the knowledge of Jesus Christ, rejoycing that ever God did send me where they were: then I began to conclude it might be so, that God had owned in his Work such a foolish one as I; and then came that Word of God to my heart with much sweet refreshment, *The blessing of them that were ready to perish is come upon me; yea, I caused the widows heart to sing for joy,* Job. 29. 13.

275. At this therefore I rejoyced, yea, the tears of those whom God did awaken by my preaching would be both solace and encouragement to me; for I thought on those Sayings, *Who is he that maketh me glad but the same that is made sorry by me?* 2 Cor. 2. 2; and again, *Though I be not an Apostle to others, yet doubtless I am unto you, for the seal of mine Apostleship are ye in the Lord,* 1 Cor. 9. 2. These things therefore were as another argument unto me that God had called me to and stood by me in this Work.

276. In my preaching of the Word, I took special notice of this one thing, namely, That the Lord did lead me to begin where his Word begins with Sinners, that is, to condemn all flesh, and to open and alledge that the curse of God, by the Law, doth belong to and lay hold on all men as they come into the World, because of sin. Now this part of my work I fulfilled with great sence; for the terrours of the Law, and guilt for my transgressions, lay heavy on my Conscience. I preached what I felt, what I smartingly did feel, even that under which my poor Soul did groan and tremble to astonishment.

277. Indeed I have been as one sent to them from the dead; I went my self in chains to preach to them in chains, and carried that fire in my own conscience that I perswaded them to beware of.

I can truly say, and that without dissembling, that when I have been to preach, I have gone full of guilt and terrour even to the Pulpit-Door, and there it hath been taken off, and I have been at liberty in my mind until I have done my work, and then imme-
5 diately, even before I could get down the Pulpit-Stairs, have been as bad as I was before. Yet God carried me on, but surely with a strong hand: for neither guilt nor hell could take me off my Work.

278. Thus I went for the space of two years, crying out against mens sins, and their fearful state because of them. After which, the
10 Lord came in upon my own Soul with some staid peace and comfort thorow Christ; for he did give me many sweet discoveries of his blessed Grace thorow him: wherefore now I altered in my preaching (for still I preached what I saw and felt;) now therefore I did much labour to hold forth Jesus Christ in all his Offices, Relations, and
15 Benefits unto the World, and did strive also to discover, to condemn, and remove those false supports and props on which the World doth both lean, and by them fall and perish. On these things also I staid as long as on the other.

279. After this, God led me into something of the mystery of
20 union with Christ: wherefore that I discovered and shewed to them also. And when I had travelled thorow these three chief points of the Word of God, about the space of five years or more; I was caught in my present practice and cast into Prison, where I have lain above as long again, to confirm the Truth by way of Suffering,
25 as I was before in testifying of it according to the Scriptures, in a way of Preaching.

280. When I have been in preaching, I thank God, my heart hath often, all the time of this and the other exercise, with great earnestness cried to God that He would make the Word effectual to the
30 salvation of the Soul; still being grieved lest the Enemy should take the Word away from the Conscience, and so it should become unfruitful: Wherefore I should labour so to speak the Word, as that thereby (if it were possible) the sin and the person guilty might be particularized by it.

35 281. Also when I have done the Exercise, it hath gone to my heart to think the Word should now fall as rain on stony places;

23-24 I have lain above as long again, to] I have lain as long to 1

still wishing from my heart, O that they who have heard me speak this day did but see as I do what sin, death, hell, and the curse of God is; and also what the grace, and love, and mercy of God is, thorow Christ, to men in such a case as they are, who are yet estranged from him; and indeed I did often say in my heart 5 before the Lord, *That if to be hanged up presently before their eyes, would be a means to awaken them, and confirm them in the truth, I gladly should be contented.*

282. For I have been in my preaching, especially when I have been engaged in the Doctrine of Life by Christ, without Works, as 10 if an Angel of God had stood by at my back to encourage me: O it hath been with such power and heavenly evidence upon my own Soul, while I have been labouring to unfold it, to demonstrate it, and to fasten it upon the Conscience of others, that I could not be contented with saying, I believe, and am sure; methought I was 15 more then sure, if it be lawful so to express my self, that those things which then I asserted, were true.

283. When I went first to preach the Word abroad, the Doctors and Priests of the Countrey did open wide against me; but I was perswaded of this, not to render rayling for rayling, but to see how 20 many of their carnal Professors I could convince of their miserable state by the Law, and of the want and worth of Christ: for thought I, *This shall answer for me in time to come, when they shall be for my hire before their face*, Gen. 30. 33.

284. I never cared to meddle with things that were controverted, 25 and in dispute amongst the Saints, especially things of the lowest nature; yet it pleased me much to contend with great earnestness for the Word of Faith, and the remission of sins by the Death and Sufferings of Jesus: but I say, as to other things, I should let them alone, because I saw they engendered strife, and because I saw they 30 neither, in doing nor in leaving undone, did commend us to God to be his: besides, I saw my Work before me did run in another channel even to carry an awakening Word; to that therefore did I stick and adhere.

285. I never endeavoured to, nor durst make use of other men's 35 lines, *Rom.* 15. 18, (though I condemn not all that do) for I verily

30 I saw] *om.* 3 5 6

thought, and found by experience, that what was taught me by the Word and Spirit of Christ, could be spoken, maintained, and stood to, by the soundest and best established Conscience: and though I will not now speak all that I know in this matter; yet my experience 5 hath more interest in that text of Scripture, *Gal.* I. 11, 12 than many amongst men are aware.

286. If any of those who were awakened by my Ministery did after that fall back, (as sometimes too many did) I can truly say their loss hath been more to me, then if one of my own Children, 10 begotten of my body, had been going to its grave; I think verily I may speak it without any offence to the Lord, nothing hath gone so near me as that, unless it was the fear of the loss of the salvation of my own Soul: I have counted as if I had goodly buildings and lordships in those places where my Children were born: my heart 15 hath been so wrapt up in the glory of this excellent work, that I counted myself more blessed and honoured of God by this, than if he had made me the Emperour of the Christian World, or the Lord of all the glory of Earth without it! O that word, *He that converteth a sinner from the error of his way, doth save a soul from death*, Jam. 5. 20. *The* 20 *Fruit of the Righteous, is a Tree of Life; and he that winneth Souls, is wise,* Prov. 11. 30. *They that be wise, shall shine as the brightness of the Firmament; and they that turn many to Righteousness, as the Stars for ever and ever,* Dan. 12. 3. *For what is our hope, or joy, or crown of rejoycing? are not even ye in the presence of our Lord Jesus Christ at his coming? For ye* 25 *are our glory and joy,* 1 Thess. 2. 19, 20. These, I say, with many others of a like nature, have been great refreshments to me.

287. I have observed, that where I have had a work to do for God, I have had first as it were the going of God upon my Spirit to desire I might preach there: I have also observed that such and 30 such Souls in particular have been strongly set upon my heart, and I stirred up to wish for their Salvation; and that these very Souls have after this been given in as the fruits of my Ministry. I have also observed, that a word cast in by the by hath done more execution in a Sermon then all that was spoken besides: sometimes also

3 the] *om.* 1   11 any] an 1   14 where] *om.* 1   18 that word]
these words 3 5 6   19–26 Jam. 5. 20 . . . me.] *add.* 3   25 I say,]
add. 5

when I have thought I did no good, then I did the most of all; and at other times when I thought I should catch them, I have fished for nothing.

288. I have also observed this that where there hath been a work to do upon Sinners, there the Devil hath begun to roar in the 5 hearts, and by the mouths of his Servants. Yea, often-times when the wicked World hath raged most, there hath been souls awakened by the Word: I could instance particulars, but I forbear.

289. My great desire in fulfilling my Ministry, was, to get into the darkest places in the *Countrey*, even amongst those people that 10 were furthest off of profession; yet not because I could not endure the light (for I feared not to shew my Gospel to any) but because I found my spirit leaned most after awakening and converting Work, and the Word that I carried did lean itself most that way; *Yea, so have I strived to preach the Gospel, not where Christ was named, lest* 15 *I should build upon another mans foundation,* Rom. 15. 20.

290. In my preaching I have really been in pain, and have as it were travelled to bring forth Children to God; neither could I be satisfied unless some fruits did appear in my work: if I were fruitless it matter'd not who commended me; but if I were fruitful, I cared 20 not who did condemn. I have thought of that, *He that winneth souls is wise,* Pro. 11. 30. and again, *Lo Children are an heritage of the Lord; and the fruit of the Womb is his Reward: as arrows in the hand of a mighty man, so are Children of the youth; happy is the man that hath filled his quiver with them, they shall not be ashamed, but they shall speak with the* 25 *Enemies in the gate,* Psal. 127. 3, 4, 5.

291. It pleased me nothing to see people drink in Opinions if they seemed ignorant of Jesus Christ, and the worth of their own Salvation, sound conviction for Sin, especially for Unbelief, and an heart set on fire to be saved by Christ, with strong breathings after 30 a truly sanctified Soul: that was it that delighted me; those were the souls I counted blessed.

292. But in this work, as in all other, I had my temptations attending me, and that of diverse kinds: as sometimes I should be assaulted with great discouragement, therein fearing that I should 35

not be able to speak the Word at all to edification, nay, that I should
not be able to speak sence unto the people; at which times I should
have such a strange faintness and strengthlessness seiz upon my
body that my legs have scarce been able to carry me to the place of
5 Exercise.

293. Sometimes again, when I have been preaching, I have been
violently assaulted with thoughts of blasphemy, and strongly
tempted to speak them with my mouth before the Congregation.
I have also at some times, even when I have begun to speak the
10 Word with much clearness, evidence, and liberty of speech, yet
been before the ending of that Opportunity so blinded, and so
estranged from the things I have been speaking, and have also bin
so straitned in my speech, as to utterance before the people, that I
have been as if I had not known or remembred what I have been
15 about, or as if my head had been in a bag all the time of the *exercise*.

294. Again, When as sometimes I have been about to preach
upon some smart and scorching portion of the *Word*, I have found
the tempter suggest, What! will you preach this? this condemns
your self; of this your own Soul is guilty; wherefore preach not of
20 it at all, or if you do, yet so mince it as to make way for your own
escape, lest instead of awakening others, you lay that guilt upon
your own soul, as you will never get from under.

295. But I thank the Lord I have been kept from consenting to
these so horrid suggestions, and have rather, as *Sampson*, bowed my
25 self with all my might, to condemn sin and transgression where
ever I found it, yea though therein also I did bring guilt upon my
own Conscience; *Let me die*, thought I, *with the Philistines*, Judg. 16.
29, 30, rather than deal corruptly with the blessed Word of God,
Thou that teachest another, teachest thou not thyself? it is far better that
30 thou do judge thy self, even by preaching plainly to others, then
that thou, to save thyself, imprison the truth in unrighteousness:
Blessed be God for his help also in this.

296. I have also, while found in this blessed work of Christ, been
often tempted to pride and liftings up of heart; and though I dare
35 not say, I have not been infected with this, yet truly the Lord of

§ *295 add.* 3
8 them] the words 5 6

his precious mercy hath so carried it towards me, that for the most part I have had but small joy to give way to such a thing: for it hath been my every-days portion to be let into the evil of my own heart, and still made to see such a multitude of corruptions and infirmities therein, that it hath caused hanging down of the head under all my Gifts and Attainments: I have felt this thorn in the flesh (2 *Cor.* 12. 8, 9.) the very mercy of God to me.

297. I have had also together with this, some notable place or other of the Word presented before me, which word hath contained in it some sharp and piercing sentence concerning the perishing of the Soul, notwithstanding gifts and parts; as for instance, that hath been of great use unto me, *Though I speak with the tongue of men and of angels, and have not charity, I am become as sounding-brass, and a tinkling cymbal,* 1 Cor. 13. 1, 2.

298. A tinkling Cymbal is an instrument of Musick with which a skilful player can make such melodious and heart-inflaming Musick, that all who hear him play, can scarcely hold from dancing; and yet behold the Cymbal hath not life, neither comes the musick from it, but because of the art of him that playes therewith: so then the instrument at last may come to nought and perish, though in times past such musick hath been made upon it.

299. Just thus I saw it was and will be with them who have Gifts, but want saving-Grace; they are in the hand of Christ, as the Cymbal in the hand of *David*; and as *David* could, with the Cymbal make that mirth in the service of God, as to elevate the hearts of the Worshippers; so Christ can use these gifted men, as with them to affect the Souls of his People in his Church, yet when he hath done all hang them by as lifeless, though sounding *Cymbals.*

300. This consideration therefore, together with some others, were for the most part as a maul on the head of pride and desire of vain-glory: What, thought I, shall I be proud because I am a sounding Brass? is it so much to be a Fiddle? hath not the least creature that hath life, more of God in it than these? besides, I knew 'twas Love should never die, but these must cease and vanish: So I concluded, a little Grace, a little Love, a little of the true Fear of God, is better then all these Gifts: Yea, and I am fully convinced of it, that it is possible for a Soul that can scarce give a man an

answer, but with great confusion as to method, I say it is possible for them to have a thousand times more Grace, and so to be more in the love and favour of the Lord, then some who by vertue of the Gift of Knowledge, can deliver themselves like Angels.

301. Thus, therefore, I came to perceive, that though gifts in themselves were good to the thing for which they are designed, to wit, the Edification of others; yet empty and without power to save the Soul of him that hath them, if they be *alone*: Neither are they, as so, any sign of a mans state to be happy, being only a dispensation of God to some, of whose improvement, or non improvement, they must, when a little life more is over, give an account to him that is ready to judge the quick and the dead.

302. This shewed me, too, that gifts being alone, were dangerous, not in themselves, but because of those evils that attend them that have them, to wit, pride, desire of vain glory, self-conceit, &c., all of which were easily blown up at the applause, and commendation of every unadvised Christian, to the endangering of a poor Creature to fall into the condemnation of the Devil.

303. I saw therefore that he that hath Gifts had need be let into a sight of the nature of them, to wit, that they come short of making of him to be in a truly saved condition, lest he rest in them, and so fall short of the grace of God.

304. He hath also cause to walk humbly with God, and be little in his own Eyes, and to remember withall, that his Gifts are not his own, but the Churches; and that by them he is made a Servant to the Church, and that he must give at last an account of his Stewardship unto the Lord Jesus; and to give a good account, will be a blessed thing!

305. Let all men therefore prize a little with the fear of the Lord, (Gifts indeed are desirable) but yet great Grace and small Gifts are better then great Gifts and no Grace. It doth not say, the Lord gives Gifts and Glory, but the Lord gives Grace and Glory! and blessed is such an one to whom the Lord gives Grace, true Grace, for that is a certain forerunner of Glory.

§§ 301–5 *add.* 3

8 save] have 5 6   9–12 being . . . the dead.] *add.* 5   11 life] love 3 5 6
33–34 true Grace, for that is a certain forerunner of Glory.] *add.* 5

306. But when Satan perceived that his thus tempting, and assaulting of me, would not answer his design, to wit, to overthrow my Ministry, and make it ineffectual as to the ends thereof: then he tryed another way, which was to stir up the minds of the ignorant and malicious, to load me with slanders and reproaches; now therefore I may say, That what the Devil could devise, and his instruments invent, was whirled up and down the Countrey against me, thinking, as I said, that by that means they should make my ministry to be abandoned.

307. It began therefore to be rumored up and down among the People, that I was a Witch, a Jesuit, a Highway-man, and the like.

308. To all which, I shall only say, God knows that I am innocent. But as for mine accusers, let them provide themselves to meet me before the tribunal of the Son of God, there to answer for these things, (with all the rest of their Iniquities) unless God shall give them Repentance for them, for the which I pray with all my heart.

309. But that which was reported with the boldest confidence, was, that I had my *Misses*, my *Whores*, my *Bastards*, yea, *two wives at once*, and the like. Now these slanders (with the other) I glory in, because but slanders, foolish, or knavish lies, and falshoods cast upon me by the Devil and his Seed; and should I not be dealt with thus wickedly by the World, I should want one sign of a Saint, and Child of God. *Blessed are ye* (said the Lord Jesus) *when men shall revile you, and persecute you, and shall say all manner of evil against you falsely for my sake; rejoyce, and be exceeding glad, for great is your Reward in Heaven; for so persecuted they the Prophets which were before you,* Mat. 5. 11.

310. These things therefore upon mine own account trouble me not, no, though they were twenty times more then they are. I have a good Conscience, and whereas they speak evil of me, as an evil doer, they shall be ashamed that falsely accuse my good Conversation in Christ.

311. So then, what shall I say to those that have thus bespattered me? shall I threaten them? Shall I chide them? shall I flatter them? shall I intreat them to hold their tongues? no, not I: were it not for that these things make them ripe for damnation that are the authors

and abettors, I would say unto them: *report it*! because 'twill increase my Glory.

312. Therefore I bind these lies and slanders to me as an ornament, it belongs to my Christian Profession, to be villified, slandered, reproached and reviled: and since all this is nothing else, as my God and my Conscience do bear me witness: I rejoyce in reproaches for Christs sake.

313. I also calling all those fools, or knaves, that have thus made it anything of their business to affirm any of the things aforenamed of me, namely, that I have been naught with other Women, or the like, when they have used to the utmost of their endeavours, and made the fullest enquiry that they can, to prove against me truly, that there is any woman in Heaven, or Earth, or Hell, that can say, I have at any time, in any place, by day or night, so much as attempted to be naught with them; and speak I thus, to beg mine Enemies into a good esteem of me? No, not I. I will in this beg relief of no man: believe, or disbelieve me in this, all is a case to me.

314. My Foes have mist their mark in this their shooting at me. I am not the man, I wish that they themselves be guiltless, if all the Fornicators and Adulterers in *England* were hang'd by the Neck till they be dead, *John Bunyan*, the object of their Envie, would be still alive and well. I know not whether there be such a thing as a woman breathing under the Copes of the whole Heaven but by their apparel, their Children, or by common Fame, except my Wife.

315. And in this I admire the Wisdom of God, that he made me shie of women from my first Convertion until now. Those know, and can also bear me witness, with whom I have been most intimately concerned, that it is a rare thing to see me carry it pleasant towards a Woman; the common Salutation of a woman I abhor, 'tis odious to me in whosoever I see it. Their Company alone, I cannot away with. I seldom so much as touch a Womans Hand, for I think these things are not so becoming me. When I have seen good men Salute those Women that they have visited, or that have visited them, I have at times made my objection against it, and when they have answered, that it was but a peice of Civilitie, I have told them, it is not a comely sight; some indeed have urged the holy kiss but then I have asked why they made baulks, why

they did salute the most hansom, and let the ill-favoured go; thus, how laudable so ever such things have been in the Eyes of others, they have been unseemly in my sight.

316. And now for a wind up in this matter, I call on not only Men, but Angels, to prove me guilty of having carnally to do with 5 any Woman save my Wife, nor am I afraid to do it a second time, knowing that I cannot offend the Lord in such a case, to call God for a Record upon my Soul, that in these things I am innocent. Not that I have been thus kept, because of any goodness in me more than any other, but God has been merciful to me, and has kept me, 10 to whom I pray that he will keep me still, not only from this, but from every evil way and work, and preserve me to his Heavenly Kingdom. Amen.

317. Now as Sathan laboured by reproaches and slanders to make me vile among my Countrymen, that, if possible, my preach- 15 ing might be made of none effect, so there was added hereto a long and tedious Imprisonment, that thereby I might be frighted from my Service for Christ, and the World terrified, and made afraid to hear me Preach, of which I shall in the next place give you a brief account.

A brief Account of the Authors Imprisonment 20

318. Having made profession of the glorious Gospel of Christ a long time, and preached the same about five year; I was appre- hended at a Meeting of good People in the Countrey, (amongst whom, had they let me alone, I should have preached that day, but they took me away from amongst them) and had me before a 25 Justice, who, after I had offered security for my appearing at the next Sessions yet committed me, because my Sureties would not consent to be bound that I should preach no more to the people.

319. At the Sessions after, I was indicted for an Upholder and Maintainer of unlawful Assemblies and Conventicles, and for not 30 conforming to the National Worship of the Church of *England*; and after some conference there with the Justices, they taking my plain dealing with them for a confession, as they termed it, of the indict- ment, did sentence me to perpetual banishment, because I refused

4 call on] calling 5 6
22 preached] had preached 1 3   32–34 they . . . did sentence me] was sentenced 1 3

to Conform. So being again delivered up to the Goalers hands, I was had home to Prison again, and there have lain now compleat twelve years, waiting to see what God would suffer these men to do with me.

5   320. In which condition I have continued with much content thorow Grace, but have met with many turnings and goings upon my heart both from the Lord, Satan, and my own corruptions; by all which, (glory be to Jesus Christ) I have also received, among many things, much conviction, instruction, and understanding, of
10 which at large I shall not here discourse; onely give you, in a hint or two, a word that may stir up the Godly to bless God, and to pray for me; and also to take encouragement, should the case be their own, *Not to fear what men can do unto them.*

321. I never had in all my life so great an inlet into the Word of
15 God as now; them Scriptures that I saw nothing in before, are made in this place and state to shine upon me; Jesus Christ also was never more real and apparent then now; here I have seen him and felt him indeed: O that word, *We have not preached unto you cunningly devised fables,* 2 Pet. 1. 16: and that, *God raised Christ from*
20 *the dead, and gave him glory, that your faith and hope might be in God,* 1 Pet. 1. 21. were blessed words unto me in this my imprisoned condition.

322. These three or four Scriptures also have been great refreshment in this condition to me: *Joh.* 14. 1,2,3,4. *Joh.* 16. 33. *Col.* 3. 3,4.
25 *Heb.* 12. 22, 23, 24. So that sometimes when I have been in the savour of them, I have been able to laugh at destruction, *and to fear neither the Horse nor his Rider.* I have had sweet sights of the forgiveness of my sins in this place, and of my being with Jesus in another world: *O the mount Zion, the heavenly Jerusalem, the innumerable com-*
30 *pany of Angels, and God the Judge of all, and the Spirits of just men made perfect, and Jesus,* have been sweet unto me in this place: I have seen that here, that I am perswaded I shall never, while in this world, be able to express; I have seen a truth in that scripture, *Whom having not seen, ye love; in whom, though now ye see him not, yet believing,*
35 *ye rejoyce with joy unspeakable, and full of glory,* 1 Pet. 1. 8.

323. I never knew what it was for God to stand by me at all

2–3 compleat twelve years] above five year and a quarter 1   3 would] will 1

turns, and at every offer of Satan to afflict me, &c., as I have found him since I came in hither; for look how fears have presented themselves, so have supports and encouragements; yea, when I have started, even as it were at nothing else but my shadow, yet God, as being very tender of me, hath not suffered me to be molested, but would with one Scripture and another strengthen me against all: insomuch that I have often said, *Were it lawful, I could pray for greater trouble, for the greater comforts sake,* Eccles. 7. 14; 2 Cor. 1. 5.

324. Before I came to Prison, I saw what was a coming, and had especially two Considerations warm upon my heart; the first was, How to be able to endure, should my imprisonment be long and tedious; the second was, How to be able to encounter death, should that be here my portion; for the first of these, that Scripture, *Col.* 1. 11, was great information to me, namely, to pray to God *to be strengthened with all might, according to his glorious power, unto all patience and long-suffering with joyfulness*: I could seldom go to prayer before I was imprisoned, but for not so little as a year together, this Sentence, or sweet Petition, would as it were thrust it self into my mind, and perswade me that if ever I would go thorow long-suffering, I must have all patience, especially if I would endure it joyfully.

325. As to the second Consideration, that Saying, 2 *Cor.* 1. 9, was of great use to me, *But we had the sentence of death in our selves, that we might not trust in our selves, but in God that raiseth the dead*: by this Scripture I was made to see, that if ever I would suffer rightly, I must first pass a sentence of death upon everything that can properly be called a thing of this life, even to reckon my Self, my Wife, my Children, my health, my enjoyments, and all, as dead to me, and my self as dead to them. *He that loveth father or mother, son or daughter, more than me, is not worthy of me,* Matt. 10. 37.

326. The second was, to live upon God that is invisible; as *Paul* said in another place, The way not to faint, is *to look not at the things that are seen, but at the things that are not seen; for the things that are seen are temporal; but the things that are not seen, they are eternal,* 2 Cor. 4. 18. And thus I reasoned with myself; If I provide only for a prison,

---

1 to afflict me] *add.* 5   11–12 How to . . . was,] *om* 6   29–30 *He that loveth . . .* Matt. 10. 37.] *add.* 5   34 2 Cor. 4. 18] *add.* 3.

then the whip comes at unawares; and so does also the pillory;
again, if I provide onely for these, then I am not fit for banishment;
further, if I conclude that banishment is the worst, then if death
come, I am surprized; so that I see the best way to go thorow
5 sufferings, is to trust in God thorow Christ, as touching the world
to come; and as touching this world, to *count the grave my house, to
make my bed in darkness, and to say to Corruption, Thou art my Father, and
to the Worm, Thou art my Mother and Sister*; that is, to familiarize
these things to me.

10   327. But notwithstanding these helps, I found myself a man,
and compassed with infirmities; the parting with my Wife and
poor Children hath oft been to me in this place as the pulling the
flesh from my bones; and that not onely because I am somewhat too
fond of these great mercies, but also because I should have often
15 brought to my mind the many hardships, miseries and wants that
my poor family was like to meet with, should I be taken from them,
especially my poor blind Child, who lay nearer my heart than all I
had besides; O the thoughts of the hardship I thought my blind one
might go under, would break my heart to pieces.

20   328. Poor Child! thought I, what sorrow art thou like to have
for thy portion in this world? Thou must be beaten, must beg,
suffer hunger, cold, nakedness, and a thousand calamities, though
I cannot now endure the wind should blow upon thee: but yet
recalling my self, thought I, I must venture you all with God,
25 though it goeth to the quick to leave you: O I saw in this condition
I was as a man who was pulling down his house upon the head of
his Wife and Children; yet thought I, I must do it, I must do it:
and now I thought of those *two milch Kine that were to carry the Ark
of God into another Country, and to leave their Calves behind them*, 1 Sam.
30 6. 10, 11, 12.

    329. But that which helped me in this temptation was divers con-
siderations, of which three in special here I will name; the first was the
consideration of those two Scriptures, *Leave thy fatherless children,
I will preserve them alive, and let thy widows trust in me*: and again, *The
35 Lord said, Verily it shall be well with thy remnant, verily I will cause the
enemy to entreat thee well in the time of evil*, &c. Jer. 49. 11. Chap. 15. 11.

330. I had also this consideration, that if I should now venture all for God, I engaged God to take care of my concernments; but if I forsook him and his ways, for fear of any trouble that should come to me or mine, then I should not only falsifie my profession, but should count also that my concernments were not so sure if left at 5 Gods feet, while I stood to and for his name, as they would be if they were under my own tuition, though with the denial of the way of God. This was a smarting consideration, and was as spurs unto my flesh: that Scripture also greatly helped it to fasten the more upon me, where Christ prays against *Judas,* that God would 10 disappoint him in all his selfish thoughts, which moved him to sell his Master. Pray read it soberly, *Psal.* 109. 6, 7, 8, &c.

331. I had also another consideration, and that was, The dread of the torments of Hell, which I was sure they must partake of, that for fear of the Cross do shrink from their profession of Christ, his Word 15 and Laws, before the sons of men: I thought also of the glory that he had prepared for those that, in faith, and love, and patience, stood to his ways before them. These things, I say, have helped me, when the thoughts of the misery that both my self and mine might, for the sake of my profession, be exposed to, hath lain pinching on my mind. 20

332. When I have indeed conceited that I might be banished for my Profession, then I have thought of that Scripture, *They were stoned, they were sawn asunder, were tempted, were slain with the sword, they wandered about in sheepskins and goatskins; being destitute, afflicted, tormented, of whom the world was not worthy,* Heb. 11. 37, 38, for all 25 they thought they were too bad to dwell and abide amongst them. I have also thought of that saying, *The Holy Ghost witnesseth in every city, that bonds and afflictions abide me*; I have verily thought that my Soul and it have sometimes reasoned about the sore and sad estate of a banished and exiled condition, how they are exposed to hunger, 30 to cold, to perils, to nakedness, to enemies, and a thousand calamities; and at last it may be to die in a ditch like a poor forlorn and desolate sheep. But I thank God, hitherto I have not been moved by these most delicate reasonings, but have rather by them more approved my heart to God.   35

7 tuition] care 5 6   16 I thought also of the glory] and of the glory 1 3
25 Heb. 11. 37, 38,] *add.* 3

333. I will tell you a pretty business: I was once above all the rest in a very sad and low condition for many weeks, at which time also I being but a young Prisoner, and not acquainted with the Laws, had this lay much upon my spirit, That my imprisonment
5 might end at the Gallows for ought that I could tell; now, therefore, Satan laid hard at me to beat me out of heart, by suggesting thus unto me: But how if when you come indeed to die, you should be in this condition; that is, as not to savour the things of God, nor to have any evidence upon your soul for a better state hereafter? (for
10 indeed at that time all the things of God were hid from my soul).

334. Wherefore when I at first began to think of this, it was a great trouble to me: for I thought with my self that in the condition I now was in, I was not fit to die, neither indeed did I think I could, if I should be called to it: besides, I thought with myself, if I should
15 make a scrabling shift to clamber up the Ladder, yet I should either with quaking or other symptoms of faintings, give occasion to the enemy to reproach the way of God and his People, for their timerousness: this therefore lay with great trouble upon me, for methought I was ashamed to die with a pale face, and tottering knees, for such
20 a Cause as this.

335. Wherefore I prayed to God that he would comfort me, and give me strength to do and suffer what he should call me to; yet no comfort appeared, but all continued hid: I was also at this time so really possessed with the thought of death, that oft I was as if I
25 was on the Ladder, with the Rope about my neck; onely this was some encouragement to me, I thought I might now have an opportunity to speak my last words to a multitude which I thought would come to see me die; and, thought I, if it must be so, if God will but convert one Soul by my very last words, I shall not count
30 my life thrown away, nor lost.

336. But yet all the things of God were kept out of my sight, and still the tempter followed me with, *But whither must you go when you die? what will become of you? where will you be found in another world? what evidence have you for heaven and glory, and an inheritance among them*
35 *that are sanctified?* Thus was I tossed for manie weeks, and knew not what to do; at last this consideration fell with weight upon me,

15 scrabling] scrambling 3 5 6

That it was for the Word and Way of God that I was in this condition, wherefore I was ingaged not to flinch a hair's breadth from it.

337. I thought also, that God might chuse whether he would give me comfort now, or at the hour of death; but I might not therefore chuse whether I would hold my profession or no: I was bound, but he was free: yea, it was my dutie to stand to his Word, whether he would ever look upon me or no, or save me at the last: Wherefore, thought I, the point being thus, I am for going on, and venturing my eternal state with Christ, whether I have comfort here or no; if God doth not come in, thought I, I will leap off the Ladder even blindfold into Eternitie, sink or swim, come heaven, come hell; Lord Jesus, if thou wilt catch me, do; if not, I will venture for thy Name.

338. I was no sooner fixed upon this resolution, but that word dropped upon me, *Doth Job serve God for nought?* as if the accuser had said, Lord, *Job* is no upright man, he serves thee for by-respects, hast thou not made a hedge about him, &c. But put forth now thy hand, and touch all that he hath, and he will curse thee to thy face: How now, thought I, is this the sign of an upright Soul, to desire to serve God when all is taken from him? is he a godlie man that will serve God for nothing rather then give out? blessed be God, then, I hope I have an upright heart, for I am resolved, (God give me strength) never to denie my profession, though I have nothing at all for my pains; and as I was thus considering, that Scripture was set before me, Psa. 44. 12. &c.

339. Now was my heart full of comfort, for I hoped it was sincere; I would not have been without this trial for much; I am comforted everie time I think of it, and I hope I shall bless God for ever for the teaching I have had by it. Many more of the Dealings of God towards me I might relate, but these out of the spoils won in Battel have I dedicated to maintain the house of God, 1 Chron. 26. 27.

The CONCLUSION

1. Of all the Temptations that ever I met with in my life, to question the being of God, and the truth of his Gospel, is the worst, and worst to be born; when this temptation comes, it takes away my girdle from me, and removeth the foundations from under me: O I have often thought of that word, *Have your loyns girt about with truth*; and of that, *When the foundations are destroyed what can the Righteous do?*

2. Sometimes, when, after sin committed, I have looked for sore chastisement from the hand of God, the very next that I have had from him hath been the discovery of his grace. Sometimes, when I have been comforted, I have called myself a fool for my so sinking under trouble. And then, again, when I have been cast down, I thought I was not wise to give such way to comfort. With such strength and weight have both these been upon me.

3. I have wondered much at this one thing, that though God doth visit my Soul with never so blessed a discoverie of himself, yet I have found again, that such hours have attended me afterwards, that I have been in my spirit so filled with darkness, that I could not so much as once conceive what that God and that comfort was with which I have been refreshed.

4. I have sometimes seen more in a line of the Bible then I could well tell how to stand under, and yet at another time the whole Bible hath been to me as drie as a stick, or rather, my heart hath been so dead and drie unto it, that I could not conceive the least dram of refreshment, though I have lookt it all over.

5. Of all tears, they are the best that are made by the Blood of Christ; and of all joy, that is the sweetest that is mixt with mourning over Christ: O 'tis a goodly thing to be on our knees, with Christ in our arms, before God: I hope I know something of these things.

6. I find to this day seven abominations in my heart: 1. Inclinings to unbelief, 2. Suddenlie to forget the love and mercie that Christ

The CONCLUSION 2. Sometimes . . . me. *add.* 3. *renumbered* § 2 5

2 being . . . Gospel] being and truth of the Gospel 1 3   25 all] *add.* 3
26 tears] fears 6

manifesteth, 3. A leaning to the Works of the Law, 4. Wandrings and coldness in prayer, 5. To forget to watch for that I pray for, 6. Apt to murmur because I have no more, and yet ready to abuse what I have, 7. I can do none of those things which God commands me, but my corruptions will thrust in themselves; When I would 5 do good, evil is present with me.

7. These things I continuallie see and feel, and am afflicted and oppressed with; yet the Wisdom of God doth order them for my good: 1. They make me abhor myself; 2. They keep me from trusting my heart; 3. They convince me of the insufficiencie of all 10 inherent righteousness; 4. They shew me the necessity of flying to Jesus; 5. They press me to pray unto God; 6. They show me the need I have to watch and be sober; 7. And provoke me to look to God thorow Christ to help me, and carry me thorow this world. *Amen.* 15

FINIS

13-14 look to God] pray unto God 6

A RELATION

OF THE

IMPRISONMENT

OF

Mr. JOHN BUNYAN,

Minifter of the Gofpel at BEDFORD,

In NOVEMBER, 1660.

His Examination before the Juftices, his Conference with the Clerk of the Peace, what paffed
between the Judges and his Wife, when fhe pre-
fented a Petition for his Deliverance, &c.

Written by himfelf, and never before publifhed.

Bleffed are ye which are perfecuted for righteoufnefs fake,
for theirs is the kingdom of Heaven.

Bleffed are ye when men fhall revile you and perfecute you,
and fhall fay all manner of evil againft you falfly for my
name's fake.

Rejoice and be exceeding glad, for great is your reward in
Heaven, for fo perfecuted they the Prophets which were
before you. MAT. v. 10, 11, 12.

LONDON:

Printed for JAMES BUCKLAND, at the Buck,
in Paternofter-Row.

MDCCLXV.

*The Relation of my Imprisonment in the month of November, 1660, when, by
the good hand of my God, I had for five or six years together, without any
great interruption, freely preached the blessed Gospel of our Lord Jesus
Christ; and had also, through his blessed Grace, some encouragement by his
blessing thereupon: The Devil, that old enemy of mans salvation, took his* 5
*opportunity to inflame the hearts of his vassals against me, insomuch that at
the last, I was laid out for by the warrant of a justice, and was taken and
committed to prison. The relation thereof is as followeth:*

Upon the 12th of this instant November, 1660, I was desired by
some of the friends in the country to come to teach at *Samsell*, by 10
Harlington, in *Bedfordshire*. To whom I made a promise, if the Lord
permitted, to be with them on the time aforesaid. The justice
hearing thereof, (whose name is Mr. *Francis Wingate*) forthwith
issued out his warrant to take me, and bring me before him, and
in the mean time to keep a very strong watch about the house 15
where the meeting should be kept, as if we that was to meet
together in that place did intend to do some fearful business, to
the destruction of the country; when alas, the constable, when he
came in, found us only with our Bibles in our hands, ready to speak
and hear the word of God; for we was just about to begin our 20
exercise. Nay, we had begun in prayer for the blessing of God upon
our opportunity, intending to have preached the Word of the Lord
unto them there present: But the constable coming in prevented
us. So that I was taken and forced to depart the room. But had I
been minded to have played the coward, I could have escaped, and 25
kept out of his hands. For when I was come to my friend's house,
there was whispering that that day I should be taken, for there was
a warrant out to take me; which when my friend heard, he being
somewhat timorous, questioned whether we had best have our
meeting or not: And whether it might not be better for me to 30
depart, lest they should take me and have me before the Justice,
and after that send me to prison, (for he knew better than I what
spirit they were of, living by them) to whom I said, no: By no
means, I will not stir, neither will I have the meeting dismissed for
this. Come, be of good chear, let us not be daunted, our cause is 35
good, we need not be ashamed of it, to preach Gods word, it is so

good a work, that we shall be well rewarded, if we suffer for that; or to this purpose—(But as for my friend, I think he was more afraid of me, than of himself.) After this I walked into the close, where I somewhat seriously considering the matter, this came into 5 my mind: That I had shewed myself hearty and couragious in my preaching, and had, blessed be Grace, made it my business to encourage others; therefore thought I, if I should now run, and make an escape, it will be of a very ill savour in the country. For what will my weak and newly converted brethren think of it? But that I was 10 not so strong in deed, as I was in word. Also I feared that if I should run now there was a warrant out for me, I might by so doing make them afraid to stand, when great words only should be spoken to them. Besides I thought, that seeing God of his mercy should chuse me to go upon the forlorn hope in this country; that is, to be the 15 first, that should be opposed, for the Gospel; if I should fly, it might be a discouragement to the whole body that might follow after. And further, I thought the world thereby would take occasion at my cowardliness, to have blasphemed the Gospel, and to have had some ground to suspect worse of me and my profession, than I 20 deserved. These things, with others, considered by me, I came in again to the house, with a full resolution to keep the meeting, and not to go away, though I could have been gone about an hour before the officer apprehended me; but I would not; for I was resolved to see the utmost of what they could say or do unto me: For 25 blessed be the Lord, I knew of no evil that I had said or done. And so, as aforesaid, I begun the meeting: But being prevented by the constable's coming in with his warrant to take me, I could not proceed: But before I went away, I spake some few words of counsel and encouragement to the people, declaring to them, that they see 30 we was prevented of our opportunity to speak and hear the word of God, and was like to suffer for the same: desiring them that they should not be discouraged: For it was a mercy to suffer upon so good account: For we might have been apprehended as thieves or murderers, or for other wickedness; but blessed be God it was 35 not so, but we suffer as christians for well doing: And we had better be the persecuted, than the persecutors, &c. But the constable and the justice's man waiting on us, would not be at quiet till they had

me away, and that we departed the house: But because the justice
was not at home that day, there was a friend of mine engaged for
me to bring me to the constable on the morrow morning. Otherwise
the constable must have charged a watch with me, or have secured
me some other ways, my crime was so great. So on the next morning 5
we went to the constable, and so to the justice.[1] He asked the
constable what we did, where we was met together, and what we
had with us. I trow, he meant whether we had armour or not; but
when the constable told him that there was only met a few of us
together to preach and hear the word, and no sign of any thing else, 10
he could not well tell what to say: Yet because he had sent for me,
he did adventure to put out a few proposals to me, which was to
this effect. Namely, What I did there? and why I did not content
myself with following my calling: For it was against the law, that
such as I should be admitted to do as I did. 15

John Bunyan. To which I answered, that the intent of my coming
thither, and to other places, was to instruct, and counsel people to
forsake their sins, and close in with Christ, lest they did miserably
perish; and that I could do both these without confusion, (to wit)
follow my calling, and preach the word also. 20

At which words, he[2] was in a chafe, as it appeared; for he said
that he would break the neck of our meetings.

Bun. I said, it may be so. Then he wished me to get me sureties
to be bound for me, or else he would send me to the jail.

My sureties being ready, I call'd them in, and when the bond for 25
my appearance was made, he told them, that they was bound to
keep me from preaching; and that if I did preach, their bonds would
be forfeited. To which I answered, that then I should break them;
for I should not leave speaking the word of God: Even to counsel,
comfort, exhort, and teach the people among whom I came; and I 30
thought this to be a work that had no hurt in it: But was rather
worthy of commendation, than blame.

Wing. Whereat he told me, that if they would not be so bound,
my mittimus must be made, and I sent to the jail, there to lie to
the quarter-sessions. 35

Now while my mittimus was a making, the justice was withdrawn;

---

[1] Justice Wingate.   [2] Ibid.

and in comes an old enemy to the truth, Dr. *Lindale,* who, when he was come in, fell to taunting at me with many reviling terms.

Bun. To whom I answered, that I did not come thither to talk with him, but with the justice. Whereat he supposing that I had 5 nothing to say for myself, triumphed as if he had got the victory. Charging and condemning me for medling with that for which I could shew no warrant. And asked me if I had taken the oaths? and if I had not, 'twas pity but that I should be sent to prison, &c.

I told him, that if I was minded, I could answer to any sober ques- 10 tion that he should put to me. He then urged me again, how I could prove it lawful for me to preach, with a great deal of confidence of the victory.

But at last, because he should see that I could answer him if I listed, I cited to him that in Peter, which saith, *As every man hath* 15 *received the gift, even so let him minister the same, &c.*

Lind. I, saith he, to whom is that spoken?

Bun. To whom, said I, why to every man that hath received a gift from God. Mark, saith the Apostle, *As every man that hath received a gift from God, &c.* And again, *You may all prophesy one by one.* 20 Whereat the man was a little stopt, and went a softlier pace: But not being willing to lose the day, he began again, and said:

Lind. Indeed I do remember that I have read of one Alexander a Coppersmith, who did much oppose, and disturb the Apostles. (Aiming 'tis like at me, because I was a Tinker.)

25   *Bun.* To which I answered, that I also had read of very many priests and pharisees, that had their hands in the blood of our Lord Jesus Christ.

Lind. I, saith he, and you are one of those scribes and pharisees, for you, with a pretence, make long prayers to devour widows houses.

30   *Bun.* I answered, that if he had got no more by preaching and praying than I had done, he would not be so rich as now he was. But that Scripture coming into my mind, *Answer not a fool according to his folly,* I was as sparing of my speech as I could, without preju- dice to truth.

35   Now by this time my mittimus was made, and I committed to the constable to be sent to the jail in Bedford, &c.

But as I was going, two of my brethren met with me by the way, and desired the constable to stay, supposing that they should prevail with the justice, through the favour of a pretended friend, to let me go at liberty. So we did stay, while they went to the justice, and after much discourse with him, it came to this; that if I would come to him again, and say some certain words to him, I should be released. Which when they told me, I said if the words was such that might be said with a good conscience, I should, or else I should not. So through their importunity I went back again, but not believing that I should be delivered: For I feared their spirit was too full of opposition to the truth, to let me go, unless I should in something or other, dishonour my God, and wound my conscience. Wherefore as I went, I lift up my heart to God, for light, and strength, to be kept, that I might not do any thing that might either dishonour him, or wrong my own soul, or be a grief or discouragement to any that was inclining after the Lord Jesus Christ.

Well, when I came to the justice again, there was Mr. *Foster* of Bedford, who coming out of another room, and seeing of me by the light of the candle (for it was dark night when I went thither) he said unto me, who is there, *John Bunyan?*[1] with such seeming affection, as if he would have leaped in my neck and kissed me, which made me somewhat wonder, that such a man as he, with whom I had so little acquaintance, and besides, that had ever been a close opposer of the ways of God, should carry himself so full of love to me: But afterwards, when I saw what he did, it caused me to remember those sayings, *Their tongues are smoother than oil, but their words are drawn swords.* And again, *Beware of men, &c.* When I[2] had answered him, that blessed be God I was well, he said, What is the occasion of your being here? or to that purpose. To whom I answered, that I was at a meeting of people a little way off, intending to speak a word of exhortation to them; the justice hearing thereof (said I) was pleased to send his warrant, to fetch me before him, &c.

Fost. So (said he) I understand: But well, if you will promise to call the people no more together, you shall have your liberty to go home: for my brother is very loath to send you to prison, if you will be but ruled.

---

[1] A right Judas.   [2] Bunyan.

Bun. Sir (said I) pray what do you mean by calling the people together? my business is not any thing among them when they are come together, but to exhort them to look after the salvation of their souls, that they may be saved, &c.

5   *Fost.* Saith he, we must not enter into explication, or dispute now; but if you will say you will call the people no more together, you may have your liberty; if not, you must be sent away to prison.

Bun. Sir, said I, I shall not force or compel any man to hear me, but yet if I come into any place where there is a people met together,
10 I should, according to the best of my skill and wisdom, exhort and counsel them to seek out after the Lord Jesus Christ, for the salvation of their souls.

Fost. He said, that was none of my work; I must follow my calling, and if I would but leave off preaching, and follow my
15 calling, I should have the justice's favour, and be acquitted presently.

Bun. To whom I said, that I could follow my calling and that too, namely, preaching the word: And I did look upon it as my duty to do them both, as I had an opportunity.

Fost. He said, to have any such meetings was against the law;
20 and therefore he would have me leave off, and say, I would call the people no more together.

Bun. To whom I said, that I durst not make any further promise: For my conscience would not suffer me to do it. And again, I did look upon it as my duty to do as much good as I could, not only in
25 my trade, but also in communicating to all people wheresoever I came, the best knowledge I had in the word.

Fost. He told me, that I was the nearest the Papists of any, and that he would convince me of immediately.

Bun. I asked him wherein?

30   *Fost.* He said, in that we understood the Scriptures literally.

Bun. I told him, that those that was to be understood literally we understood them so; but for those that was to be understood otherwise, we endeavoured so to understand them.

Fost. He said, which of the Scriptures do you understand literally?

35   *Bun.* I said, this, *He that believes shall be saved.* This was to be understood, just as it is spoken; that whosoever believeth in Christ, shall, according to the plain and simple words of the text, be saved.

Fost. He said, that I was ignorant, and did not understand the Scriptures; for how (said he) can you understand them, when you know not the original Greek? &c.

Bun. To whom I said, that if that was his opinion, that none could understand the Scriptures, but those that had the original Greek, &c. then but a very few of the poorest sort should be saved, (this is harsh) yet the Scripture saith, *That God hides his things from the wise and prudent,* (that is from the learned of the world) *and reveals them to babes and sucklings.*

Fost. He said there was none that heard me, but a company of foolish people.

Bun. I told him that there was the wise as well as the foolish that do hear me; and again, those that are most commonly counted foolish by the world, are the wisest before God. Also that God had rejected the wise, and mighty and noble, and chosen the foolish, and the base.

Fost. He told me, that I made people neglect their calling; and that God had commanded people to work six days, and serve him on the seventh.

Bun. I told him, that it was the duty of people, (both rich and poor) to look out for their souls on them days, as well as for their bodies: And that God would have his people exhort one another daily, while it is called to day.

Fost. He said again, that there was none but a company of poor simple ignorant people that come to hear me.

Bun. I told him, that the foolish and the ignorant had most need of teaching and information; and therefore it would be profitable for me to go on in that work.

Fost. Well, said he, to conclude, but will you promise that you will not call the people together any more? and then you may be released, and go home.

Bun. I told him, that I durst say no more than I had said. For I durst not leave off that work which God had called me to.

So he withdrew from me, and then came several of the justices servants to me, and told me, that I stood so much upon a nicity. Their[1] master, they, said was willing to let me go; and if I would

---

[1] Justice's servants.

but say I would call the people no more together, I might have my liberty, &c.

Bun. I told them, there was more ways than one, in which a man might be said to call the people together. As for instance, if 5 a man get upon the market-place, and there read a book, or the like, though he do not say to the people, Sirs, come hither and hear; yet if they come to him because he reads, he, by his very reading, may be said to call them together; because they would not have been there to hear, if he had not been there to read. And seeing this 10 might be termed a calling the people together, I durst not say, I would not call them together; for then, by the same argument, my preaching might be said to call them together.

Wing. and Fost. Then came the Justice and Mr. Foster to me again (we had a little more discourse about preaching, but because 15 the method of it is out of my mind, I pass it) and when they saw that I was at a point, and would not be moved nor perswaded,

Mr. Foster[1] told the justice, that then he must send me away to prison. And that he would do well also, if he would present all them that was the cause of my coming among them to meetings. 20 Thus we parted.

And verily as I was going forth of the doors, I had much ado to forbear saying to them, that I carried the peace of God along with me: But I held my peace, and blessed be the Lord, went away to prison with God's comfort in my poor soul.

25 After I had lain in the jail five or six days, the brethren sought means again to get me out by bondsmen, (for so run my mittimus, that I should lie there till I could find sureties). They went to a justice at Elstow, one Mr. Crumpton, to desire him to take bond for my appearing at the quarter-sessions. At the first he told them 30 he would, but afterwards he made a demur at the business, and desired first to see my mittimus, which run to this purpose; That I went about to several conventicles in this county, to the great disparagement of the government of the church of England, &c. When he had seen it, he said that there might be something more against 35 me, than was expressed in my mittimus: And that he was but a young man, therefore he durst not do it. This my jailor told me.

---

[1] This is the man that did at the first express so much love to me.

Whereat I was not at all daunted, but rather glad, and saw evidently that the Lord had heard me, for before I went down to the justice, I begged of God, that if I might do more good by being at liberty than in prison, that then I might be set at liberty: But if not, his will be done; for I was not altogether without hopes, but that my imprisonment might be an awakening to the Saints in the country, therefore I could not tell well which to chuse. Only I in that manner did commit the thing to God. And verily at my return, I did meet my God sweetly in the prison again, comforting of me and satisfying of me that it was his will and mind that I should be there.

When I came back again to prison, as I was musing at the slender answer of the Justice, this word dropt in upon my heart with some life, *For he knew that for envy they had delivered him.*

Thus have I in short, declared the manner, and occasion of my being in prison; where I lie waiting the good will of God, to do with me, as he pleaseth; knowing that not one hair of my head can fall to the ground without the will of my Father which is in Heaven. Let the rage and malice of men be never so great, they can do no more, nor go no farther than God permits them: But when they have done their worst, we know all things shall work together for good to them that love God.

Farewell.

Here is the Sum of my Examination, before Justice Keelin, Justice Chester, Justice Blundale, Justice Beecher, and Justice Snagg, &c.

After I had lain in prison above seven weeks, the quarter-sessions was to be kept in Bedford, for the county thereof; unto which I was to be brought; and when my jailor had set me before those Justices, there was a bill of indictment preferred against me. The extent thereof was as followeth: That John Bunyan of the town of Bedford, labourer, being a person of such and such conditions, he hath (since such a time) devilishly and perniciously abstained from coming to church to hear divine service, and is a common upholder of several unlawful meetings and conventicles, to the great disturbance and distraction of the good subjects of this kingdom, contrary to the laws of our sovereign lord the king, &c.

The Clerk. When this was read, the clerk of the sessions said unto me; What say you to this?

Bun. I said, that as to the first part of it, I was a common frequenter of the church of God. And was also, by grace, a member with them people, over whom Christ is the Head.

Keelin. But saith Justice *Keelin* (who was the judge in that court) 5 Do you come to church (you know what I mean) to the parish church, to hear divine service?

Bun. I answered, no, I did not.

Keel. He asked me, why?

Bun. I said, because I did not find it commanded in the word of 10 God.

Keel. He said, we were commanded to pray.

Bun. I said, but not by the Common Prayer-book.

Keel. He said, how then?

Bun. I said with the spirit. As the Apostle saith, *I will pray with* 15 *the spirit and with understanding.* 1 Cor. xiv. 15.

Keel. He said, we might pray with the spirit, and with understanding, and with the Common Prayer-book also.

Bun. I said that those prayers in the Common Prayerbook, was such as was made by other men, and not by the motions of the 20 Holy Ghost, within our Hearts; and as I said the Apostle saith, he will pray with the spirit and with understanding; not with the spirit and the Common Prayerbook.

Another Justice. What do you count prayer? Do you think it is to say a few words over before, or among a people?

25 *Bun.* I said, no, not so; for men might have many elegant, or excellent words, and yet not pray at all: But when a man prayeth, he doth through a sense of those things which he wants (which sense is begotten by the spirit) pour out his heart before God through Christ; though his words be not so many, and so excellent 30 as others are.

Justices. They said, that was true.

Bun. I said, this might be done without the Common Prayer-book.

Another. One of them said, (I think it was Justice *Blundale,* or Justice *Snagg*) How should we know, that you do not write out 35 your prayers first, and then read them afterwards to the people? This he spake in a laughing way.

15 *and*] om. 1765   16 *and*] *om.* 1765

Bun. I said, it is not our use, to take a pen and paper and write a few words thereon, and then go and read it over to a company of people.

But how should we know it, said he?

Bun. Sir, it is none of our custom, said I.

Keel. But said Justice Keelin, it is lawful to use Common Prayer, and such like forms: For Christ taught his disciples to pray, as John also taught his disciples. And further, said he, cannot one man teach another to pray? Faith comes by hearing: And one man may convince another of sin, and therefore prayers made by men, and read over, are good to teach, and help men to pray.

While he was speaking these words, God brought that word into my mind, in the eighth of the Romans, at the 26th verse: I say God brought it, for I thought not on it before: but as he was speaking, it came so fresh into my mind, and was set so evidently before me, as if the Scripture had said, Take me, take me; so when he had done speaking,

Bun. I said, Sir, the Scripture saith, that *it is the spirit as helpeth our infirmities*; for we know not what we should pray for as we ought: But the spirit itself maketh intercession for us, with sighs and groanings which cannot be uttered. Mark, said I, it doth not say the Common Prayer-book teacheth us how to pray, but the spirit. And it is the spirit that helpeth our infirmities, saith the Apostle; he doth not say it is the Common Prayer-book.

And as to the Lord's Prayer, although it be an easy thing to say *Our Father, &c.* with the mouth; yet there is very few that can, in the spirit, say the two first words of that Prayer; that is, that can call God their Father, as knowing what it is to be born again, and as having experience, that they are begotten of the spirit of God: Which if they do not, all is but babbling, &c.

Keel. Justice *Keelin* said, that that was a truth.

Bun. And I say further, as to your saying that one man may convince another of sin, and that faith comes by hearing, and that one man may tell another how he should pray, &c. I say men may tell each other of their sins, but it is the spirit that must convince them.[1]

---

[1] If any say now that God useth means; I answer, but not the Common Prayer-book, or that is none of his institution, 'tis the spirit in the word that is Gods ordinance.

L

And though it be said that *faith comes by hearing*: Yet it is the spirit that worketh faith in the heart through hearing, or else[1] *they are not profited by hearing*.

And that though one Man may tell another how he should pray: Yet, as I said before, he cannot pray, nor make his condition known to God, except the spirit help. It is not the Common Prayer-book that can do this. It is the[2] *spirit that sheweth us our sins*, and the[3] *spirit that sheweth us a Saviour*: And the spirit that stireth up in our hearts desires to come to God, for such things as we stand in need of, even sighing out our souls unto him for them with *groans which cannot be uttered*. With other words to the same purpose. At this they were set.

Keel. But says Justice *Keelin*, what have you against the Common Prayer-book?

Bun. I said, Sir, if you will hear me, I shall lay down my reasons against it.

Keel. He said I should have liberty; but first, said he, let me give you one caution; take heed of speaking irreverently of the Common Prayer-book: For if you do so, you will bring great damage upon yourself.

Bun. So I proceeded, and said, my first reason was; because it was not commanded in the word of God, and therefore I could not do it.

Another. One of them said, where do you find it commanded in the Scripture, that you should go to *Elstow*, or *Bedford*, and yet it is lawful to go to either of them, is it not?

Bun. I said, to go to *Elstow* or *Bedford*, was a civil thing, and not material, though not commanded, and yet God's word allowed me to go about my calling, and therefore if it lay there, then to go thither, &c. But to pray, was a great part of the divine worship of God, and therefore it ought to be done according to the rule of God's word.

Another. One of them said, he will do harm; let him speak no further.

Just. Keel. Justice *Keelin* said, No, no, never fear him, we are better established than so; he can do no harm, we know the Common

---

[1] Heb. iv. 2.   [2] John xv. 16.   [3] Matth. iii. 16–17.

Prayer-book hath been ever since the Apostles time, and is lawful
to be used in the church.

Bun. I said, shew me the place in the epistles, where the Common
Prayer-book is written, or one text of Scripture, that commands me
to read it, and I will use it. But yet, notwithstanding, said I, they 5
that have a mind to use it, they have their liberty; that is,[1] I would
not keep them from it, but for our parts, we can pray to God without it. Blessed be his name.

With that one of them said, who is your God? Beelzebub? Moreover, they often said, that I was possessed with the spirit of delusion, 10
and of the Devil. All which sayings, I passed over, the Lord forgive
them! And further, I said, blessed be the Lord for it, we are encouraged to meet together, and to pray, and exhort one another;
for we have had the comfortable presence of God among us, for
ever blessed be his holy name. 15

Keel. Justice *Keeling* called this pedlers French, saying that I must
leave off my canting. The Lord open his eyes!

Bun. I said, that we ought to exhort one another daily, while it
is called to-day, &c.

Keel. Justice *Keeling* said, that I ought not to preach. And 20
asked me where I had my authority? with many other such like
words.

Bun. I said, that I would prove that it was lawful for me, and
such as I am, to preach the word of God.

Keel. He said unto me, by what Scripture? 25

I said, by that in the first epistle of *Peter*, the ivth chap., the
11th ver. and *Acts* the xviiith, with other Scriptures, which he would
not suffer me to mention. But said, hold; not so many, which is the
first?

Bun. I said, this. *As every man hath received the gift, even so let him* 30
minister the same unto another, as good stewards of the manifold grace of
God: If any man speak, let him speak as the oracles of God, &c.

Keel. He said, let me a little open that Scripture to you. *As every*
man hath received the gift; that is, said he, as every man hath received
a trade, so let him follow it. If any man have received a gift of 35

---

[1] It is not the spirit of a Christian to persecute any for their religion; but to pity
them; and if they will turn, to instruct them.

tinkering, as thou hast done, let him follow his tinkering. And so other men their trades. And the divine his calling, &c.

Bun. Nay, Sir, said I, but it is most clear, that the Apostle speaks here of preaching the word; if you do but compare both the verses
5 together, the next verse explains this gift what it is; saying, *If any man speak, let him speak as the oracles of God*: So that it is plain, that the Holy Ghost doth not so much in this place exhort to civil callings, as to the exercising of those gifts that we have received from God. I would have gone on, but he would not give me leave.

10 *Keel.* He said, we might do it in our families but not otherways.

Bun. I said, if it was lawful to do good to some, it was lawful to do good to more. If it was a good duty to exhort our families, it is good to exhort others: But if they held it a sin to meet together to seek the face of God, and exhort one another to follow Christ, I
15 should sin still; For so we should do.

Keel. He said he was not so well versed in Scripture as to dispute, or words to that purpose. And said, moreover, that they could not wait upon me any longer; but said to me, then you confess the indictment, do you not? Now, and not till now, I saw I was indicted.

20 *Bun.* I said, this I confess, we have had many meetings together, both to pray to God, and to exhort one another, and that we had the sweet comforting presence of the Lord among us for our encouragement, blessed be his name therefore. I confessed myself guilty no otherwise.

25 *Keel.* Then said he, hear your judgment. You must be had back again to prison, and there lie for three months following; at three months end, if you do not submit to go to church to hear divine service, and leave your preaching, you must be banished the realm: And if, after such a day as shall be appointed you to be gone, you
30 shall be found in this realm, *&c.* or be found to come over again without special licence from the King, *&c.* you must stretch by the neck for it, I tell you plainly; and so he bid my jailor have me away.

Bun. I told him, as to this matter, I was at a point with him: For if I was out of prison to day, I would preach the Gospel again
35 to-morrow, by the help of God.

Another. To which one made me some answer: But my jailor pulling me away to be gone, I could not tell what he said.

Thus I departed from them; and I can truly say, I bless the Lord *Jesus Christ* for it, that my heart was sweetly refreshed in the time of my examination, and also afterwards, at my returning to the prison: So that I found *Christ's* words more than bare trifles, where he saith, he *will give a mouth and wisdom, even such as all the adversaries* 5 *shall not resist, or gainsay.* And that his peace no man can take from us.

Thus have I given you the substance of my examination. The Lord make these profitable to all that shall read or hear them.

Farewell.

The Substance of some Discourse had between the Clerk of the Peace and 10
myself; when he came to admonish me, according to the tenor of that Law,
by which I was in Prison.

When I had lain in prison other twelve weeks, and now not know-ing what they intended to do with me, upon the third of *April,* comes Mr. *Cobb* unto me, (as he told me) being sent by the Justices 15 to admonish me, and demand of me submittance to the church of *England, &c.* The extent of our discourse was as followeth.

Cobb. When he was come into the house he sent for me out of my chamber; who, when I was come unto him, he said, Neighbour *Bunyan,* how do you do? 20

Bun. I thank you Sir, said I, very well, blessed be the Lord.

Cobb. Saith he, I come to tell you, that it is desired, you would submit yourself to the laws of the land, or else at the next sessions it will go worse with you, even to be sent away out of the nation, or else worse than that. 25

Bun. I said, that I did desire to demean myself in the world, both as becometh a man and a christian.

Cobb. But, saith he, you must submit to the laws of the land, and leave off those meetings which you was wont to have: For the statute law is directly against it; and I am sent to you by the 30 Justices to tell you that they do intend to prosecute the law against you, if you submit not.

Bun. I said, Sir, I conceive that that law by which I am in prison at this time, doth not reach or condemn, either me, or the meetings which I do frequent: That law was made against those, that being 35 designed to do evil in their meetings, make the exercise of religion their pretence to cover their wickedness. It doth not forbid the private meetings of those that plainly and simply make it their only end to worship the Lord, and to exhort one another to edification. 5 My end in meeting with others is simply to do as much good as I can, by exhortation and counsel, according to that small measure of light which God hath given me, and not to disturb the peace of the nation.

Cobb. Every one will say the same, said he; you see the late 10 insurrection at *London*, under what glorious pretences they went, and yet indeed they intended no less than the ruin of the kingdom and commonwealth.

Bun. That practice of theirs, I abhor, said I; yet it doth not follow, that because they did so, therefore all others will do so. I 15 look upon it as my duty to behave myself under the King's government, both as becomes a man and a christian; and if an occasion was offered me, I should willingly manifest my loyalty to my Prince, both by word and deed.

Cobb. Well, said he, I do not profess myself to be a man that can 20 dispute; but this I say truly, neighbour *Bunyan*, I would have you consider this matter seriously, and submit yourself; you may have your liberty to exhort your neighbour in private discourse, so be you do not call together an assembly of people; and truly you may do much good to the church of Christ, if you would go this way; 25 and this you may do, and the law not abridge you of it. It is your private meetings that the law is against.

Bun. Sir, said I, if I may do good to one by my discourse, why may I not do good to two? And if to two, why not to four, and so to eight, &c.

30 *Cobb.* I, saith he, and to a hundred, I warrant you.

Bun. Yes, Sir, said I, I think I should not be forbid to do as much good as I can.

Cobb. But, saith he, you may but pretend to do good, and indeed, notwithstanding, do harm, by seducing the people; you are there- 35 fore denied your meeting so many together, lest you should do harm.

Bun. And yet, said I, you say the law tolerates me to discourse with my neighbour; surely there is no law tolerates me to seduce any one; therefore if I may by the law discourse with one, surely it is to do him good; and if I by discoursing may do good to one, surely, by the same law, I may do good to many.

Cobb. The law, saith he, doth expresly forbid your private meetings, therefore they are not to be tolerated. 5

Bun. I told him, that I would not entertain so much uncharitableness of that parliament in the 35th of *Elizabeth,* or of the Queen herself, as to think they did by that law intend the oppressing of any of God's ordinances, or the interrupting any in the way of God; but men may, in the wresting of it, turn it against the way of 10 God, but take the law in itself, and it only fighteth against those that drive at mischief in their hearts and meetings, making religion only their cloak, colour, or pretence; for so are the words of the statute. *If any meetings, under colour or pretence of religion,* &c.

Cobb. Very good; therefore the King seeing that pretences are 15 usual in, and among people, as to make religion their pretence only; therefore he, and the law before him, doth forbid such private meetings, and tolerates only public; you may meet in public.

Bun. Sir, said I, let me answer you in a similitude; set the case that, at such a wood corner, there did usually come forth thieves to 20 do mischief, must there therefore a law be made, that every one that cometh out there shall be killed? May not there come out true men as well as thieves, out from thence? Just thus is it in this case; I do think there may be many, that may design the destruction of the commonwealth: But it doth not follow therefore that all private 25 meetings are unlawful; those that transgress, let them be punished: And if at any time I myself, should do any act in my conversation as doth not become a man and christian, let me bear the punishment. And as for your saying I may meet in public, if I may be suffered, I would gladly do it: Let me have but meetings enough in 30 public, and I shall care the less to have them in private. I do not meet in private because I am afraid to have meetings in public. I bless the Lord that my heart is at that point, that if any man can lay any thing to my charge, either in doctrine or practice, in this particular, that can be proved error or heresy, I am willing to dis- 35 own it, even in the very market-place. But if it be truth, then to

stand to it to the last drop of my blood. And Sir, said I, you ought to commend me for so doing. To err, and to be a heretic, are two things; I am no heretic, because I will not stand refractorily to defend any one thing that is contrary to the word; prove any thing
5 which I hold to be an error, and I will recant it.

Cobb. But goodman *Bunyan,* said he, methinks you need not stand so strictly upon this one thing, as to have meetings of such public assemblies. Cannot you submit, and, notwithstanding do as much good as you can, in a neighbourly way, without having such meetings?
10 *Bun.* Truly Sir, said I, I do not desire to commend myself, but to think meanly of myself; yet when I do most despise myself, taking notice of that small measure of light which God hath given me, also that the people of the Lord (by their own saying) are edified thereby: Besides, when I see that the Lord, through grace, hath in
15 some measure blessed my labour, I dare not but exercise that gift which God hath given me, for the good of the people. And I said further, that I would willingly speak in public if I might.

Cobb. He said, that I might come to the public assemblies and hear. What though you do not preach? you may hear: Do not think
20 yourself so well enlightened, and that you have received a gift so far above others, but that you may hear other men preach. Or to that purpose.

Bun. I told him, I was as willing to be taught as to give instruction, and I looked upon it as my duty to do both; for, said I, a man
25 that is a teacher, he himself may learn also from another that teacheth; as the Apostle saith: *We may all prophecy one by one, that all may learn.* That is, every man that hath received a gift from God, he may dispense it, that others may be comforted; and when he hath done, he may hear, and learn, and be comforted himself of others.
30 *Cobb.* But, said he, what if you should forbear awhile; and sit still, till you see further, how things will go?

Bun. Sir, said I, *Wickliffe* saith, that he which leaveth off preaching and hearing of the word of God for fear of excommunication of men, he is already excommunicated of God, and shall in the day of
35 judgment be counted a traitor to Christ.

Cobb. I, saith he, they that do not hear shall be so counted indeed; do you therefore hear.

Bun. But Sir, said I, he saith, he that shall leave off either preaching or hearing, &c. That is, if he hath received a gift for edification, it is his sin, if he doth not lay it out in a way of exhortation and counsel, according to the proportion of his gift; as well as to spend his time altogether in hearing others preach.   5

Cobb. But, said he, how shall we know that you have received a gift?

Bun. Said I, let any man hear and search, and prove the doctrine by the Bible.

Cobb. But will you be willing, said he, that two indifferent per- 10 sons shall determine the case, and will you stand by their judgment.

Bun. I said, are they infallible?

Cobb. He said, no.

Bun. Then, said I, it is possible my judgment may be as good as theirs: But yet I will pass by either, and in this matter be judged by 15 the Scriptures; I am sure that is infallible, and cannot err.

Cobb. But, said he, who shall be judge between you, for you take the Scriptures one way, and they another.

Bun. I said, the Scripture should, and that by comparing one Scripture with another; for that will open itself, if it be rightly 20 compared. As for instance, if under the different apprehensions of the word *Mediator*, you would know the truth of it, the Scriptures open it, and tell us, that he that is a mediator, must take up the business between two, and a mediator is not a mediator of one, *but God is one, and there is one mediator between God and man, even the man* 25 *Christ Jesus.* So likewise the Scripture calleth Christ a *compleat*, or perfect, or able *high-priest*. That is opened in that he is called man, and also God. His blood also is discovered to be effectually efficacious by the same things. So the Scripture, as touching the matter of meeting together, &c. doth likewise sufficiently open itself and 30 discover its meaning.

Cobb. But are you willing, said he, to stand to the judgment of the Church?

Bun. Yes Sir, said I, to the approbation of the church of God: the church's judgment is best expressed in Scripture. We had much 35 other discourse, which I cannot well remember, about the laws of the nation, submission to governments; to which I did tell him, that I did look upon myself as bound in conscience to walk according to all righteous laws, and that whether there was a King or no; and if I did any thing that was contrary, I did hold it my duty to bear patiently the penalty of the law, that was provided against 5 such offenders; with many more words to the like effect. And said, moreover, that to cut off all occasions of suspicion from any, as touching the harmlessness of my doctrine in private, I would willingly take the pains to give any one the notes of all my sermons: For I do sincerely desire to live quietly in my country, and to submit 10 to the present authority.

Cobb. Well, neighbour *Bunyan*, said he, but indeed I would wish you seriously to consider of these things, between this and the quarter-sessions, and to submit yourself. You may do much good if you continue still in the land: But alas, what benefit will it be to 15 your friends, or what good can you do to them, if you should be sent away beyond the seas into *Spain*, or *Constantinople*, or some other remote part of the world? Pray be ruled.

Jaylor. Indeed, Sir, I hope he will be ruled.

Bun. I shall desire, said I, in all godliness and honesty to behave 20 myself in the nation whilst I am in it. And if I must be so dealt withall, as you say, I hope God will help me to bear what they shall lay upon me. I know no evil that I have done in this matter, to be so used. I speak as in the presence of God.

Cobb. You know, saith he, that the Scripture saith, *the powers that* 25 *are, are ordained of God.*

Bun. I said, yes, and that I was to submit to the King as supreme, also to the governors, as to them that are sent by him.

Cobb. Well then, said he, the King then commands you, that you should not have any private meetings; because it is against his law, 30 and he is ordained of God, therefore you should not have any.

Bun. I told him, that *Paul* did own the powers that were in his day, as to be of God; and yet he was often in prison under them for all that. And also, though *Jesus Christ* told *Pilate*, that he had no power against him, but of God, yet he died under the same *Pilate*; 35 and yet, said I, I hope you will not say, that either *Paul*, or Christ, was such as did deny magistracy, and so sinned against God in slighting the ordinance. Sir, said I, the law hath provided two ways of obeying: The one to do that which I in my conscience do believe that I am bound to do, actively; and where I cannot obey actively, there I am willing to lie down, and to suffer what they shall do unto me. At this he sate still and said no more; which when he had done, I did thank him for his civil and meek discoursing with me; and so we parted.

O! that we might meet in Heaven!

Farewell. *J.B.*

Here followeth a Discourse between my Wife and the Judges, with others, touching my Deliverance at the Assises following: the which I took from her own Mouth.

After that I had received this sentence of banishing, or hanging, from them, and after the former admonition, touching the determination of Justices, if I did not recant; just when the time drew nigh, in which I should have abjured, or have done worse (as Mr. *Cobb* told me) came the time in which the King was to be crowned. Now at the coronation of Kings, there is usually a releasement of divers prisoners, by virtue of his coronation; in which privilege also I should have had my share; but that they took me for a convicted person, and therefore, unless I sued out a pardon, (as they called it) I could have no benefit thereby, notwithstanding, yet forasmuch as the coronation proclamation did give liberty from the day the King was crowned, to that day twelvemonth to sue them out: Therefore, though they would not let me out of prison, as they let out thousands, yet they could not meddle with me, as touching the execution of their sentence; because of the liberty offered for the suing out of pardons. Whereupon I continued in prison till the next assizes, which are called *Midsummer* assizes, being then kept in *August*, 1661.

Now at that assizes, because I would not leave any possible means unattempted that might be lawful; I did, by my wife, present a petition to the Judges three times, that I might be heard, and that they would impartially take my case into consideration.

The first time my wife went, she presented it to Judge *Hales*, who very mildly received it at her hand, telling her that he would do her and me the best good he could; but he feared, he said, he could do

none. The next day again, least they should, through the multitude
of business, forget me, we did throw another petition into the coach
to Judge *Twisdon*; who, when he had seen it, snapt her up, and angrily
told her that I was a convicted person, and could not be released,
5 unless I would promise to preach no more, *&c.*

Well, after this, she yet again presented another to Judge *Hales* as
he sate on the bench, who, as it seemed, was willing to give her
audience. Only Justice *Chester* being present, stept up and said, that
I was convicted in the court, and that I was a hot spirited fellow
10 (or words to that purpose) whereat he waved it, and did not
meddle therewith. But yet, my wife being encouraged by the High
Sheriff, did venture once more into their presence (as the poor
widow did to the unjust Judge) to try what she could do with them
for my liberty, before they went forth of the town. The place where
15 she went to them, was to the *Swan Chamber*, where the two Judges,
and many Justices and Gentry of the country, was in company
together. She then coming into the chamber with a bashed face,
and a trembling heart, began her errand to them in this manner.

Woman. My Lord, (directing herself to Judge *Hales*) I make bold
20 to come once again to your Lordship to know what may be done
with my husband.

Judge Hales. To whom he said, Woman, I told thee before I could
do thee no good; because they have taken that for a conviction
which thy husband spoke at the sessions: And unless there be
25 something done to undo that, I can do thee no good.

Woman. My Lord, said she, he is kept unlawfully in prison, they
clap'd him up before there were any proclamation against the
meetings; the indictment also is false: Besides, they never asked
him whether he was guilty or no; neither did he confess the
30 indictment.

One of the Justices. Then one of the Justices that stood by, whom
she knew not, said, My Lord, he was lawfully convicted.

Wom. It is false, said she; for when they said to him, do you confess the indictment? He said only this, that he had been at several
35 meetings, both where there was preaching the word, and prayer,
and that they had God's presence among them.

Judge Twisdon. Whereat Judge Twisdon answered very angrily, saying, what, you think we can do what we list; your husband is a breaker of the peace, and is convicted by the law, *&c.* Whereupon Judge *Hales* called for the Statute Book.

Wom. But said she, my Lord, he was not lawfully convicted.

Chester. Then Justice *Chester* said, my Lord, he was lawfully con- 5
victed.

Wom. It is false, said she; it was but a word of discourse that they took for a conviction (as you heard before.)

Chest. But it is recorded, woman, it is recorded, said Justice *Chester.* As if it must be of necessity true because it was recorded. 10
With which words he often endeavoured to stop her mouth, having no other argument to convince her, but it is recorded, it is recorded.

Wom. My Lord, said she, I was a-while since at *London,* to see if I could get my husband's liberty, and there I spoke with my Lord *Barkwood,* one of the house of Lords, to whom I delivered a petition, 15
who took it of me and presented it to some of the rest of the house of Lords, for my husband's releasement; who, when they had seen it, they said, that they could not release him, but had committed his releasement to the Judges, at the next assises. This he told me; and now I come to you to see if any thing may be done in this business, 20
and you give neither releasement nor relief. To which they gave her no answer, but made as if they heard her not.

Chest. Only Justice *Chester* was often up with this, He is convicted, and it is recorded.

Wom. If it be, it is false, said she. 25

Chest. My Lord, said Justice *Chester,* he is a pestilent fellow, there is not such a fellow in the country again.

Twis. What, will your husband leave preaching? If he will do so, then send for him.

Wom. My Lord, said she, he dares not leave preaching, as long 30
as he can speak.

Twis. See here, what should we talk any more about such a fellow? Must he do what he lists? He is a breaker of the peace.

Wom. She told him again, that he desired to live peaceably, and to follow his calling, that his family might be maintained; and 35
moreover said, my Lord, I have four small children, that cannot

16 it²] *om.* 1765

help themselves, of which one is blind, and have nothing to live upon, but the charity of good people.

Hales. Hast thou four children? said Judge *Hales*; thou art but a young woman to have four children.

5   *Wom.* My Lord, said she, I am but mother-in-law to them, having not been married to him yet full two years. Indeed I was with child when my husband was first apprehended: But being young and unaccustomed to such things, said she, I being smayed at the news, fell into labour, and so continued for eight days, and then was 10 delivered, but my child died.

Hales. Whereat, he looking very soberly on the matter, said, Alas poor woman!

Twis. But Judge *Twisdon* told her, that she made poverty her cloak; and said, moreover, that he understood, I was maintained better by 15 running up and down a preaching, than by following my calling.

Hales. What is his calling? said Judge *Hales*.

Answer. Then some of the company that stood by, said, A Tinker, my Lord.

Wom. Yes, said she, and because he is a Tinker, and a poor man; 20 therefore he is despised, and cannot have justice.

Hales. Then Judge *Hales* answered, very mildly, saying, I tell thee, woman, seeing it is so, that they have taken what thy husband spake, for a conviction; thou must either apply thyself to the King, or sue out his pardon, or get a writ of error.

25   *Chest.* But when Justice *Chester* heard him give her this counsel; and especially (as she supposed) because he spoke of a writ of error, he chaffed, and seemed to be very much offended; saying, my Lord, he will preach and do what he lists.

Wom. He preacheth nothing but the word of God, said she.

30   *Twis.* He preach the word of God! said *Twisdon* (and withal, she thought he would have struck her) he runneth up and down, and doth harm.

Wom. No, my Lord, said she, it's not so, God hath owned him, and done much good by him.

35   *Twis.* God! said he, his doctrine is the doctrine of the Devil.

Wom. My Lord, said she, when the righteous judge shall appear, it will be known, that his doctrine is not the doctrine of the Devil.

Twis. My Lord, said he, to Judge *Hales*, do not mind her, but send her away.

Hales. Then said Judge *Hales*, I am sorry, woman, that I can do thee no good; thou must do one of those three things aforesaid, namely; either to apply thyself to the King, or sue out his pardon, 5 or get a writ of error; but a writ of error will be cheapest.

Wom. At which *Chester* again seemed to be in a chaffe, and put off his hat, and as she thought, scratched his head for anger: But when I saw, said she, that there was no prevailing to have my husband sent for, though I often desired them that they would send 10 for him, that he might speak for himself, telling them, that he could give them better satisfaction than I could, in what they demanded of him; with several other things, which now I forget; only this I remember, that though I was somewhat timerous at my first entrance into the chamber, yet before I went out, I could not 15 but break forth into tears, not so much because they were so hard-hearted against me, and my husband, but to think what a sad account such poor creatures will have to give at the coming of the Lord, when they shall there answer for all things whatsoever they have done in the body, whether it be good, or whether it 20 be bad.

So, when I departed from them, the book of Statute was brought, but what they said of it, I know nothing at all, neither did I hear any more from them.

Some Carriages of the Adversaries of God's Truth with me at the next 25
Assises, which was on the nineteenth of the first Month, 1662.

I Shall pass by what befel between these two assizes, how I had, by my Jailor, some liberty granted me, more than at the first, and how I followed my wonted course of preaching, taking all occasions that was put into my hand to visit the people of God, exhorting them to 30 be stedfast in the faith of Jesus Christ, and to take heed that they touched not the Common Prayer, *&c.* but to mind the word of God, which giveth direction to Christians in every point, being able to make the man of God perfect in all things through faith in Jesus Christ, and thoroughly to furnish him up to all good works. 35

Also how I having, I say, somewhat more liberty, did go to see Christians at *London*, which my enemies hearing of, was so angry, that they had almost cast my Jailor out of his place, threatning to indite him, and to do what they could against him. They charged 5 me also, that I went thither to plot and raise division, and make insurrection, which, God knows, was a slander; whereupon my liberty was more straightened than it was before; so that I must not look out of the door. Well, when the next sessions came, which was about the 10th of the 11th month, I did expect to have been very 10 roundly dealt withal; but they passed me by, and would not call me, so that I rested till the assises, which was the 19th of the first month following; and when they came, because I had a desire to come before the judge, I desired my Jailor to put my name into the Kalender among the felons, and made friends to the Judge and 15 High Sheriff, who promised that I should be called; so that I thought what I had done might have been effectual for the obtaining of my desire: But all was in vain; for when the assises came, though my name was in the kalender, and also though both the Judge and Sheriff had promised that I should appear before them, 20 yet the Justices and the Clerk of the peace, did so work it about, that I, notwithstanding, was defered, and might not appear: And though I say, I do not know of all their carriages towards me, yet this I know, that the Clerk of the peace did discover himself to be one of my greatest opposers: For, first he came to my Jailor, and 25 told him that I must not go down before the Judge, and therefore must not be put into the kalender; to whom my Jailor said, that my name was in already. He bid him put me out again; my Jailor told him that he could not: For he had given the Judge a kalender with my name in it, and also the Sheriff another. At which he was 30 very much displeased, and desired to see that kalender that was yet in my Jailor's hand, who, when he had gave it him, he looked on it, and said it was a false kalender; he also took the kalender and blotted out my accusation, as my Jailor had writ it. (Which accusation I cannot tell what it was, because it was so blotted out) and 35 he himself put in words to this purpose: That *John Bunyan* was committed in prison; being lawfully convicted for upholding of unlawful meetings and conventicles, &c. But yet for all this, fearing that what he had done, unless he added thereto, it would not do, he first run to the Clerk of the assises; then to the Justices, and afterwards, because he would not leave any means unattempted to hinder me, he comes again to my Jailor, and tells him, that if I did go down before the Judge, and was released, he would make him 5 pay my fees, which he said was due to him; and further, told him, that he would complain of him at the next quarter sessions for making of false kalenders, though my Jailor himself, as I afterwards learned, had put in my accusation worse than in itself it was by far. And thus was I hindred and prevented at that time also from appear- 10 ing before the Judge: And left in prison. Farewell.

JOHN BUNYAN.

NOTE

The notes at the foot of the page in *A Relation of My Imprisonment* appear thus in the edition of 1765; it seems likely from comparison with those in the early editions of *The Pilgrim's Progress* that they were intended for the margin and so appeared in Bunyan's manuscript.

M

NOTES

A PREFACE

p. 1, Title. *those whom God hath counted him worthy to beget to Faith.* Those whom his preaching had converted, largely members of the church at Bedford and its sister churches in the neighbourhood.

p. 1, ll. 1–2. *I being taken from you in presence, and so tied up.* Bunyan is writing from prison. Since the *Church Book* provides evidence that he was able to enjoy the liberty to visit meetings of the congregation in the early stages of his imprisonment, and as late as September 1661, this suggests that *Grace Abounding* was written between the later date and 1666 (Introduction, p. xxv).

p. 1, ll. 9–10. *while I stick between the Teeth of the Lions in the Wilderness.* The lions represent persecution, as do those guarding the House Beautiful, *P.P.*, pp. 45–46, 218–19. 'The lions, the wicked people of the world that fear not God' (*Fear of God*, i. 469).

p. 1, l. 17. *a drop of that honey* (Judges xiv. 5–9.)

p. 1, ll. 21–22. *The Philistians understand me not.* Samson's Philistine companions were unable to solve his riddle: 'Out of the strong came forth sweetness' (Judges xiv. 12–14).

p. 2, ll. 4–5. *I lay so long at Sinai.* Mount Sinai represents the domination of the old law before grace has come to the soul; cf. *P.P.*, p. 20, when the mountain threatens Christian with thunder and lightning after his surrender to the merely moral Christianity recommended by Mr. Worldly Wiseman (*Of the Law and the Christian*, ii. 387–8.)

p. 2, l. 24. *hill Mizar* (Ps. xlii.)

p. 3, ll. 20–21. *Have you forgot the Close, the Milk-house, the Stable, the Barn, and the like, where God did visit your Soul?* A passage vividly evoking the rural way of life followed by many members of Bunyan's congregation. For precision in marking the exact place and time when the work of grace began in his soul cf. his later meeting with the poor women of Bedford, 'sitting at a door in the sun' (§ 37). Cf. '. . . their was scarce A Corner in the house, or Barnes, or Cowhousen, or Stable, or Closes, under the hegges, or in the wood, but I was made to poure out my soul to God' (*Narrative of Agnes Beaumont*, p. 5).

GRACE Abounding to the chief of Sinners

2. p. 5, ll. 7–9. *of that rank that is meanest, and most despised of all the families in the Land.* Cf. Introduction, p. xii, and Colonel John Okey on the gallows,

19 April 1662: 'I shall not trouble you with what is superfluous, which is to tell you of my Family, which of all the Families in Israel was the least, and I was the least of that Family.' (His family was armigerous and well-to-do.)

3. p. 5, ll. 15–16. *to put me to School*. Cf. 'I never went to school to Aristotle or Plato, but was brought up at my father's house in a very mean condition, among a company of poor countrymen' (*Law and Grace*, i. 495). In the *Scriptural Poems* Bunyan speaks of himself as

> a mechanic guided by no rule
> But what I gained in a grammar school
> In my minority.

12. p. 7, l. 30. *But God did not utterly leave me*. Cf. '. . . though I thought it nothing yet still the all-seeing watched my ways, and he called to me, though I knew him not, yet he kept me, and his banner over me was love; and though my nature was as corrupt as any, a child of wrath as well as others . . . yet still I was under the awaking of Jehovah' (Anna Trapnel, *A Legacy for Saints; being several experiences of the dealings of God with Anna Trapnel, in, and after her Conversion*, 1654, p. 1).

p. 7, l. 33. *Bedford-River*: the Ouse.

p. 8, l. 3. *stounded*: altered in the sixth edition to the more familiar 'stunned'.

13. Cf. Introduction, pp. xv–xvi. The anonymous author of *A Continuation of Mr. Bunyan's Life* (in *Grace Abounding*, 7th ed. 1692, pp. 157–8) associates the incident with the siege of Leicester in 1645 and assigns Bunyan to the Royalist side, perhaps merely on the grounds that the Royalists were the besiegers. The evidence of the Muster Rolls of the Newport garrison suggests that he spent the greater part of his period of service, from November 1644 to July 1647, on garrison duty at Newport. The fact that he was mustered in Major Boulton's company on 27 May 1645 makes it unlikely that he took any part in the operations at Leicester. (*P.R.O. Commonwealth Exchequer Papers*, xxviii. 121 B) However, several other detachments were drawn off from Newport to reinforce Aylesbury and other places during 1645 (*C.S.P.D. Charles I, 1645*, 453, 460, 472). The governor of Newport was Sir Samuel Luke, the hero of Butler's *Hudibras* (Brown, pp. 46–50; H. G. Tibbutt, *Bedfordshire and the First Civil War with a Note on the Military Service of John Bunyan*, 1956).

15. p. 8, l. 20. *household-stuff*. The insertion of this word in the third edition suggests a scrupulous desire for accuracy. 'Not having so much as a dish or spoon betwixt us both', might have seemed to indicate a state of total beggary; the qualifying phrase suggests that Bunyan and his wife had a livelihood and a cottage, but nothing to furnish it with.

p. 8, l. 22. The Plain Man's Path-way to Heaven: the celebrated handbook of popular piety written by Arthur Dent, minister of Shoeburyness, and first published in 1601. By 1640 it had run through twenty-five editions. Its piety is homely and proverbial, often dramatic and humorous, and has its roots in medieval popular treatises like the *Nuns' Rule* or the sermon given by Chaucer's Parson. It is in the form of a dialogue: Asunetos, the ignorant man, learns about evangelical Christianity from Theologus, who resists the objections and counter-arguments of Antilegon, the scoffer. *The Practice of Piety* (3rd ed. 1613) by Lewis Bayley, who after being chaplain to Henry, Prince of Wales, became bishop of Bangor (1616–32), is a manual of devotion with a strong Calvinistic bias, setting out 'the knowledge of Gods Majesty and Mans Misery as the first and chiefest grounds of the Practice of Piety'. See L. B. Wright, *Middle Class Culture in Elizabethan England* (1935), pp. 253–5; J. B. Wharey, *M.L.N.* xxxvi (1921), 65–79; Maurice Hussey, *M.L.R.* xliv (1949), 26–34; and J. E. Bailey, *Papers of the Manchester Literary Club*, ix (1883), 201–19.

16. p. 8, ll. 33–34. *the Religion of the times.* Though the whole passage, with its reference to 'High place, Priest, Clerk, Vestments, Service', suggests the performance of a ritual, Bunyan is speaking of a period when the Puritans were in power and the national church was controlled by the decisions of the Westminster Assembly of Divines. The use of the Book of Common Prayer had been abolished by Act of Parliament in 1643 and a new Directory of Public Worship published. Christopher Hall, the vicar of Elstow, retained his living throughout the Interregnum, which proves that he must have conformed to the requirements of Parliament; his 'Vestments' would presumably be a plain Geneva gown (*V.C.H. Bedford*, i. 340–5).

The style of language is that of the extremist sects who condemned all ordained clergy as idolatrous; 'Priest' is the term favoured by the early Quakers even for independent ministers (see Fox, *Journal*, passim).

p. 8, l. 34. *to go to Church twice a day*: to morning and evening prayer.

20. p. 9, ll. 31–32. *of the Sabbath-day, and of the evil of breaking that.* The legal toleration of Sunday pastimes by the Act of James I called the *Book of Sports* (1618) was a major cause of Puritan discontent before the Civil War. In 1644 an Act was passed prohibiting 'all wrestling, shooting, bowling, bell-ringing (except to call people to church), dancing, and all games whatsoever' on Sundays. Bunyan's story shows that even the denunciation of the local clergy could not stop this traditional merrymaking of the common people. Richard Baxter describes the Sunday dancing in his boyhood in Shropshire before the Civil War:

> In the Village where I lived the Reader read the Common-Prayer briefly and the rest of the Day even until dark Night almost, excepting Eating time, was spent in Dancing under a May-Pole, and a great Tree, not far from my Father's Door; where all the Town did meet together: And though one of my Father's own Tenants was

the Piper, he could not restrain them, or break the Sport: so that we could not read the Scripture in our Family without the great disturbance of the Taber and Pipe and Noise in the Street! (*Reliquiae Baxterianae*, 1690, i. 3).

Puritan biography affords numerous examples of the work of sermons in first arousing the conscience and preparing the way for conversion. Thomas Goodwin, the Cambridge preacher, was moved by a funeral sermon preached by the Master of Christ's College, Thomas Bainbridge, to adopt in his own preaching a plain, spiritual style. He records in his diary the date when he heard this sermon: 'Monday the second of Octob. 1620 in the afternoon', *Works* (1704), V, pp. v–xix. Anna Trapnel, who was associated with the South-wark open-communion church of Henry Jessey, and was converted about the same time as Bunyan, was awakened to a sense of sin after hearing a sermon by Hugh Peters on the nature of the covenanted people: 'My Spirit was filled with horror, and the terrors of the Law exceedingly oppressed me. . . .', *A Legacy for Saints* (1654), p. 2. Jane Turner, another Baptist, describes how she was stirred to repentance by a sermon, *Choice Experiences* (1653), pp. 22–23, and the Quaker John Crook gives a similar account of an awakening sermon succeeded by temptations to despair, *A Short History of the Life of John Crook* (1706), p. 13. Cf. Arise Evans, *An Eccho to the Voice from Heaven, or A Narration of the Life, and Manner of the special Callings and Visions of Arise Evans* (1652), p. 14.

21. p. 10, ll. 7–8. *benum the sinews of my best delights.* The first edition reading, 'cut the sinews' (from ham-stringing a horse), is not appropriate, since his pleasures were only embittered for a time (then 'my heart returned to its old course'). The revision appears in the third and subsequent editions.

22. p. 10, l. 16. *a game at Cat.* Sometimes called tipcat.

The game of cat is played with a cudgel. Its denomination is derived from a piece of wood about six inches long, and two thick, diminished from the middle to form a double cone. When the cat is placed on the ground the player strikes it smartly—it matters not at which end—and it must rise with a rotatory motion high enough for him to strike it. If he misses, another player takes his place. If he hits, he calls for a number to be scored to his game. If that number is more than as many lengths of his cudgel, he is out. If not, they are scored, and he plays again (Joseph Strutt, *Sports and Pastimes of the People of England*, 1801, II. iii. 101).

p. 10, l. 17. *the hole.* The place on the ground where the cat was laid.

Bunyan has bounced the cat into the air by hitting it at one end, and is preparing to hit it again when he hears the voice.

24. p. 11, l. 12. *delicates:* delicacies, luxuries.

25. p. 11, ll. 20–21. *a scurvie and seared frame of heart.* The word 'seared' is applied by other sectarian writers on spiritual experience to the condition of the soul under conviction of sin. 'I apprehended Divine displeasure, leaving me in a seared condition . . .' (Anna Trapnel, *A Legacy for Saints*, pp. 2, 7, 16).

29. p. 12, l. 22. *the historical part . . . Paul's Epistles*. The Pauline epistles, especially the classical statements of the doctrine of grace in Romans and Galatians, provided crucial texts for the Puritan doctrine of conversion.

30–32. pp. 12–13. Bunyan's experience represents a stage common to all Puritan autobiographies: the attempt to attain salvation by conformity with the moral law. This phase of his religious development, with its air of public respectability, corresponds to the episode of Mr. Worldly Wiseman in *P.P.*, pp. 17–28. On 'The attempt to earn salvation by formalism and self righteousness' see J. H. Taylor, 'Some Seventeenth-Century Testimonies', *Trans. Cong. Hist. Soc.* xvi. 2 (1949), 64–77.

32. p. 13, l. 10. *Tom of Bethlem*. I.e. a madman; from the Hospital of St. Mary of Bethlehem outside London Wall where the insane were confined. The less violent patients were released and licensed to beg about the country. The Bedlam beggar would be a familiar figure to anyone like Bunyan who spent much time on the roads:

Before the Civil Warres Tom a Bedlams went about a begging. They had been such as had been in Bedlam and there recovered and come to some degree of soberness (Aubrey, B.M. Lansdowne MS. 231).

Cf. Edgar in *King Lear*, III. iv.

33. p. 13, l. 21. *delight in ringing*. The tower of Elstow church was built in the fifteenth century, and as in some other Bedfordshire churches, stands detached from the main body of the church, to the north of the west end. There are five bells. The treble was cast by Christopher Graie in 1655; the second, inscribed with 'Praise the Lord, 1602', by Hugh Watts; the third by John Keene; the fourth is an alphabet bell, and the tenor is by Newcombe of Leicester (*V.C.H. Bedford*, iii. 282–3).

There is abundant evidence in Bunyan's books of his love of music and especially of bell-ringing. When Christian and Hopeful enter the Celestial City, 'All the Bells in the City Rang again for joy'; and as Valiant-for-truth passed over the river of death, 'all the Trumpets sounded for him on the other side'. In the scenes of triumph in *The Holy War* silver trumpets are sounded and bells are rung (*P.P.*, pp. 162, 309; *H.W.*, p. 295).

As well as for change-ringing, bells were used to summon people to football matches and other Sunday games; The Puritan party was bitterly hostile to their recreational use. A parallel to Bunyan's prevarication is found in the autobiography of Vavasor Powell, the Baptist preacher and evangelist of Wales. Powell had reached the point before his conversion when he would not take part in Sabbath games but still remained as an onlooker. When a friend remonstrated with him for breaking the commandment, he replied:

Wherein do I break it: you see me only stand by but I do not play at all; to which he replyed, but you find your own pleasure herein by looking on, and this God forbids in his holy Word (*The Life and Death of Mr. Vavasor Powell, that Faithful Minister and Confessor of Jesus Christ*, 1671, p. 2).

p. 14, ll. 2–4. *Steeple . . . Steeple door.* The word 'steeple' was current among the Quakers to describe any church building (see Fox, *Journal,* p. 291 and *passim*). For other resemblances in thought and usage between Bunyan and the early Friends see Introduction, pp. xx–xxi.

35. p. 14, l. 6. *my dancing.* Another recreation which the mature Bunyan seems to have looked back on with pleasure in a more mellow mood. Ready-to-halt and Mistress Much-afraid dance in the road after the destruction of Doubting Castle (*P.P.,* p. 283). Cf. 'the Bells ringed, the Minstrils played, the people danced' (*H.W.,* p. 320).

37. p. 14, l. 18. *to work on my calling*: i.e. as a travelling tinker.

p. 14, l. 19. *three or four poor women.* These women were members of John Gifford's congregation and played an important part in its life; since it was only founded in 1650 the incident must have occurred in its earliest days. The original list of members in the *Church Book,* which runs from the foundation in 1650 up to and including the church meeting in December 1663 includes 142 members and of these ninety-five are women (*Church Book,* p. 5).

p. 14, l. 22. *a brisk talker.* Like Talkative the son of Saywell of Prating Row: 'He talketh of Prayer, of Repentance, of Faith, and of the New-Birth but he knows but only to talk of them' (*P.P.,* p. 83).

38. p. 15, ll. 4–5. As in other Biblical references the quotation is inaccurate and does not correspond exactly with either Geneva or A.V.

42. p. 15, ll. 32–33. *like a Horseleach at the vein.* As elsewhere, Bunyan reapplies a scriptural metaphor in a totally different context. The image of the horse-leach in Proverbs xxx. 15 introduces the four things that will not be satisfied: the grave, the barren womb, the earth, and the fire; according to the Geneva commentary the horse-leech stands for the 'covetous extortioners insatiable'.

43. p. 16, ll. 7–8. *a young man in our Town . . .* The story of Harry is later introduced as a cautionary tale into *Badman* (p. 45).

44. p. 16, l. 17. *some Ranters Books.* The Ranters, or antinomians, were the most fanatical of the extreme sectaries in the Commonwealth period. They carried to its logical extreme the Calvinist doctrine of free, undeserved grace by giving themselves up to sexual promiscuity in the belief that the elect were entirely outside the moral law. Lawrence Clarkson ran through the whole gamut of the sects from Anglican through Presbyterian, Independent, Baptist, Seeker, and Ranter to rest as a disciple of Reeve and Muggleton, who proclaimed themselves the Two Witnesses of the Book of Revelation. In *A Single Eye All Light* (1650) he claims that to be freed from sin a man must act it 'in purity'. In *The Lost Sheep Found*

(1660) he describes his successive conversions and how he travelled up and down the country feasting and drinking with his concubine. Abiezar Coppe, another celebrated Ranter, had just published *A Fiery Flying Roule* and *A Second Fiery Flying Roule* (1649). See Lawrence Clarkson, *The Lost Sheep Found, or, the Prodigal returned to his Fathers house, after many a sad and weary Journey through many Religious Countreys*, printed for the Author (1660); Thomas Edwards, *Gangraena* (2nd ed. 1646), pp. 104–5; C. E. Whiting, *Studies in English Puritanism 1660–1688* (1931), pp. 272–7.

p. 16, l. 19. *several old Professors.* 'Professor': one who makes open profession of religion; a Puritan usage: *O.E.D.*, s.v. 3*b*.

51. p. 19, l. 2. *horse pads.* The tracks in the muddy road made by the horses' hoofs. *O.E.D.*, sb. 2. 1. Celia Fiennes, travelling forty years later, found the Bedfordshire roads particularly bad (Celia Fiennes, *Journeys*, ed. Christopher Morris, 1947 and cf. *V.C.H. Bedford*, ii, 1908, 98–99).

53. p. 19, l. 18. *in a kind of Vision.* The reading of the first edition, 'in a Dream or Vision', does not indicate clearly whether the vision took place within an ordinary dream or whether it was a hallucination; the change in the third removes the ambiguity and shows that it was a visual hallucination comparable to the auditory impressions, as of voices over his shoulder, which affected Bunyan later.

The idea of forcing himself through the little door in the wall reflects the obsession with violent physical activity especially pushing or pulling, which is a feature of Bunyan's psychological experience (see E. Marcault, 'Le cas "Bunyan" et le Tempérament psychologique', *Mélanges littéraires et philosophiques*, Clermont-Ferrand, 1910). The passage, often attended with difficulty, through a small door, is a widely diffused symbol for the initiation into the religious life or into a higher stage of human development; and an echo of it may be detected in Alice's painful squeeze through the door into the garden in *Alice in Wonderland*. Bunyan, of course, did not need to look further than the 'strait gate' of the New Testament (Matt. vii. 13, 14). But this imaginative treatment of the biblical image anticipates the Wicket Gate in the wall called Salvation in *P.P.*, p. 25. Cf. also the sermon treatment of the same metaphor in *The Strait Gate* (1676).

For the vagueness of the topography ('a Wall that did compass about this Mountain', and the presence of frost and snow on one side and sunshine on the other) cf. 'a wide field full of dark mountains' in *P.P.*, p. 42; as a dweller in a flat, featureless countryside Bunyan had no knowledge of any more varied landscape.

55. p. 20, ll. 8–9. *the gap which was in this wall, I thought was Jesus Christ.* Although the reformers had laid down the superiority of the literal sense of the Bible to any figurative interpretation, there were some passages in which Protestants were still compelled to resort to the older moral and allegorical mode of exegesis; such were Christ's parables and metaphors, and the love poetry of the *Song of Solomon*. In addition, the traditional multifold interpretation of straightforward narrative was sometimes employed (e.g. Jonah's three days and three nights in the whale's belly was interpreted as a type of the interval between the Crucifixion and the Resurrection). Bunyan's mind, rich in conceiving imagery, profited from this survival of the medieval habit of assigning significances to almost any feature of narrative. The detailed working out of the allegory in this paragraph owes something both to the inspiration of the parables, and to the traditional mode of exposition as he had learnt it from sermons and from discourse with members of the Bedford church. The most complete repository of the Puritan interpretation of scripture metaphors is provided by the two volumes of Benjamin Keach (1640–1704), a Baptist who was, like Bunyan, a popular preacher and a writer of religious novels: *Tropologia, or, a Key to open Scripture Metaphors* (1681), and *Tropes and Figures* (1682). In the former there is a section on Christ as a door with reference to John x. 1, 2, 7, 9 (Bunyan's reference to John xiv. 6 is perhaps less pertinent):

A Door is the place of legal Entrance; no Men are allowed by Law to climb up to Windows, or break down any part of the Walls for entrance.
Jesus Christ is the legal way of entrance, whether into the visible Church, or into the Kingdom of Heaven. Whosoever shall attempt to enter into either of these, otherwise than by Christ, will be look'd upon as Thieves and Robbers (*Tropologia*, ii. 129, and cf. i. 177).

It is noteworthy that in *The Pilgrim's Progress*, after Christian has passed through the Wicket Gate, he is received in the Interpreter's House, where the significance of various allegorical scenes and pictures is explained to him; some of these are scriptural, while others are based on emblem books or traditional proverbs (*P.P.*, pp. 28–33). Cf. the allegorical interpretation of Revelation in *Holy City* (1665), iii. 400–459, and of various texts in *Solomon's Temple Spiritualised* (1688).

56. p. 20, ll. 21–22. *O Lord, consider my distress.* The first line of Psalm li as given in the familiar metrical version by Sternhold and Hopkins:

> O Lord consider my distress,
> And now with speed some pitie take:
> My sinnes deface, my faultes redresse,
> Good Lord for thy great mercies sake.
> (*The Whole Booke of Psalmes*, 1609)

58. p. 21, l. 3. *Rom. 9. 16.* The quotation conforms more closely to Geneva than to A.V.

61. p 21, l. 20. *close*: come to terms with, agree.

65. p. 22, l. 14. *the promises*: texts giving promise of salvation. Cf. Tyndale, *Doctrinal Treatises* (Parker Society, Cambridge, 1848), p. 399: 'Seek therefore in the Scripture as thou readest it, first the *law*, what God commandeth us to do; and secondarily the *promises* . . . in Christ Jesus our lord.'

66. p. 22, ll. 18–19. *How if you have over-stood the time of mercy?* have let the opportunity go past; 'to over-stand one's market' is to postpone selling one's goods until there are not enough customers to buy them (*Badman*, pp. 116–17).

71. p. 23, ll. 25–26. *something concerning the Beasts that Moses counted clean and unclean.* This exegesis of Lev. xi and Deut. xiv which first appears in the third edition recalls Faithful's comment on Talkative in *The Pilgrim's Progress*: 'And this [the hare] truly resembleth Talkative; he cheweth the Cud, he seeketh knowledge, he cheweth upon the Word, but he divideth not the Hoof, he parteth not with the way of sinners; but, as the Hare, retaineth the foot of a Dog, or Bear, and therefore he is unclean' (*P.P.*, p. 80).

78. p. 25, l. 21. *Mr. Gifford*: John Gifford, the first pastor of the independent congregation at Bedford; he had been a major in the Royalist forces, and escaped from prison when he was awaiting execution for his part in the Kentish rising of 1648. He came to Bedford and practised as a physician, while living the life of a gamester and debauchee. After conversion, he soon revealed his gifts in preaching and exhortation to the local saints, and was their natural choice as leader when it was decided to gather a church together. The principle they based their worship on was of his choice: 'faith in Christ and holiness of life, without respect to this or that circumstance or opinion in outward or circumstantiall things'. A letter of Gifford to the congregation, written on his deathbed, upheld this liberal principle; it was customary for it to be read out from time to time at meetings of the church. Though adult or believers' baptism was administered by Gifford and his successor John Burton to those who desired it, it was not a condition of communion with the church; as Gifford's letter says:

> Concerning separation from the Church about Baptisme, laying on of hands, Anoynting with Oyls, Psalmes [i.e. whether it was right to sing psalms] or any externalls; I charge every one of you respectively, that none of you be found guilty of this great evill (*Church Book*).

There were many groups of a similar mixed-communion character in which Congregationalists and Baptists met together, including the Bury St. Edmunds, Cambridge, and Southwark churches. Cf. Bunyan's *Differences in Judgment about Water-Baptism no Bar to Communion* (1673), *The Life and Death of Mr. Henry Jessey* (1671), p. 87, and G. F. Nuttall, *Visible Saints* (Oxford, 1957), pp. 118–21.

p. 26, ll. 2–3. *a clog on the leg of a Bird to hinder her from flying*: a piece of wood or metal tied to the leg of a bird to impede its flight; used in taming hawks for falconry. The metaphor is found in Quarles's *Emblemes*, a work which Bunyan knew and from which some of his emblems in the Interpreter's House are taken.

> Ev'n like the Hawlk (whose keeper's wary hands
> Have made a prisner to her wethring stock),
> Forgetting quite the pow'r of her fast bands,
> Makes a rank Bate from her forsaken Block.
> But her too faithfull Leash does soon restraine
> Her broken flight, attempted oft in vaine;
> It gives her loynes a twitch, and tugs her back againe.
>
> *Emblemes* (1635), p. 278.

79. p. 26, l. 11. *the Cananites would dwell in the Land.* An image for the state of the soul before conversion, since the Canaanites were the inhabitants of the Promised Land before the Israelites entered it (Judges i. 27.)

82. p. 26, ll. 32–33. *I durst not take a pin:* '. . . afraid lest he sins in every word he speaketh and in every thought, and every look, and every meal he eateth.' (Baxter, *Christian Directory*, 1673, p. 313.)

p. 27, l. 2. *a miry bog.* Cf. the Slough of Despond, *P.P.*, pp. 14–15.

88. p. 29, ll. 2–4. *Man Indeed is the most noble, by creation, of all the creatures in the visible World; but by sin he has made himself the most ignoble.* The familiar paradox of the traditional view, medieval and Renaissance, of the nature of man: 'I know myselfe a Man, Which is a *proud*, and yet a *wretched* thing' (Sir John Davies, *Nosce Teipsum*, in *Complete Poems*, ed. Grosart, i. 24, and cf. *Hamlet*, II. ii. 295–300).

89. p. 29, l. 10. *the Song:* the Song of Solomon.

p. 29, l. 16. *dissertion.* The spelling also used by Bunyan in *P.P.* (p. 103, 'disserting'). The word is applied frequently to spiritual despair, for instance in Richard Sibbes, *Bowels Opened* (3rd ed. 1648), p. 386.

91. p. 29, l. 27. *My Love.* He recalls the two words quoted at the end of § 90; 'Thou art my Dove', in the third edition, instead of the repetition of 'Thou art my Love', is followed by all the subsequent editions and is certainly a slip. Cf. 'Oh, this word "Beloved" made such Mellody in my heart' (*Narrative of Agnes Beaumont*, p. 24).

92. p. 30, l. 9. *. . . I would write this down . . .* This suggests that even during the period of his conversion Bunyan was beginning to record his spiritual experience.

93. p. 30, ll. 18–19. *thinking verily that some man had behind me called to me.* The same experience is mentioned by Anna Trapnel:

sometimes as I have been going along the streets, I have looked behind me, thinking I heard some locall voice, a voice without me . . . I oft-times turned back when I have been going along the streets, to see who it was that spake . . . (*A Legacy for Saints*, pp. 7–8).

97. p. 31, ll. 18–27. Mingled with Bunyan's Calvinistic fears of reprobation there are these sceptical arguments, modern and relativist in tone and savouring more of the post-Restoration intellectual atmosphere. But even the relativist argument against Christian belief appears to Bunyan as the temptation of a personal devil.

100. p. 32, ll. 11–12. *to swallow my spittle.* See *O.E.D.*, s.v. 'swallow' and cf. Job vii. 19.

p. 32, l. 13. *these temptations would drown and over-flow.* Cf. 'temptations comming on me like waves of the Sea' (Jane Turner, *Choice Experiences*, 1653, p. 28).

104. p. 33, ll. 21–22. *That Scripture did also tear and rend my soul.* '. . . when any one is a little awakened, O what work will one verse, one line, nay one word of the Holy Scriptures make in his heart' (*Sighs from Hell*, iii. 915).

106. p. 34, l. 1. *Ordinances*: the Puritan term for the sacraments.

117. p. 37, l. 7. *those false and unsound rests.* Gifford is counselling his hearers not to take any form of spiritual consolation (rest) upon trust, but to seek assurance of its validity in prayer; otherwise, if they submit to superficial cures for a troubled mind, they will not be able to withstand temptations when they come. Cf. § 86:

> And that which made me the more afraid of this, was, Because I had seen some, who though when they were under Wounds of Conscience, then they would cry and pray; but they seeking rather present Ease from their Trouble, then Pardon for their Sin, cared not how they lost their guilt, so they got it out of their minde; and, therefore, having got it off the wrong way, it was not sanctified unto them; but they grew harder, and blinder, and more wicked after their trouble.

The frequent employment of the word in the plural throughout Baxter's *The Saints Everlasting Rest* illustrates current Puritan usage; and cf. Stephen Crisp, *Memorable Account of the Christian Experiences* (1694), p. 6. Later editions alter to 'tests'.

119–21. This period of education in the Bible corresponds to the episode of the House Beautiful in Bunyan's allegory where Christian is prepared for the trials that await him in the Valley of the Shadow of Death and beyond (*P.P.* pp. 45–56).

p. 37, l. 30. *Even from the birth and cradle of the Son of God . . .* : 'the Lord, just before the men called Quakers came into the country, did set me down so blessedly in the truth of the doctrine of Jesus Christ, . . . how Jesus Christ was born of a virgin, walked in the world awhile with his disciples, afterwards hanged on the cross, spilt his blood, was buried, rose again, ascended above the clouds and heavens, there lives to make intercession, and that he also will come again at the last day to judge the world . . .' (*Law and Grace*, i. 549).

121. p. 38, ll. 14–15. *a man on the right-hand of God the Father for me*: i.e. Christ is to intercede with the Father on his behalf, and to use His human nature as a pledge to redeem man's fallen nature; as does the Son in *Paradise Lost*, iii. 294–5.

> So Man, as is most just,
> Shall satisfie for Man, be judg'd and die.

According to the Calvinist view of the Atonement, God's justice demands the sacrifice of the innocent Son as a price for human sin; see Calvin, *Institutes*, trans. John Allen (1813), vol. i, book ii, chap. xii, pp. 492–3.

124. p. 39, l. 5. *The errors that this people then maintained . . .* All the errors enumerated spring from a hostile interpretation of the early Quaker doctrine of the inner light according to which the Holy Spirit worked within every man and the whole work of the Bible and every mystery of the Christian religion (the Resurrection, &c.) were re-enacted within the individual soul. The language of the early Quakers is often loose and extravagant; it was difficult for them to rebut charges of heresy from those who chose to read it in an exact theological sense; cf. *Reliquae Baxterianea* (1696), i. 77. Fox committed himself to statements like 'He that hath the same spirit that raised up Jesus is equal with God' (Braithwaite, *The Beginnings of Quakerism*, p. 109). There was also a pronounced lunatic fringe of the movement: the fanatic James Nayler was treated by his disciples as the Messiah when he entered Bristol in triumph in 1656. Bunyan's first controversy was with the Quaker Edward Burrough in the same year, and led to his first book, *Some Gospel-truths Opened* (1656).

128. p. 40, ll. 9–10. *my salvation . . . with many golden Seals thereon.* An assurance of his salvation, but seventeenth-century Calvinists looked not for one but for several such assurances, and between them bouts of despair or doubt might well intervene. There is a parallel in the incident in *P.P.* when, at the Cross, Christian's burden falls from his shoulders, and he receives a scroll signifying his election (*P.P.*, p. 38).

The image is probably suggested by a legal document with many seals on it; such as Bunyan's father's will in the County Records Office at Bedford.

p. 40, ll. 30–31. *Luther. . . on the Galathians.* The translation published by Thomas Vautrollier in 1575, with an address 'To the Reader' by Thomas Sandys, Bishop of London. There were eight other editions before 1640. Bunyan's praise of the book in § 131 echoes the words of Sandys: 'amongst many other godly English books in these our days printed and translated, thou shalt find but few wherein thy time shall seem better bestowed . . .'; the Preface is addressed 'to all afflicted consciences', and there is a passage in it which may have provided a suggestion for the vision of his salvation handed down from heaven in the previous section: 'In which thou mayest see. . . in the heavens being opened . . . thy salvation freely and only by faith in Christ.

The climax of Bunyan's ensuing struggle with temptations to despair comes when he hears the words 'Thy righteousness is in heaven' (§ 230) and here both his language and thought are close to Luther's comment on Gal. v. 5. See note on § 230.

132-3. The new and severe period of temptation that now begins is described in Bunyan's allegory in the episode of Doubting Castle; Bunyan is impelled to sell or abandon Christ, and thinks he has committed the sin against the Holy Ghost; he becomes a prisoner of Giant Despair.

134. p. 42, l. 1. *were once effectually in Christ.* Characteristic of sectarian usage and especially of that of Baptist and 'gathered' churches. In a sermon preached in December 1661 Robert South says

> Some you shall have amusing their Consciences with a set of Phantastical New-Coin'd Phrases, such as *Laying hold on Christ, getting into Christ,* and *rolling themselves upon Christ,* and the like . . . it is all but a *Jargon* of empty, senseless Metaphors (*Twelve Sermons upon Several Subjects and Occasions,* 1697–8, ii. 203).

p. 42, l. 5. *a Christ.* The address by the indefinite article or by demonstratives is also employed by Anna Trapnel throughout her autobiography *A Legacy for Saints.*

136. p. 42, l. 17. *Sell him, sell him.* 'The very pain of their fears draws them to what they fear. . . . And oft-times they feel a vehement urgency, as if something within them urged them to speak such or such a blasphemous or foolish word, and they can have no rest unless they yield' (Baxter, *A Christian Directory: or, a Summ of Practical Theologie and Cases of Conscience,* 1673, p. 314).

137. p. 42, l. 28. *by way of pushing or thrusting.* Cf. Marcault, 'Le cas "Bunyan" ', *ut supra.*

139–41. This is the crisis of the temptation; Bunyan believes that his surrender to these neurotic compulsions constitutes a real betrayal of Christ; the ensuing period of despair lasts for two years (§ 143) and corresponds in *P.P.* to the imprisonment of Christian and Hopeful in Doubting Castle by Giant Despair. It is later made clear that Bunyan's fault is spiritual diffidence or inexperience; he does not rely upon the promises of divine grace already given to him: it is partly intellectual error, partly weakness or cowardice, not the grievous sin against the Holy Ghost which at the time he imagines it to be (§§ 246, 248). On the unpardonable sin and the delusions of many scrupulous believers about it see Thomas Collier, *The Body of Divinity* (1674), pp. 210–11; Baxter, *Christian Directory* (1673), p. 356.

143 p. 44, ll. 6–7. *about ten or eleven a Clock one day, as I was walking under a Hedge.* The precision of the reference to time and place is characteristic. The mention of an interval of 'several months together' since the morning when he had given in to his voices while lying in bed shows that the change to 'that day', occurring first in the fifth edition, is unauthoritative (it would mean that these words of comfort were heard on the very same morning when he was completely prostrated with despair).

144. p. 44, l. 14. *lear and steal away.* To look away or aside; to slink away, to turn away in shame (O.E. *hleor*, the cheek, face). Faithful reports that when he met Pliable in the street 'he leered away on the other side, as one ashamed of what he had done' (*P.P.*, p. 68).

p. 44, l. 18. *clot.* Used in the seventeenth century interchangeably with clod for a lump of something solid as well as for coagulated liquid. But the choice of the form may be influenced by the presence of 'Blood of Christ' in the same sentence.

148. p. 45, l. 17. *that sin unpardonable.* The case-books of Puritan moral theology all discuss the nature of the sin against the Holy Ghost and give directions against the unwarranted despair which tender consciences were liable to feel in connexion with this sin. The Calvinist stress on the mysterious and immutable character of election and reprobation caused much agony of mind on this score; so did the dramatic and lurid treatment of particular historical reprobates in popular homiletic literature (the classic example is Francis Spira, whose story made Bunyan's sufferings more fearful, § 163).

Richard Baxter, in giving 'Directions against sinful Despair', defines the implications of the same verse in the Epistle to the Hebrews which tormented Bunyan (xii. 17):

> If I did repent, it is too late because the day of Grace is past ... sometime by the day of grace is meant, that day in which God moveth the hearts of the impenitent more strongly towards conversion than formerly he did; And this is it that Divines mean when they talk of the day of Grace being past with men before their death (Richard Baxter, *Christian Directory*, 1673, p. 356).

Thomas Collier, the principal contemporary Baptist theologian, mentions how frequently righteous people are distressed by this sin through ignorance:

> In this matter, to depart from the Faith, and to reject Christ crucified, and Salvation by him, is the unpardonable sin. . . .
> Many gracious souls trouble themselves about this sin, fearing themselves to be guilty thereof, through their ignorance of the sin what it is: all sin (it's true) is against the Holy Spirit, but the unpardonable sin, or sin unto death, consists especially in . . . 1. a wilful departing from the Faith . . . 2. a wilful and malicious opposing of the Spirits working. . . . (Thomas Collier, *The Body of Divinity*, 1674, pp. 210–11).

Numerous cases of men and women labouring for many years under these anxieties are to be found in the collections of experience:

> Then was I repulsed in all duties by Satan, terrifying my soul to perswade me, that it was in vaine for me to seek for salvation, because I had committed the sin against the holy ghost (which God by his word hath declared shall never be forgiven

neither in this world nor in the world to come . . . (*Spirituall Experiences of sundry Beleevers*, 1653, p. 145).

151. p. 46, ll. 8–9. *David's Adultery and Murder.* Cf. § 170, *P.P.*, p. 66.

152. p. 46, l. 15. *racked upon the Wheel.* To be broken on the wheel was the common method of executing criminals in France.

p. 46, l. 18. *the great transgression.* 'Keep back thy servant also from presumptuous sins; let them not have dominion over me: then shall I be upright, and I shall be innocent from the great transgression' (Ps. xix. 13).

154. p. 46, l. 31. *Peters sin.* '. . . suppose a man should deny his God . . . Let him come again with Peter's tears, and no doubt but he shall obtain Peter's forgiveness . . . Peter was pardoned his horrible revolt from his Master' (*The Jerusalem Sinner Saved*, i. 97, and cf. *P.P.*, pp. 139–40).

156. p. 47, l. 22. *places:* i.e. texts of Scripture.

157. p. 48, ll. 3–4. *abide under the shaddow of the Almighty* (Ps. xci. 1).

158. p. 48, l. 20. *like the Locusts* (Ps. cix. 23).

161. p. 49, ll. 5–6. *that there should be no such thing as a Day of Judgment.* . . . Cf. note on § 44, and Alexander Barclay, *The Inner Life of the Religious Sects of the Commonwealth* (1876) pp. 409–74.

163. p. 49, l. 28. *Francis Spira.* Bunyan's source is Nathaniel Bacon, *A Relation of the Fearful Estate of Francis Spira, in the year 1548* (1649; eleven editions by 1695). Spira was a Protestant who became a Catholic for worldly motives and died in despair; there are further references to him in *The Greatness of the Soul*, i. 118, and *The Barren Fig-tree*, iii. 582: 'This was the burden of Spira's complaint, "I cannot do it! O! now I cannot do it!"' Cf. Richard Baxter, *Christian Directory* (1673), p. 312: 'The reading of Spira's case causeth or increaseth melancholy for many.' But the terror of Spira's case must have been more vividly brought home to Bunyan by its repetition in the life of his Bedford associate John Child (1638–84), who conformed for fear of persecution and afterwards hanged himself (see *The Mischief of Persecution Exemplified: by a true narrative of the Life and Deplorable End of Mr. John Child*, 1688, and the account appended to later editions of the life of Spira, *A Relation of the Fearful Estate of John Child*, 1710, pp. 63–122). He is referred to as disputing on Bunyan's part against the Quakers (Edward Burrough, *Memorable Works of a Son of Thunder and Consolation*, 1672, p. 305); in February 1658–9 Bunyan was asked to serve notice on him to attend a full meeting to give reasons for dissociating himself from the Church (*Church Book*, p. 22). He appears as the Man in the Iron Cage (of despair) in the Interpreter's House in *P.P.*, pp. 34–53.

169. p. 51, l. 12. *David shed blood* (2 Sam. xi. 2–27).

170. p. 51, l. 19. *Solomon* (1 Kings xi. 1–8).

171. p. 51, l. 26. *Manasseh* (2 Kings xxi. 1–16).

p. 51, l. 28. *was a Witch.* Used in both masculine and feminine; but altered to 'Wizzard' in the sixth edition, perhaps to conform with the A.V. account of Manasseh, who 'dealt with Wizards' (2 Kings xxi. 6).

173. p. 52, l. 25. *hollow. Sc.* 'holla'; 'Hollow me like a hare' (*Coriolanus,* I. viii. 7).

175. p. 52, l. 29–p. 54, ll. 1–2. *Once, as I was walking . . . began to mistrust and to despair again.* The whole section appears for the first time in the fifth edition. Bunyan is loath to make too much of this revelation because of its sensory accompaniment (the 'noise of wind . . . but very pleasant'). A similar extreme scrupulosity in the reporting of spiritual experience is reflected in other Puritan autobiographers. 'If there were any thing which was clear to my remembrance, that I could not bring in without something which was doubtfull, I would rather leave out the one, than write the other, much less write any thing which was a plain addition, and in this resolution I set upon it . . .' (Jane Turner, *Choice Experiences,* 1653, pp. 4–5).
Cf. the experience recounted by Lord Herbert of Cherbury, who, when in doubt whether to publish his work *De Veritate,* prayed for a sign from heaven to guide him: 'A loud but gentle noise came from heaven (for it was like nothing on earth) which did so comfort and cheer me that I took my petition as granted' (*Autobiography,* 1764, p. 171).

p. 53, l. 35. *savour.* A common expression of spiritual comfort in Puritan usage.

175. p. 54, l. 4. *which way I should tip*: i.e. whether I should tip the scales. Cf. Quarles, *Emblemes* (1635), pp. 17–19.

178. p. 55, l. 5. *I can but die.* Hopeful shows a like resolution in the face of despair: 'And therefore thought I with my self, If I leave off, I die; and I can but die at the Throne of Grace' (*P.P.,* p. 142).

179. p. 55, l. 21. *Man knows the beginning of sin . . . A Relation of the Fearful Estate of Francis Spira* (1710), pp. 10–11.

182. p. 56, ll. 4–5. *He is of one mind, and who can turn him?* (Job xxiii 13).

p. 56, l. 10. *rent.* The same present tense is found in the A.V.: 'lest they trample them under their feet, and turn again, and rent you' (Matt. vii. 6).

186. p. 58, l. 7. *my Soul, like a broken Vessel.* Bunyan wrongly interprets Ps. xxxi. 12 where the broken vessel is a pot; he would have found the image of the storm-tossed ship put to spiritual use in Quarles, *Emblemes* (1635), Book

N

iii, Emblem 11, where the motto is taken from Ps. lxix. 15: 'Let not the water
floods overflow me, neither let the deeps swallow me up':

> The world's a Sea; my flesh, a ship that's man'd
> With lab'ring Thoughts, and steer'd by Reason's hand:
> My heart's the Sea-man's Card, whereby she sailes,
> My loose Affections are the greater Sailes . . .
> My seas are stormy, and my Ship doth leake.

The same metaphor is found drawn out to elaborate length in Anna Trapnel,
A Legacy for Saints (1654), p. 17.

p. 58, ll. 15–16. *the man that hath his dwelling among the Tombs.* The same text
is used to illustrate the plight of the victims of Giant Despair as described to
Christian and Hopeful by the Shepherds: 'he at last did put out their eyes, and
led them among those Tombs, where he has left them to wander to this very
day, that the saying of the wise Man might be fulfilled, *He that wandereth out
of the way of understanding, shall remain in the Congregation of the dead*' (*P.P.*,
p. 121).

187. p. 59, l. 5. *every creature over I was!* 'I thought every Man or Woman
to be in a better Condition than my self' (*A Short History of the Life of John
Crook*, 1706, p. 14).

189. p. 60, l. 1. *a Mill-post.* The strong wooden post on which a windmill
stands and on which the whole body of the mill turns.

193. p. 61, l. 5. *If thou, Lord,* &c. As in some of the other quotations from
Scripture, Bunyan reproduces the text of the A.V. with slight inaccuracies,
apparently quoting from memory: 'If thou, Lord, shouldest mark iniquities,
O Lord, who shall stand? But there is forgiveness with thee, that thou
mayest be feared' (Ps. cxxx. 3, 4).

198. p. 62, ll. 21–22. *a Mill-pit.* The place where the wheel of a water-mill is
fixed; being walled in, it would offer no means of escape.

p. 62, ll. 27–28. *well-nigh two years and an half.* Bunyan later states that this
period of his greatest temptation to despair began one and a half years after
the time when his wife was with child (§ 240); his first child, Mary, was baptized on 20 July 1650, and the temptation, therefore, probably began in
the early or middle months of 1651. He resisted 'for the space of a year' before
abandoning himself to the belief that he had rejected Christ (§ 133) and in
an earlier section he declares that the subsequent spiritual torment lasted
'for two years together', thus roughly confirming the chronology of the
present paragraph and assigning the period of intense suffering to about
1652–4.

200. p. 63, l. 4. *the 18 of Luke.* '. . . that men ought always to pray and not to faint'.

p. 3, ll. 9–10. *Well, said I, I will pray. 'Tis no boot, said he.* There are many such short interchanges between the soul and its tempter in Bunyan's published sermons: e.g. 'Says Satan, dost thou not know that thou hast sinned horribly? yes, says the soul, I do . . . Well, says Satan, now will I come upon thee with my appeals. Art thou not a graceless wretch? Yes. Hast thou an heart to be sorry for this wickedness? No, not as I should' (*The Saints' Knowledge of Christ's Love*, ii. 37; cf. *Christ a Complete Saviour*, i. 223).

204. p. 64, l. 23. *My Grace is sufficient.* Cf. Hopeful's account of his conversion: 'But I replyed, Lord, I am a great, a very great sinner; and he answered *My grace is sufficient for thee*' (*P.P.*, p. 152); 'the Devil came in with this Suggestion, *That my Sins were too big to be pardoned*; but the Lord came with these words, *My Grace is sufficient for you*' (Charles Doe, *A Collection of Experience of the Work of Grace*, 1700, p. 17); there may, however, be conscious or unconscious reminiscence of Bunyan's language in the autobiography of Doe, his disciple.

p. 64, ll. 22–23. *that piece of a sentence darted in upon me.* '. . . that Scripture would often dart into my mind' (*Narrative of Agnes Beaumont*, p. 8).

206. p. 65, l. 16. *a Meeting of Gods People.* One of the, usually monthly, meetings of the Bedford church. Doe says: 'He lit on to the dissenting congregation of Christians at Bedford, and was, upon confession of faith, baptized about the year 1651, or 52, or 53' ('The Struggler' in *Works*, iii. 765). The author of *A Continuation of Mr. Bunyan's Life* gives 1655 as the year of his baptism; this later date is confirmed by the *Church Book*, p. 15, where his name occurs twenty-sixth in a list of members under that year. It is clear that his doubts and temptations continued for some time after his admission into the church: 'I went my self in chains to preach to them in chains' (§ 277).

207. p. 65, ll. 32–33. *as in a pair of Scales.* The image of the soul weighed in the balance is common in the religious emblem books, e.g. Quarles, *Emblemes* (1635), pp. 17–19.

210. p. 66, l. 23. *trembling at their Gate for deliverance.* Cf. Christiana and Mercy at the Wicket Gate: 'Now all this while, poor *Mercie* did stand without, trembling and crying for fear that she was rejected' (*P.P.*, Part Two, p. 189).

226. p. 71, l. 23. *in a New-Testament stile and sence.* By interpreting Old Testament episodes as types of the new law.

229. p. 72, ll. 17–18. *Thy righteousness is in Heaven.* 'Moreover, they know that God is then most nere unto them, when he seemeth to be farthest of, and that he is then a most mercifull and louing Saviour, when he semeth to be most angry, to afflict, and destroy. Also they know that they haue an euerlasting righteousnes, which they wait for through hope, as a certain and sure possession laid up for them in heauen, euen when they feele the horrible terrours of sinne and death . . .' (Luther, *A Commentary on the Epistle to the Galatians*, 1575, f. 233); and cf. reminiscence of the passage in *Law and Grace*, l. 545.

230. p. 72, ll. 26–27. *chains . . . irons . . .* Cf. Christian in Doubting Castle: I have a *Key* in my bosom, called *Promise*, that will . . . open any Lock in *Doubting-Castle*' (*P.P.*, p. 118).

232. p. 73, l. 14. *crack'd-Groats and Four-pence-half-pennies.* The groat was a fourpenny piece. A proclamation of 8 April 1603 fixed the value of the Irish twelvepence at ninepence English; the Irish sixpence was correspondingly valued at fourpence-halfpenny in England. This was to avoid confusion of the 'silver harp money' of Ireland with English shillings and sixpences (see Rogers Ruding, *Annals of the Coinage of Great Britain*, 1840, i. 359–64).

237. p. 74, l. 22. *the Temptation that went before.* The 'very great storm' of temptation lasting 'about a year' (§§ 97–132).

p. 74, l. 23. All the editions punctuate incorrectly with a full stop in the middle of the sentence after 'me'.

p. 75, l. 8. *Reader, that thou learn to beware.* 'I hope the same will be a plain patterne for all those which shall read my book' (James Hunt, *A Sermon Gathered and set forth by that Divine Spirit which God hath given to me*, 1648, p. 1, Dedication).

240. p. 75, ll. 12–13. *my Wife was great with Child.* See note to § 198.

243. p. 76, l. 5. *Gideon tempted God.* 'And Gideon said unto God, If thou wilt save Israel by mine hand, as thou hast said, Behold, I will put a fleece of wool in the floor; and if the dew be on the fleece only, and it be dry upon all the earth beside, then shall I know that thou wilt save Israel by mine hand, as thou hast said. And it was so: for he rose up early on the morrow, and thrust the fleece together, and wringed the dew out of the fleece, a bowlful of water. And Gideon said unto God, Let not thine anger be hot against me, and I will speak but this once: let me prove, I pray thee, but this once with the fleece; let it now be dry only upon the fleece, and upon all the ground let there be dew. And God did so that night: for it was dry upon the fleece only, and there was dew on all the ground' (Judges vi. 36–40).

245. p. 75, ll. 27–28. *the Keys of the Kingdom of Heaven.* Cf. again the key called Promise that will open 'any Lock in *Doubting-Castle*' (*P.P.*, p. 118).

249. p. 77, l. 32. *2 Sam. 7. 28*. 'And now, O Lord God, thou art that God, and thy words be true, and thou hast promised this goodness unto thy servant.' The editions give incorrectly '2 Sam. 3. 28'.

250. p. 77, l. 34. *flounce*: to flounder, rather than to move ostentatiously. Cf. *Badman*, p. 140.

252. p. 78, l. 19. *heights and depths*. A common phrase with the enthusiastic preachers: it is found in the title of the Ranter Joseph Salmon's autobiography *Heights in Depths and Depths in Heights* (1651). The biblical origins are Isa. vii. 11 and Rom. viii. 39.

253. p. 79, ll. 3–4. *joyn in fellowship with the People of God in Bedford*. See note to § 206.

p. 79, l. 13. *that Ordinance*. The central importance of the communion ordinance in the Bedford church, as in other independent congregations, is shown by entries in the *Church Book*, e.g. under 4 December 1669: 'Brother Bunyan to reason with Mr. Sewster about his desire of breaking bread with this congregation, without sitting downe as a member with us' (*Church Book*, p. 29), and see, on the general Puritan respect for the communion service, G. F. Nuttall, *The Holy Spirit in Puritan Faith and Experience* (1946), pp. 90–101.

255. p. 79, l. 30. *a Consumption*. 'Also, at another time, having contracted guilt upon my soul, and having some distemper of body upon me, I supposed that death might now so seize upon me as to take me away from among men; then, thought I, what shall I do now? Is all right with my soul? (*Law and Grace*, i. 545).

261. p. 81, l. 29. *savoury in my spirit*. Cf. 'savour', § 174.

p. 81, l. 34. *as if my loyns were broken*. Cf. 'such a clogging and heat at my stomach . . . as if my breast-bone would have split asunder', § 165; for attempts to provide a pathological account of Bunyan's terrors see William James, *Varieties of Religious Experience* (1902), pp. 157 f.; E. Marcault, 'Le cas "Bunyan" et le tempérament psychologique', in *Mélanges littéraires et philosophiques* (Clermont-Ferrand, 1910).

262. p. 82, l. 11. *came bolting in upon me*. Cf. 'that Scripture came in upon my mind' (*Narrative of Agnes Beaumont*, p. 24).

p. 82, l. 12. *Hebrews the twelfth*. The passage is alluded to in *The Pilgrim's Progress* by the angels who meet Christian and Hopeful when they have crossed the river: 'There, said they, is the Mount *Sion*, the heavenly *Jerusalem*, the inumerable company of Angels, and the Spirits of Just Men made perfect' (*P.P.*, p. 169). Heb. xii is a crucial chapter for Bunyan and for his associates in the gathered churches: v. 17 on the rejection of Esau provides the theme

of despair for the central episode of the autobiography; the intervening
vv. 18–21 contain the significant image of the old law, Mount Sinai with its
thunder and fire, which is frequently used in the sermons and is the subject
of the short summary of doctrine printed posthumously by Doe in the Folio,
Of the Law and the Christian (*Works*, ii. 387–8); it is later embodied in Bunyan's
allegory as the climax of the Worldly Wiseman episode (pp. 21–22, 25–26).
See also Walter Cradock, *Divine Drops Distilled from the Fountain of Holy
Scriptures* (1650), pp. 188 ff.; John Owen, *A Continuation of the Exposition of the
Epistle of Paul the Apostle to the Hebrews* (1684), pp. 237–9.

264. p. 82, l. 23. *The words are these.* The quotation is from A.V. except for
Heb. xii. 24 where 'Mediator of the New Testament' instead of '. . .
of the new covenant' appears to follow Geneva. But there are none of the
other features peculiar to Geneva (e.g. 'celestial Jerusalem'), so the departure
from A.V. may be due as in other cases to quotation from memory.

265. p. 83, l. 3. *about five or six years awakened.* 'NB Mr. Bunyan began to
preach some time in the year 1656' (*Church Book*, p. 15). This confirms other
evidence in the text, especially § 78, that the beginning of his conversion,
after the short period of 'legal Christianity', was about 1650. Cf. '. . . when
the set time was come, the Lord, just before the men called Quakers came
into the country, did set me down so blessedly in the truth of the doctrine of
Jesus Christ' (*Law and Grace*, i. 549). This would seem to refer to the beginning of Quaker activities about 1650 and not to the period of full Quaker
evangelizing in Bedfordshire in 1655 when Fox stayed with the magistrate
John Crook at Beckrings Park, or to William Dewsbury's mission in 1654
(Fox, *Journal*, pp. 207–9; Elisabeth Brockbank, *Edward Burrough, A Wrestler
for Truth*, 1949, p. 105).

p. 83, l. 31. *preaching the Word.* An account of the author's ministry
usually follows that of conversion in the autobiographies of pastors; cf. *The
Life and Death of Mr. Henry Jessey, Late Preacher of the Gospel* (1671), pp. 25–31;
The Life and Death of Mr. Vavasor Powell (1671), pp. 10–19.

268. p. 83, l. 35. *I was most sorely afflicted.* This and other passages suggest
that the final period of temptation, lasting as it did at least until 1655, may
in its last stages have overlapped with the beginning of his ministry.

270. p. 84, l. 9. *Gifts and Abilities.* Bunyan, like other mechanics, speaks out
for the uneducated and unordained preacher's right to exercise his gift. Cf.
the shoemaker Samuel Howe's *The Sufficiency of the Spirit's Teaching* (1645).
He would become familiar with the case made out against humane learning
by Puritan extremists through his friendship with William Dell, rector of
Yelden till 1662, who declared that he would 'rather chuse to be in fellowship
with poor plain Husbandmen and Tradesmen, who believe in Christ, and
have received his Spirit, then with the Heads of Universities, and highest,
and stateliest of the Clergy' (*The Tryal of Spirits*, 1653, Preface).

p. 84, l. 17. *Fox*. Acknowledgement is made to the *Acts and Monuments* in *Come and Welcome*, i. 295-6, and *The House of the Forest of Lebanon*, iii. 532; in the former passage reference is made to the edition of 1632. The martyrdoms of Ignatius, Romanus, and Polycarp are described in *P.P.*, Part Two, p. 260, in terms similar to those in the passage in *Come and Welcome*. Bunyan had his copy of Foxe's book with him in prison: 'There also I survey'd his Library, the least and yet the best, that e'er I saw, consisting only of two books, a Bible and the *Book of Martyrs*' (*An Account of the Life and Death of Mr. John Bunyan* (appended to *The Heavenly Footman*, 2nd ed. 1700), p. 128). A copy of the three-volume 1641 edition of the *Acts and Monuments* with a signature purporting to be Bunyan's in the third volume was sold to the Pierpont Morgan Library by the Bedford Scientific and Literary Institute in 1911. The writing differs from that of the other Bunyan signatures and its genuineness has been doubted by Sir Hilary Jenkinson and others (*Bedfordshire Magazine*, vi, 1957, 47-49).

272. p. 84, l. 27. *bowels*. Cf. 'Bowels becometh Pilgrims' (*P.P.*, Part Two, p. 186). Pity, compassion (Isa. lxiii. 15.)

274. p. 85, l. 15. *Job. 29. 13*. A.V. 'of him' is altered to 'of them' and 'yea', added to the second sentence.

276. p. 85, ll. 29-30. *the terrours of the Law*. From these early sermons, written before his own distress of conscience was at an end, were composed *Sighs from Hell, or the Groans of a Damned Soul* (1658) and portions of *The Doctrine of the Law and Grace Unfolded* (1660).

278. p. 86, l. 8. *the space of two years*. c. 1656-8.

p. 86, ll. 14-15. *Jesus Christ in all his Offices, Relations, ana Benefits . . .*, referring to the field covered in *Law and Grace*.

279. p. 86, l. 23. *cast into Prison*. Bunyan was arrested by a magistrate, Francis Wingate, at Lower Samsell on 12 November 1660. The time reference of the first edition implies that he is writing c. 1665 ('have lain as long to confirm the Truth . . . as I was before in testifying of it').

283. p. 87, ll. 18-19. *Doctors and Priests*. The established clergy; the usage is that of the early Quakers (Fox, *Journal*, passim).

p. 87, l. 23. *they shall be for my hire*. Jacob's words to Laban, when bargaining over the cattle he was to have as his wages, are here adopted and spiritualized (Gen. xxx. 33).

284. p. 87, l. 25. *things that were controverted*. John Gifford in his testament to the Bedford church at his death in 1655 warns specifically against disputes over inessential points: 'Concerning separation from the Church about Baptisme, Laying on of hands, Anoynting with Oyls, Psalmes, or any externalls; I charge every one of you respectively, as you will give an account for it to our Lord Jesus Christ who shall judge both quick, and dead at his coming, that none of you be found guilty of this great evill: which whiles some have committed, and through a zeale for God, yet not according to knowledge; they have erred from the Lawe of the Love of Christ; and have made a rent from the true Church which is but one . . . In your assemblies avoide all disputes which gender to strifes; as questions about externals, and all doubtful disputations' (*Church Book*, p. 3). Bunyan followed this tradition of toleration in matters not pertaining to salvation: 'Fly Seducers' company; keep company with the soundest Christians, that have most experience of Christ; and be sure thou have a care of Quakers, Ranters, Freewillers; also do not have too much company with some Anabaptists, though I go under that name myself' (*The Heavenly Footman*, iii. 383). But the controversy with the Quaker, Edward Burrough, which led to the publication of his first book, *Some Gospel Truths Opened* (1656), was regarded by Bunyan as a dispute over fundamentals involving the question whether the historical Christ whom the Quakers called 'the man who died at Jerusalem' was to be abandoned for an indwelling Christ.

285. p. 87, ll. 35–36. *other men's lines.* Bunyan gives his own figurative interpretation of 'to boast in another man's line of things made ready to our hand' (2 Cor. x. 16). Cf. the misunderstanding of 'vessel' in § 187. Resentment at the charge of plagiarism is frequent throughout his work, and in spite of the amount of traditional material which the allegories and sermons contain, he is always scrupulous in acknowledging the few instances of conscious borrowing, from the *Acts and Monuments*, Clarke's *A Mirrour or Looking-glasse both for saints and sinners*, and Dod's *A Plaine and Familiar Exposition of the Ten Commandments* (e.g. *Come and Welcome*, i. 295–6; *Badman*, pp. 60, 142, 154, 155; *Law and Grace*, i. 502). Cf. the indignant Advertisement to the Reader at the end of *H.W.* (1682):

> Some say the *Pilgrims Progress* is not mine,
> Insinuating as if I would shine
> In name and fame by the worth of another . . .
> . . . *John* such dirt-heap never was . . .
> It came from mine own heart, so to my head,
> And thence into my fingers trickled;
> Then to my Pen, from whence immediately
> On Paper I did dribble it daintily.
>
> (*H.W.*, p. 432).

290. p. 89, l. 18. *to bring forth Children to God.* Cf. the description of the picture of Evangelist, the first emblem in the Interpreter's House: 'he can beget Children, Travel in birth with Children, and Nurse them himself when they are born' (*P.P.*, p. 29).

296. p. 90, l. 34. *pride and liftings up of Heart.* 'The truth is, as himself sometimes acknowledged, he always needed the thorn in the flesh . . . lest, under his extraordinary circumstance, he should be exalted above measure; which perhaps was the evil that did more easily beset him than any other' (George Cokayne, 'A Preface to the Reader', 21 Sept. 1688, in *The Acceptable Sacrifice,* i. 685).

298. p. 91, ll. 16–17. *melodious and heart-inflaming Musick.* Bunyan's appreciation of music, vocal and instrumental, is shown by references scattered throughout the works, especially in *P.P.*; the King's trumpeters welcome Christian and Hopeful into the Celestial City (an episode added in the second edition, pp. 160–1); in the Second Part Prudence sings to 'a pair of Excellent Virginals' (p. 233), Christiana plays the viol and Mercy the lute (p. 283); the many hymns in the Second Part provide indirect advocacy of congregational singing (cf. *Solomon's Temple Spiritualized,* 1688, iii. 496 and *Trans. Bapt. Hist. Soc.* vi, 1918–19, 277). A flute, said to have been made by Bunyan in prison from a chair leg, is preserved at Bunyan Meeting, Bedford; its authenticity was accepted by Joseph Whiting, Frank Mott Harrison, and others (see Percy A. Scholes, *The Puritans and Music in England and New England,* Oxford, 1934, p. 385).

302. p. 92, ll. 5–12. The caution against gifts of nature agrees with the general tenor of sectarian criticism of worldly learning in the Commonwealth period; cf. 'Hath not the Lord long ago told us by his prophet, and wished his people to behold it, That he would do a marvellous work? and then he doubles it again, even a marvellous work and a wonder; and then all comes to this, "That he would cause to perish, and destroy the wisdom of the wise, and cast away the understanding of the prudent." Isa. 29. 14' (Samuel Howe, *The Sufficiency of the Spirit's Teaching,* 8th ed. 1792, p. 39); 'Let the faithful examine every thing that is taught by the word of God, and not receive doctrines upon trust, from their Teachers, who, through the reputation of their learning and holiness, may easily lead them unawares into error' (William Dell, *The Way of true Peace and Unity* in *Several Sermons and Discourses of William Dell, Minister of the Gospel,* 1652, p. 216).

p. 92, l. 11. *life.* The early editions all print 'love', presumably influenced by its occurrence in the preceding paragraph.

306–17. These sections, replying to accusations of immoral conduct, appear for the first time in the fifth edition (1680); they may, of course, have been added in the fourth. The passage refers to the Agnes Beaumont affair of 1674. Agnes Beaumont was the daughter of John Beaumont of Edworth and was twenty-one at the time; she had joined the sister church of the Bedford meeting at Gamlingay, but her father was violently opposed to her attending it. In February Bunyan was persuaded against his will to take her behind him on his horse to the meeting in the absence of her usual escort. John Beaumont saw this and was so enraged that he forbade her to return to the house; two days after her return had been permitted he died, and a lawyer named Farrow, a rejected suitor, spread the story that she had poisoned her father and that Bunyan had furnished her with the means of doing it. Meanwhile, a Bedford clergyman Lane was spreading slander about her relations with her pastor. A sensible coroner's jury found her innocent of murder and the affair died down. It is told in her own words in B.M. MS. Egerton 2414 which has been published by G. B. Harrison as *A Narrative of the Persecution of Agnes Beaumont in the Year 1674* (1929). See Appendix C.

307. p. 93, l. 11. *a Witch.* The masculine use is common; cf. Simon Magus, 'Simon the Witch', *P.P.*, p. 112; 'He is a witch asking counsel at soothsayers', see note on § 171.

313. p. 94, l. 15. *to be naught.* Cf. *King Lear*, II. iv. 136: 'Thy sister's naught'.

p. 94, l. 17. *all is a case*: i.e. one and the same case.

p. 94, l. 20. *hang'd by the Neck.* This recalls the prescription of the death penalty for fornication under the law of 1657.

314. p. 94, l. 23. *under the Copes.* 'Under the cope of heaven' would be more common usage. See *O.E.D.*, s.v. 'cope'.

315. p. 94, l. 29. *the common Salutation.* Kissing as a form of greeting, described by several foreign travellers in England, for instance Van Meteren, *Nederlandtshe Historie.*

p. 94, l. 37. *baulks.* Omissions, exceptions; from the ridge between two furrows left in ploughing.

318. p. 95, l. 22. *about five year.* Bunyan's high reputation at this period (*c.* 1659–60) is shown by the fact that a letter from Alexander Parker to George Fox, '4th day of the 3rd month 1659', speaks of the Bedford congregation as 'Bunian his society' (Dr. Williams's Library, *Swarthmore Transcripts*, iii. 45).

p. 95, ll. 25–26. *a Justice.* Francis Wingate of Harlington Hall. His father's death at the outbreak of the Civil War had made him a ward of the Crown, but his mother took him to the Royalist headquarters at Oxford and for this offence had to compound with Parliament for her estate and to pay a fine. His prosecution of Bunyan was one of the first proceedings against Nonconformists after the Restoration: 'It may be doubted whether there was another Justice the country through in such eager haste as was Francis Wingate' (Brown, p. 134). His son Francis was knighted in 1672 and married the fourth daughter of the Earl of Anglesey (*Royalist Composition Papers*, G53, No. 146, p. 163; Brown, pp. 132–9).

319. p. 95, ll. 29–30. *Upholder . . . of unlawful Assemblies and Conventicles.* At the time of the arrest in November 1660 there was no fresh legislation against Nonconformists; the Declaration of Breda had promised liberty of conscience and Charles II's settlement of the Church was still incomplete; an Act against conventicles was not passed until 1662. Wingate proceeded under the old statute of 35 Elizabeth, c. i, which sentenced any person who attended any 'unlawful assembly, conventicle, or meeting' to be imprisoned without bail until he conformed and submitted in the parish church. For a third offence such a person could be transported for seven years and if he escaped or returned to England was to suffer death as a felon.

p. 95, l. 34. *perpetual banishment.* A confused recollection of the terms of the statute as it was reissued in 1662: 'And for the third offence he shall be sent to the jail or house of correction, there to remain until the next session or assizes, and then to be indicted; and being thereupon found guilty, the court shall enter judgment of transportation against such offenders, to some of the foreign plantations (Virginia and New England only excepted) there to remain seven years . . .' (14 Car. II, c. 2; *Statutes at Large*, iii. 218).

p. 96, ll. 2–3. *compleat twelve years.* The third edition (1679) reading; altered from 'above five year and a quarter' in the first (1666); the third presumably reprints the reading of the missing second of 1672.

322. p. 96, ll. 26–27. *to fear neither the Horse nor his Rider* (Rev. ix; the horsemen of the Apocalypse).

324. p. 97, l. 16. *long-suffering.* A misunderstanding of the meaning 'patience' in the passage quoted from Col. i. 11. Cf. 2 Cor. vi. 4, 6; 2 Tim. iii. 10; James v. 10, 11.

327. p. 98, l. 17. *my poor blind Child.* His first child, Mary, baptized 20 July 1650; she died before him.

333. p. 100, ll. 3–4. *not acquainted with the Laws:* i.e. he thought that the sentence of death, prescribed only for those already transported who should return to England, was an immediate threat; cf. 'if Death come', § 327. Twelve Baptists of Aylesbury were sentenced to death for Nonconformity but pardoned by Charles II (*Some Remarkable Passages in the Life of William Kiffin, Written by Himself*, ed. William Orme, 1823, pp. 118–20); a Cambridgeshire minister, Francis Holcroft, was sentenced to be hanged under the same Act by which Bunyan was prosecuted, for refusing the oath of abjuration; he received a royal pardon (Oliver Heywood, *His Autobiography, Diaries, Anecdote and Event Books*, Brighouse and Bingley, 1882–5, iii. 83, 88).

334. p. 100, l. 15. *scrabling.* The provincial form is altered to 'scrambling' in the third edition; cf. 'to scrabble on his way' in *P.P.*, p. 134.

338. p. 101, l. 15. *by-Respects.* Cf. By-ends in *P.P.*, pp. 98, 272–3.

A Relation of My Imprisonment

p. 105, l. 10. *Samsell, by Harlington.* A village about thirteen miles south of Bedford beyond Ampthill.

p. 106, l. 3. *the close.* An enclosed field under the village system of enclosure farming.

p. 107, l. 8. *armour or not*: i.e. arms; the insinuation that Nonconformists met for subversive ends was common: 'I told him this Act did not concern us, which was made against seditious meetings that met under colour of religion to contrive insurrections' (Fox, *Journal*, p. 563).

p. 107, l. 23. *sureties.* Other dissenting preachers objected to the use of sureties to prevent their effectiveness in their pastoral duties; cf. Edmund Calamy, *A Continuation of the Account of the Ministers who were Ejected after the Restoration* (1727), i. 331.

p. 108, l. 1. *Dr. Lindale.* William Lindall or Lyndall. He matriculated as a sizar at Trinity, Cambridge, in 1618, subsequently becoming Fellow and D.D. in 1637. He became vicar of Blythe, Notts., in 1633, curate of Hitchin, and then vicar of Harlington; by his marriage to the widow of Dr. Stephen Pierce, vicar of Hitchin, he became Wingate's father-in-law. He died in 1674 (Brown, p. 135; J. A. Venn, *Alumni Cantabrigienses*, Part I, vol. iii, p. 121, which wrongly gives *c.* 1665 as the date of his presentation to the living of Harlington).

p. 108, l. 7. *the oaths.* Some Baptists as well as Quakers refused to take the oaths in court and could under a statute of James I be involved in a charge of praemunire. See Gerald R. Cragg, *Puritanism in the Period of the Great Persecution 1660–1688* (Cambridge, 1957), p. 51.

p. 109, ll. 17–18. *Mr. Foster of Bedford.* William Foster, a lawyer of Bedford, who became commissary and later chancellor of the diocese of Lincoln; he was LL.B. of Clare, Cambridge, in 1663, and died in 1708. He was Wingate's brother-in-law, having married his sister Amy *c.* 1653. The Act Books of the Archdeacon's Court during this period show that he was assiduous in prosecuting Dissenters and distraining their goods (see also *A true and Impartiall Narrative of Some Illegal Arbitrary proceedings by certain Justices of the Peace and others . . . in and near the Town of Bedford*, 1670). The warrant of 1675 for Bunyan's arrest was signed by him as justice of the peace. In 1687 he was the only Bedford justice to submit to James II's proposals concerning the Test Acts in their entirety and was a leading spirit in the new modelling of the corporation in that year under Tory auspices (Brown, pp. 136, 140, 318, 348–9; *V.C.H. Bedford*, ii. 59, 167, 387–9; *Bedfordshire Notes and Queries*, i. 275).

p. 108, ll. 22–23. *Alexander a Coppersmith.* 'Alexander the coppersmith did me much evil; the Lord reward him according to his works' (2 Tim. iv. 14).

p. 109, ll. 26–27. Ps. lv. 21, Matt. x. 17.

p. 109, l. 35. *my brother*: his brother-in-law Wingate.

p. 111, l. 3. *the original Greek.* 'As Mr. Bunyan was upon the road near Cambridge, there overtakes him a scholar that had observed him a preacher, and said to him, How dare you preach, seeing you have not the original, being not a scholar? Then said Mr. Bunyan, Have you the original? Yes, said the scholar, Nay, but, said Mr. Bunyan, have you the very self-same original copies that were written by the penmen of the scripture, prophets and apostles? No, said the scholar but we have the true copies of those originals. How do you know that? said Mr. Bunyan. How? said the scholar. Why, we believe what we have is a true copy of the original. Then, said Mr. Bunyan, so do I believe our English Bible is a true copy of the original. Then away rid the scholar' (Charles Doe, 'The Struggler', in *Works*, iii. 767). This is presumably an incident in the dispute between Bunyan and Thomas Smith, Professor of Arabic at Cambridge described in the latter's *The Quaker Disarm'd, or A True Relation of a Late Publick Dispute Held at Cambridge. With a Letter in Defence of the Ministry and Against Lay-Preachers* (1659). Bunyan was defended by Henry Denne in *The Quaker No Papist* (1659).

p. 112, l. 25. *the brethren*: his fellow members of the Bedford church.

p. 112, l. 28. *Mr. Crumpton.* It was from this Crompton that Josias Ruff head purchased the orchard and barn in Mill Lane, Bedford, which served as a meeting-house for the church after Bunyan's release in 1672. There are Crompton arms in Elstow church (Brown, p. 215; *V.C.H. Bedford*, iii. 283)

p. 113, l. 13. Matt. xxvii. 18.

p. 113, l. 23. *my Examination.* The terrifying experience of confronting his opponents in a court of law when he was completely ignorant of its procedure left a vivid impression on Bunyan's mind; his awe at the ceremonies and formulae of quarter-sessions and assize has found its way into his writings; as well as the trial scenes in *P.P.* (Mr. Justice Hategood at Vanity Fair) and in *H.W.* (the trial of the Diabolonians) there is this passage on the Last Judgement: ' . . . there was never any quarter-sessions, nor general jail-delivery more publicly foretold of, than this day. You know that the judges before they begin their assizes, do give to the country in charge, that they take heed to the laws and statutes of the king' (*Of the Resurrection of the Dead*, ii. 123).

p. 113, l. 23. *Justice Keelin.* Sir John Kelynge of Southhill was a prominent local Royalist: Clarendon describes him as 'a person of eminent learning and eminent suffering, who never wore his gown after the Rebellion, but was always in gaol'. He was one of the new batch of serjeants in 1660, and was vigorous in the prosecution of Fifth Monarchy men and regicides, showing himself harsh and insulting to Sir Henry Vane and others. He helped to prepare the Act of Uniformity and was member for Bedford in Charles II's first Parliament. He became chief justice in 1665; there were many complaints against his want of temper and discretion (in 1670 he was compelled to appear at the bar of the House of Lords to answer for his conduct towards Lord Hollis in the King's Bench) (*D.N.B.*, *Fasti Oxonienses*, i. 404; Foss, *Biographia Juridica*, 1870, pp. 381–2; Pepys, *Diary*, ed. H. B. Wheatley, 1904, vii. 223–4).

p. 113, l. 23. *Justice Chester*. Sir Henry Chester of Tilsworth and Lidlington was created Knight of the Bath at the coronation a few months later; he was Francis Wingate's uncle; he died in 1666 and his monument is in Tilsworth church (*V.C.H. Bedford*, iii. 434).

p. 113, l. 24. *Justice Blundale*. Sir George Blundell of Cardington Manor was, like the other magistrates, a Royalist landowner who had suffered from fines and sequestrations during the Commonwealth. His family was associated with that of Snagg (see *infra*) in the office of hereditary almoner of Bedford.

p. 113, l. 24. *Justice Beecher*. Sir William Beecher of Howbury was knighted in the same week Bunyan was arrested; he was one of the signatories to the warrant for Bunyan's arrest in 1675, and became member of Parliament for the borough of Bedford under James II.

p. 113, l. 24. *Justice Snagg*. Thomas Snagg of Marston Manor near Kempston became high sheriff of the county in 1665; he died in 1675 (Feet of Fines Beds. Hil., 23 & 24 Chas. II).

p. 116, ll. 11–12. *they were set*: checked, rebuffed.

p. 117, l. 16. *pedlers French*. The jargon of thieves and vagabonds; the canting tongue:

> 'Twere fitter
> Such honest lads as myself had it, that instead
> Of pedlar's French gives him plain language for his money,
> Stand and deliver!'

(Beaumont and Fletcher, *The Faithful Friends*, I. ii. 76–79).
   'A sort of Gibrish . . . used by Gypsies &c. Also the Beggers Cant.' (*Dictionary of the Canting Crew*, 1700).

p. 117, l. 30. *As every man hath received the gift*. 'First, the Spirit doth gift the men, and qualifie them for the work . . .' (William Strong, *XXXI Select Sermons*, ed. Thomas Manton, 1656, p. 113). 'Nothing at all can be done without these Spiritual Gifts; and therefore a Ministry devoid of them, is a Mock-ministry, and no ordinance of Christ' (John Owen, *Two Discourses concerning the Holy Spirit*, 1693, p. 228).

p. 119, l. 2. *Christ's words* (Luke xxi. 15).

p. 119, l. 14. *Mr. Cobb.* Paul Cobb, the clerk of the peace; his seal is found on the warrant of 1675 (Brown, p. 268). He was later Mayor of Bedford and as an alderman was concerned in 1687 in the surrender of the old charter at the instigation of James II and Lord Bruce.

p. 119, l. 23. *worse than that.* This vague threat of capital punishment would serve to foster the fears Bunyan confesses to in §§ 324, 333.

p. 120, ll. 9–10. *the late insurrection at London.* Thomas Venner, a wine-cooper, led an outbreak of Fifth Monarchy enthusiasts in the streets of London in January 1661. 'The king had not been many days at Whitehall, when one Venner, a Fifth Monarchy man, who thought it was not enough to believe that Christ was to reign on earth, and to put the saints in possession of the kingdom, but added to this that the saints were to take the kingdom themselves. He gathered some of the most furious of the party to a meeting in Coleman Street . . . they had prepared standards and colours with their devices on them, and furnished themselves with very good arms . . . they resolved to venture out into the streets, and cry out, No king but Christ. They scoured the streets before them, and made a great progress. . . . They killed a great many, but were at last mastered by numbers; and were all either killed or taken and executed' (Burnet, *History of His Own Time*, ed. O. Airy, Oxford, 1897–1900, i. 278–9, and cf. Reresby, *Travels and Memoirs*, 1813, p. 166). The outbreak was a disaster for moderate dissenters since it gave the authorities an excuse for stricter measures against the sects. The minister of St. Stephen, Coleman Street, had formerly been the radical John Goodwin (of whom Burnet says: 'He was for liberty of all sorts').

p. 120, l. 17. *my loyalty.* Bunyan remained a staunch and consistent supporter of civil obedience: 'It is a false report then that the governors of the nations have received against the city, this new Jerusalem, if they believe, that according to the tale that is told them, she is and hath been of old a rebellious city, and destructive to kings, and a diminisher of their revenues' (*Holy City*, ed. 1669, p. 55); and cf. *Seasonable Counsel: or, Advice to Sufferers*, ii. 706–9.

p. 122, l. 32. *Wickliffe saith.* Foxe, *Acts and Monuments*, ed. Stephen Reed Cattley, 1837, iii. 21.

p. 124, l. 8. *the notes of all my sermons.* The arrangement of *A Few Sighs from Hell* shows how formal in structure Bunyan's early sermons must have been; mid-seventeenth-century Puritan sermons were rarely extempore except those of the Quakers and extreme enthusiasts (see Caroline F. Richardson, *English Preachers and Preaching, 1640–1670*, 1928, pp. 36, 74).

p. 125, l. 15. *the King was to be crowned.* Charles II was crowned in Westminster Abbey, 23 April 1661.

p. 125, l. 33. *Judge Hales.* Sir Matthew Hale (1609–76) was a judge celebrated for his learning and probity; after sitting for Gloucestershire in the Convention Parliament, he had been appointed chief baron of the exchequer and knighted; he was created chief justice of the king's bench in 1671. Himself of puritan inclinations, he was lenient towards dissenters and favoured their comprehension in the national church. His conduct on this occasion merits the high praise of his friend Baxter: 'He was most precisely just; insomuch as I believe he would have lost all that he had in the World rather than do an unjust Act: Patient in hearing the tediousest speech which any Man had to make for himself. The pillar of Justice, the Refuge of the subject who feared Oppression, and one of the greatest Honours of his Majestie's Government' (*Reliquiae, Baxterianae*, 1696, iii. 47). See also *D.N.B.*; Gilbert Burnet, *Life and Death of Sir Matthew Hale* (1682); Campbell, *Lives of the Chief Justices* (1858), i. 512–88.

p. 125, ll. 12–13. *the poor widow* (Luke xviii. 1–8).

p. 125, l. 15. *Swan Chamber.* The chief room in the inn of that name near the bridge over the Ouse (now pulled down and rebuilt).

p. 127, ll. 15–16. *my Lord Barkwood.* Probably a mistake for Bedford. William, 5th Earl, 1616–1700 (Duke from 1694), had Puritan and Parliamentary sympathies and, though he did not become Lord Lieutenant till the change of monarchy, is the local grandee to whom Bunyan's wife is most likely to have appealed. See *Complete Peerage*, 1912, ii. 79–80.

p. 128, l. 5. *but mother-in-law to them.* Stepmother: 'If she becomes a mother in law, there is no difference betwixt her carriage to her own and her second husbands children' (Fuller, *The Holy State and the Profane State*, 1642, I. x. 26).

p. 128, l. 24. *a writ of error.* In the English criminal courts in the late seventeenth century extreme precision was necessary in the wording of the indictment, otherwise the defence, by a plea of misnomer—inaccurate naming or entitling of the prisoner—could prove the whole indictment invalid; Hale's own testimony was that 'More offenders escape by the over-easy ear given to indictments than by any other means' (Blackstone, *Commentaries*, 1766–9, IV. iii. 328; Sir William Holdsworth, *History of English Law*, 1923, iii. 614–31).

p. 129, l. 28. *some liberty granted me.* Entries in the *Church Book* during this period show that on at least two occasions Bunyan was sent to admonish absent brethren: on 28 August 1661: 'Our brother Bunyan to brother Robert Nelson and sister Manly'; 26 September 1661: 'We desire brother Bunyan and John Fenne to go againe to sister Pecock' (p. 24); after this his imprisonment must have become more rigorous: the August entry had already noted 'Our meetings having bene for some time neglected, through the increase of trouble.'

p. 130, l. 3. *Christians at London.* The Bedford church was closely associated with the London congregations of Southwark and All Hallows the Great. The pastors of both, Henry Jessey and John Simpson, held open-communion principles like those of Bunyan and his predecessors Burton and Gifford. Evidence of the connexion is provided by correspondence and letters of dismission in the *Church Book* (e.g. 'The Church of Christ in Bedford to the Church of Christ in London wher of our honored brother Henry Jesse was pastor', p. 57, and cf. Geoffrey F. Nuttall, *Visible Saints: the Congregational Way 1640–1660*, Oxford, 1957, p. 97).

p. 130, l. 19. *the kalender.* The list of prisoners for trial at the assizes.

APPENDIX A

Extracts from the *Bedford Church Book*
(Bunyan Meeting, Bedford)

(f. 15) NB Mr Bunyan began to preach some time in the year 1656:
But was not ordained Pastor till 21st of October 1671.
He entered into the joy of his Lord 31st of August 1688.
So that he was a preacher of the gospel 32 years—&
Pastor of this Church 17 years.

(f. 18) At a meeting of the Church the 28th of the 3rd moneth (28 May 1657).
It was agreed that brother John Crane be admitted a member of this congregation, upon his profession that he joyneth with us, as we are in union with Christ, though differing in judgement about some outward things.

Whereas brother Maxy and his wife desire to have communion with us, we appoint brother Breeden, and Brother John Fenne, to discourse with them in order thereunto. Sister Child also, and sister Beech were appointed to go to sister Maxy, and to give an account to the Church next meeting. Upon the same account sister Spencer and sister Bluit, were appointed to speake with sister Croote of Kempston. And brother Bunyan, brother Childe and brother John Fenne were appointed to go to friend Stratton, junior, of Houghton (Conquest). Sister Boughton's desire also of joyning with us was propounded to be considered of.

(f. 19) At a meeting of the Church the 27th of the 6th moneth (27 August 1657).
Whereas there hath heretofore bene time spent in seeking God to direct us in the choyce of officers necessary for the congregation, according to the order of the Gospell, and whereas heretofore there were no nominated and appointed for tryall, our brother Spensely, brother Bunyan, brother Coventon and brother Robert Wallis, to exercise the office of deacons, and brother Bunyan being taken off by the preaching of the Gospell, we are agreed that, our brother Bunyan being otherwise imployed, our other three brethren beforenamed be continued; and upon farther debate and good consideration, have also made free choice of our brother John Fenne to be joined with them. . . .

(f. 20) At a meeting of the Church the 25th of the 12th moneth (25 February 1657–8).

Upon the relation of the brethren sent to brother Skelton, the Church still remaining dissatisfyed, did appoint brother Bunyan and brother Childe farther to speake with him.

And brother Bunyan and brother Samuel Fenne were appointed to go againe to sister Chamberlaine, the Church, upon the relation of the brethren before sent to her, remaining dissatisfyed.

It is also agreed that the 3rd day of the next moneth be set apart to seeke God in the behalf of our brother Wheeler who hath bene long ill in body, whereby his ministery hath been hindred, and also about the Church affaires, and the affaires of the Nation, and for our brother Whitbread, who hath bene long ill, and also for counsaile what to doe with respect to the indictment against brother Bunyan at the Assizes, for preaching at Eaton.[1]

(f. 21) At a meeting of the Church the 30th of the 7th moneth (30 September 1658).

... And for the continuing of unity and preventing of differences among the congregations walking with Mr. Donne Mr. Wheeler and Mr. Gibbs, and ourselves it was agreed that brother Burton, brother Grew, brother Harrington, brother Whiteman and brother Bunyan, should within few days meet together to consider of some things that may conduce to love and unity amongst us all.

(f. 22) At a meeting of the Church the latter part of the 12th moneth (February 1658–9).

Whereas our brother Bunyan hath spoken with brother John Childe to come and render a reason of his withdrawing, to some of the brethren, and he refuseth to do it unless he may come before the whole congregation, we are agreed that he have notice given him to come to the next church meeting. . . .

At a meeting of the Church at Bedford the 31th of the 1st moneth (31 March 1659).

Our brother Bunyan having since the last meeting spoken to brother Childe to come to the meeting according to the church's appointment, and his (implyed) promise, and he refusing so to doe, it is agreed by us, according to the 8th proposall agreed on

[1] Eaton Socon.

by the messengers of the Churches, that in this business the advice and assistance of the other churches be desired.

(f. 24) At a meeting of the Church the 25th of the 2d moneth (25 April 1660).

It was ordered according to our agreement, that our brother Bunyan do prepare to speake a word to us the next Church meeting, and that our brother Whiteman faile not to speake to him of it.

(f. 25) Our meetings having bene for some time neglected through the increase of trouble, the 28th of the 6th moneth 1661 (28 August) the Church through mercy againe met.

Agreed that whereas certaine of our friends have not onely withdrawne themselves but also otherwaies failed, some of our friends be sent to admonish them of the same *viz.*

Our brother Bunyan to brother Robert Nelson and sister Manly.

At a meeting of the Church at Bedford the 26th of the 7th moneth (26 September 1661).

We desire brother Bunyan and John Fenne to go againe to sister Peacock.

(f. 27) At a meeting of the Church at Bedford the 30th day of the 8th moneth (30 October 1668).

Many of the friends having in these troublous times withdrawne themselves from close walking with the Church, and not being reclaimed by those admonitions that, as time would serve, had bene sent to them formerly; some also being guilty of more grosse miscarriages, the congregation having kept certaine dayes with fasting and prayer bewailed their fall, did now agree in a solemne way to renew their admonitions, and did agree:—

. . . that brother Bunyan and brother Harrington send for brother Merrill and admonish him concerning his withdrawing from the Church, and his conformity to the world's way of worship.

And brother Bunyan and brother Cooper were appointed to go to brother Coventon to admonish him, and endeavour his conviction for his sin in withdrawing from the Church assemblyes.

(f. 28) At a meeting of the Church at Bedford the 14th of the 7th moneth (14 September 1669).

... They found not Robert Wallis at home, nor Robert Nelson: therefore brother Bunyan and brother John Fenne were againe appointed to admonish him.

(ff. 29–50) (In the entries for 1669–71, when Bunyan was still technically a prisoner, there are frequent records of his being chosen to visit brethren for purposes of admonition or to give advice in cases of scruple. Also his signature appears on most of the pastoral letters of this period reproduced in the *Church Book*.)

(ff. 50–51) At a full assembly of the Church at Bedford the 21th of the 10th moneth (21 December 1671).

After much seeking God by prayer, and sober conference formerly had, the congregation did at this meeting with joynt consent (signifyed by solemne lifting up of their hands) call forth and appoint our brother John Bunyan to the pastorall office or eldership. And he accepting therof gave up himself to serve Christ and his church in that charge, and received of the elders the right hand of fellowship.

APPENDIX B

A CONTINUATION OF MR. BUNYAN'S LIFE; BEGINNING
WHERE HE LEFT OFF, AND CONCLUDING WITH THE TIME
AND MANNER OF HIS DEATH AND BURIAL; TOGETHER
WITH HIS TRUE CHARACTER, &c.

(*Grace Abounding,* 7th ed., 1692, pp. 157–71)

Reader, The painful and industrious Author of this Book, has already
given you a very moving Relation, of the beginning and middle of the
days of his Pilgrimage on Earth, and since there yet remains somewhat
worthy of Notice and Regard, which occurred in the last Scene of his
Life; the which for want of time; or fear some over censorious People
should impute it to him, as an Earnest covering praise from Men; he
has not left behind him in writing. Wherefore as a true Friend, and long
acquaintance of Mr. *Bunyan*; that his good end may be known as well
as his evil beginning; I have taken upon me from my knowledge, and the
best account given by other of his Friends, to piece this to the Thread,
too soon broke off, and so lengthen it out to his entering upon Eternity.

He has told you at large, of his Birth and Education; the evil Habits
and Corruptions of his youth; the Temptations he struggled, and con-
flicted so frequently with; the Mercies, Comforts, and Deliverances he
found; how he came to take upon him the preaching of the Gospel; the
Slanders, Reproaches, and Imprisonments that attended him, and the
progress he notwithstanding made (by the assistance of God's Grace)
no doubt to the saving of many Souls: Therefore take these things as
he himself has methodically laid them down in the words of verity; and
so I pass on, as to what remains. After his being freed from his Twelve
years Imprisonment and upwards, for Nonconformity: wherein he had
time to furnish the World with sundry good books, *&c.* and by his
patience, to move Dr. *Barlow* the then Bishop of *Lincoln,* and other
Churchmen, to pity his hard and unreasonable sufferings, so far as to
stand very much his Friends, in procuring his Enlargement; or there
perhaps he had died, by the Noysemness and ill Usage of the Place.
Being now I say, again at Liberty, and having through mercy shaken
off his bodily Fetters; for those upon his Soul were broken before, by
the Abounding Grace that filled his heart, he went to visit those that
had been a comfort to him in his Tribulation, with a Christian-like
acknowledgment of their kindness, and enlargement of Charity; giving

encouragement by his Example, if it happened to be their hard haps to fall into affliction or trouble, then to suffer patiently for the sake of a good Conscience, and for the Love of God in Jesus Christ, towards their Souls; and by many cordial perswasions, supported some whose Spirits began to sink low through the fear of danger that threatned their worldly concernment, so that the people found a wonderful Consolation in his Discourse and Admonitions.

As often as opportunity would admit, he gather'd them together, though the Law was then in force against Meetings, in convenient places, and fed them with the sincere Milk of the word, that they might grow up in grace thereby. To such as were anywhere taken and imprison'd upon these accounts, he made it another part of his business, to extend his Charity, and gather relief for such of them as wanted.

He took great care to visit the Sick, and strengthen them against the suggestions of the Tempter, which at such times are very prevalent; so that they had cause for ever to bless God, who had put into his heart, at such a time, to rescue them from the power of the Roaring Lyon, who sought to devour them; nor did he spare any pains or labour in Travel, though to Remote Counties, where he knew, or imagined any people might stand in need of his Assistance, insomuch, that on some of these visitations that he made, which was two or three every year, some, though in jeering manner no doubt, gave him the Epethete of *Bishop Bunyan,* whilst others envied him for his so earnestly labouring in Christ's Vinyard, yet the Seed of the Word (he all this while) sowed in the hearts of his Congregation, Watered with the Grace of God, brought forth in abundance, in bringing in Disciples to the Church of Christ.

Another part of his time he spent in reconciling differences, by which he hindered many mischiefs, and saved some Families from Ruine; and, in such fallings out, he was uneasie, till he found a means to labour a Reconciliation, and become a peace-maker, on whom a Blessing is promised in Holy Writ: and indeed in doing this good Office, he may be said to sum up his days; it being the last undertaking of his Life, as will appear in the close of this Paper.

When in the late Reign, Liberty of Conscience was unexpectedly given and indulged to Dissenters of all Perswasions; his piercing wit penetrated the Veil, and found it was not for the Dissenters sake they were so suddenly freed from the Prosecutions that had long lain heavy upon them, and set, in a manner, on an equal foot with the Church of

20 on *om.* 1692

England, which the Papists were undermining, and about to subvert: he foresaw all the advantages that could have redounded to the Dissenters, would have been no more than what *Poliphemus* the monstrous giant of *Sicily* would have allowed *Ulysses,* viz., That he would Eat his Men first, and do him the favour of being Eaten last; for although Mr. *Bunyan,* following the Examples of others, did lay hold of this Liberty, as an acceptable thing in it self, knowing that God is the only Lord of Conscience, and that it is good at all times to do according to the dictates of a good Conscience, and that the Preaching the glad Tidings of the Gospel is beautiful in the Preacher; yet, in all this, he moved with caution and a Holy fear, earnestly praying for averting the impendent judgments, which he saw like a black Tempest hanging over our Heads, for our Sins, and ready to break upon us, and that the *Ninivites* Remedy was now highly necessary. Hereupon, he gathered his Congregation at *Bedford,* where he mostly lived, and had lived, and had spent the greatest part of his life; and there being no convenient place to be had, for the Entertainment of so great a Confluence of people as followed him, upon the Account of his Teaching, he consulted with them, for Building a Meeting House; to which they made their voluntary contributions, with all chearfulness and alacrity; and the first time he appeared there to Edifie, the place was so thronged, that many was constrained to stay without, though the House was very spacious, every one striving to partake of his Instructions, that were of his perswasion; and show their good will towards him, by being present at the opening of the place; and here he lived in much Peace and quiet of Mind, contenting himself with that little God had bestowed upon him, and sequestering himself from all secular imployments, to follow that of his Call to the Ministry; for, as God said to *Moses*; he that made the Lips and Heart, can give Eloquence and Wisdom, without extraordinary acquirements in an University.

During these things, there were Regulators sent in to all Cities and Towns corporate, to new model the Government in the Magistracy, &c., by turning out some, and putting in others; against this, Mr. *Bunyan* expressed his Zeal with some weariness, as foreseeing the bad consequence that would attend it, and laboured with his Congregation, to prevent their being imposed on in this kind, and when a great man in those days coming to *Bedford,* upon some such errand, sent for him, as 'tis supposed, to give him a place of publick Trust; he would by no means come at him, but sent his Excuse.

When he was at leisure from Writing and Teaching, he often came up to *London*, and there went among the Congregations of the Non-conformists, and used his Talent to the great good liking of the Hearers; and even some, to whom he had been misrepresented, upon the account of his Education, were convinced of his Worth and Know-ledge in Sacred Things, as perceiving him to be a man of sound Judg-ment, delivering himself, plainly and powerfully; insomuch that many who came meer Spectators, for novelty sake, rather than to edifie and be improved, went away well satisfied with what they heard, and wondered, as the *Jews* did at the Apostles, viz., whence this Man should have these things; perhaps not considering that God more immediately assists those that make it their business industriously and chearfully to labour in his Vineyard.

Thus he spent his latter years in imitation of his great Lord and Master, the ever-blessed Jesus; he went about doing good, so that the most prying Critick, or even Malice herself is defied to find, even upon the narrowest search or observation, any sully or stain upon his Reputation with which he may be justly charged; and this we note as a challenge to those that have had the least regard for him, or them of his Perswasion, and have one way or other appeared in the Front of those that oppressed him, and for the turning whose hearts in obedi-ence to the Commission and Commandment given him of God, he frequently prayed; and sometimes sought a Blessing for them, even with tears, the effects of which they may peradventure, though un-deservedly have found in their Persons, Friends, Relations or Estates; for God will hear the prayers of the Faithful, and Answer them, even for those that vex them; as it happened in the case of *Job*'s praying for the three Persons that had been grievous in their reproach against him, even in the day of his sorrow.

But yet let me come a little nearer to particulars, and periods of time, for the better refreshing the memories of those that knew his Labour and Suffering; and for the satisfaction of all that shall read this Book.

After he was sensibly convicted of the wicked State of his Life, and converted; he was Baptized into the Congregation, and admitted a member thereof, *viz.*, in the year 1655, and became speedily a very zealous professor; but upon the return of king *Charles* to the crown in 1660 he was on the twelfth of *November* taken, as he was Edifying some good People, that were got together to hear the Word, and confined in *Bedford* Goal for the space of six Years, till the Act of Indulgence to Dissenters being allowed, he obtained his Freedom by the Intercession of some in Trust and Power, that took pity on his Sufferings; but within six Years afterwards he was again taken up, viz., in the Year 1666, and was then confined for six years more, when even the Goaler took such pity of his rigorous Sufferings that he did as the *Egyptian* Goaler did to *Joseph*, put all the care and trust into his Hands. When he was taken this last time he was Preaching on these Words, viz., *Dost thou believe on the Son of God?* and this Imprisonment continued six Years; and when this was over, another short affliction, which was an Imprisonment of half a Year fell to his share. During these confinements he wrote these following Books, viz., *Of Prayer by the Spirit*; *The Holy City*; *Resurrection*; *Grace Abounding*; *Pilgrim's Progress, 1st part.*

In the last Year of his twelve Years Imprisonment the Pastor of the Congregation at *Bedford* died; and he was Chosen to that Care of Souls, on the twelfth of *December* 1671. And in this his Charge, he often had disputes with Scholars, that came to oppose him, as supposing him an Ignorant person, and though he Argued plainly and by Scripture without Phrases and Logical Expressions; yet he nonplussed one who came to oppose him in his Congregation; by demanding whether or no, we had the true Copies of the Original Scriptures; and another, when he was Preaching Accused him of uncharitableness, for saying, *it was very hard for most to be saved,* saying, by that he went about to exclude most of his Congregation; but he confuted him, and put him to silence, with the Parable of the Stony ground, and other texts out of the 13 of *Matt.* in our Saviours Sermon out of a Ship; all his method being to keep close to the Scriptures; and what he found not warranted there, himself would not warrant or determine, unless in such cases as were plain; wherein do doubts or scruples did arise.

But not to make any further mention of this kind; it is well known, that this person managed all his affairs with such exactness as if he had made it his study above all other things, not to give occasion of offence, but rather suffer many inconveniences to avoid, being never heard to Reproach, or Revile any, what injury soever he received, but rather to Rebuke those that did; and as it was in his Conversation, so it is manifested in those Books he has caus'd to be Published to the World; where, like the Arch Angel disputing with Satan, about the Body of *Moses,* as we find it in the Epistle of St. *Jude*, [he] brings [no] Railing Accusation; but leaves the Rebukers, (those that persecuted him,) to the Lord. In his Family he kept up a very strict Discipline, in Prayer and Exhortations; being in this like *Joshua*, as that good Man Expresses it, viz., *Whatsoever others did; as for me and my House, we will serve the Lord;*

and indeed a Blessing waited upon his Labours and Endeavours, so that his Wife as the *Psalmist* says, *Was like a pleasant Vine upon the Walls of his House, and his Children like Olive Branches round his Table; for so shall it be with the Man that fears the Lord*; and though by Reason of the many Losses he sustained by Imprisonment and Spoil and his chargeable Sickness, *&c.*, his Earthly Treasures swelled not to excess, he always had sufficient to live decently and creditably, and with that he had the greatest of all Treasures, which is content; for as the Wise Man says, *That is a continual Feast.*

But where content dwells, even a poor Cottage is a Kingly Palace; and this Happiness he had all his Life long, not so much minding this World, as knowing he was here as a Pilgrim and Stranger and had no tarrying City, but looking for one not made with Hands, Eternal in the Highest Heavens; but at length worn out with Sufferings, Age, and often Teaching, the day of his Dissolution drew near, and Death that unlocks the Prison of the Soul, to inlarge it for a more glorious Mansion, put a stop to his Acting his part on the Stage of Mortality; Heaven like Earthly Princes when it threatens War, being always so kind as to call home it's Ambassadors, before it be denounced; and even the last Act, or Undertaking of his, was a Labour of Love and Charity; for it so falling out, that a young Gentleman a Neighbour to Mr. *Bunyan* happening into the displeasure of his Father, and being much troubled in mind upon that Account, as also for that he had heard his father purposed to disinherit him, or otherwise deprive him of what he had to leave, he pitched upon *Mr. Bunyan* as a fit man to make way for his submission, and prepare his Fathers mind to receive him, and he as willing to do any good Office, as it could be requested, as readily undertook it; and so riding to *Redding* in *Barkshire*, he then there used such pressing Arguments and Reasons against Anger and Passion, as also for Love and Reconciliation, that the Father was mollified, and his Bowels yern'd towards his returning Son.

But Mr. *Bunyan* after he had disposed all things to the best, for accommodation, returning to London, and being overtaken with excessive Rains, coming to his lodging extream Wet, fell sick of a violent Feavor, which he bore with much constancy and patience, and expressed himself as if he desired nothing more than to be dissolved, and to be with Christ in that case, esteeming Death as gain, and Life only a tedious delaying felicity expected; and finding his Vital Strength decay, having settled his mind and affairs, as well as the shortness of his time, and the violence of his disease would permit, with a constant and

Christian patience, he resign'd his Soul into the hands of his most merciful Redeemer, following his Pilgrim from the City of Destruction, to the New *Jerusalem,* his better part having been all along there, in holy contemplation, pantings and breathings after the hidden *Manna,* and Water of Life, as by many holy and humble Consolations exprest in his Letters, to several Persons in Prison, and out of Prison, too many to be here incerted at present. He died at the House of one Mr. *Straddocks,* a *Grocer,* at the *Star* on *Snow hill,* in the parish of St. *Sepulchers, London,* on the 12 of *August* 1688 and in the 60 Year of his Age, after ten days Sickness; and was buried in the New burying Place, near the Artillery Ground, where he sleeps to the Morning of the Resurrection, in hopes of a glorious rising to an incorruptible immortality of Joy and Happiness, where no more Trouble and Sorrow shall afflict him, but all tears be wiped away, when the Just shall be incorrupted, as Members of Christ their Head, and reign with him, as Kings and Priests for ever.

A Brief Character of Mr. John Bunyan

He appeared in Countenance, to be of a stern and rough Temper; but in his conversation mild and affable, not given to loquacity or much Discourse in company, unless some urgent occasion required it; observing never to boast of himself, or his parts, but rather seem low in his own Eyes, and submit himself to the Judgment of others, abhoring Lying and Swearing, being just in all that lay in his Power to his word, not seeming to revenge Injuries, loving to reconcile differences, and make friendship with all; he had a sharp quick Eye, accomplished with an Excellent discerning of Persons, being of good Judgment and quick Wit. As for his Person he was Tall of Stature, strong Boned, though not Corpulent, somewhat of a Ruddy Face, with Sparkling Eyes, wearing his Hair on his upper Lip after the Old *British* fashion; his Hair Reddish, but in latter days, time had sprinkled it with Grey, his Nose well set, but not declining or bending, and his Mouth moderate Large; his Forehead somewhat high, and his Habit always plain and modest. And thus have we impartially described the internal and external Parts of a Person, whose death hath been much Regretted, a person who had tryed the Smiles and Frowns of Time; not puffed up in Prosperity, nor shaken in Adversity, always holding the Golden Mean.

> *In him at once did three great Worthies Shine;*
> Historian, Poet, *and a Choice* Divine;
> *Then let him Rest in undisturbed Dust,*
> *Until the Resurrection of the Just.*

Postscript

In this his Pilgrimage, God Blessed him with four Children, one of which named *Mary* was blind, and died some years before; his other Children are *Thomas*, *Joseph* and *Sarah*; and his wife *Elizabeth* having lived to see him overcome his Labour and Sorrow, and pass from this Life to receive the reward of his Works, long Survived him not, but 1692 she died; to follow her faithful pilgrim from this World to the other, whether he was gone before her, whilst his Works, which consist of Sixty Books, remain for the edifying of the Reader, and the Praise of the Author. *Vale.*

FINIS.

9 remain] which remain 1692

APPENDIX C

Extracts from *The Narrative of the Persecution of Agnes Beaumont in 1674*

(B.M. Egerton MS. 2414)

In those dayes I was Alwayes laying up many a Prayre in heaven, Against I came to the Lords Table, where I often found a very plentifull returne. I could say A greate deale more what I have mett with, and how I have been in y^t Ordinance, But I shall for beare.

Well, It did please ye Lord to grant mee those two things; One in a large manner indeed when I came to the Lords table. And the day before ye meeting I asked my ffather to lett me goe to it, And he seemd as if he was not very willing; but pleading wth him, I tould him I would doe what I had to doe in the morneing before I went, and come home Againe at night. At last he was willing. Soe on friday morneing, wch was the day the meeting was to bee, I made me ready to goe. My ffather asked me whoe caried mee. I said I thought Mr Wilson, whoe was to call at my Brothers y^t morneing as he went, and I would pray him to Cary mee; for my Brother spake wth him the Tuesday before, whoe tould him he had thought to Call at his house on friday morne to goe wth him to Gamgy,[1] Soe my ffather said nothing to these things.

Soe when I was ready, I went to my Brothers, Expectin to meet w^th *Mr Wilson* to ride behind him. And their I waited some time; And noe body came. At last my heart began to ake, and I fell A Crying for feare I should not goe, for my Brother tould mee he could not let me have A horse to go for they was all at worke, and he was to Cary my Sister beehind him to the Meeting, soe y^t he could noe wayes helpe me thither. And it was the deep of Winter, I could not goe on foott.

Now I was Afraid all my prayers would be lost upon that Account. Thought I, I prayed to god to make my father willing to let me goe, and y^t I might have the p^rsence of god in y^t meeting, But now my way is hedged up wth thornes. And their I weighted, and lookt, many a long looke, wth A broken heart.

Said my Brother to me, 'Mr Wilson said he would come this way and Cary you.' But he did not come. 'Oh,' thought I, 'that god would please to put it into the heart of some body to come this way and Cary mee, and make some way or other for my goeing.' Well, still I waighted, wth my heart full of feares least I should not goe.

[1] Gamlingay.

At last un Expected came *M*ʳ *Bunyan*, and cald at my Brothers as he went to the meeting; but the sight of him caused sorrow, and Ioy, in me; I was glad to see him but I was afraid he would not Cary mee to the meeting behind him; and how to Aske him I did not know, for feare he should deny mee, Soe I got my Brother to aske him.

Soe my Brother said to him, 'I must desire you to Cary my Sister today behind you.'

And he Answered my Brother very roughly, and said, 'Noe not I, I will not Cary her.' These was Cutting words to me indeed, wᶜʰ made mee weepe bitterly.

My Brother sᵈ to him Againe, 'If yow doe not Cary her, yow will breake her heart.'

And he replyed wᵗʰ the same words Againe, that he would not cary me, that he would not Cary mee. And he said to me, 'If I should cary yow, yoʳ father would be greivous Angrey wᵗʰ me.' Said I, 'If you please to carry me, I will venture that.' Soe wᵗʰ a great many intreatyes, at last my Brother did prevaile with him, and I did git up behind him. But oh, how glad was I that I was goeing.

But I had beene but just on horsebacke, as I heard afterwards, But my father Came to my brothers, to some of the men that was at worke, And askt them whoe his daughter rode behind. They Answered such An one, wᵗʰ yᵗ my father fell into a passion, And ran downe to the Close End, thincking to have mett me in the feilds, where he intended to have pulled mee off of the horse backe, he was soe Angry, because some had incenst him Against *M*ʳ *Bunyan*—But we was gone by first.

But to speake the truth I had not gone ferr behind him, but my heart was pufft up wᵗʰ pride, And I began to have high thoughts of my selfe, and proud to thincke I should ride behind Such A man as he was; and I was pleased that any body did looke after me as I rode a long. And sometimes he would be speaking to mee About the things of god as we went Along. And indeed I thought my selfe a happy body that day; First that it did please god to make way for my goeing to the meeting; & then yᵗ I should have the honour to ride behind him. But, as yow will understand, my pride had a fall.

Soe Comeing to the townes End, their meet wᵗʰ us A priest one *M*ʳ *Lane* whoe, as I remember, lived then at *Bedford*, but was use to preach at *Edworth*; and he knew us both, and spake to us, and lookt of us, as wee rode Along the way as if he would have staird his Eyes Out; and afterwards did scandalise us after a base maner, and did raise a very wicked report of us, which was altogether false, blessed be god.

Soe we Came to *Gamgy*; and after A while the meeting began, and god made it a blessed meeting to my soul indeed. Oh, it was a feast of ffatt things to me! My soul was filled wth Consolation, and I sat under his Shaddow, wth great delight, and his fruit was pleasant to my tast when I was at the Lords table. I found such a returne of prayre that I was scarse able to beare up under it. Oh, I had such a sight of Iesus Christ y^t brake my heart to peeces. Oh, how I longed that day to bee wth Iesus Christ; how faine would I have dyed in the place, y^t I might have gone the next way to him, my blessed Saviour. A sence of my sinns, and of his dying love, made me love him, and long to be with him; and truly it was infinite Condesention in him, and I have often thought of his grace and goodness to me, that Jesus Christ should soe gratiously visit my poore Soul that day. He knew what tryalls and temptations I had to meet with that night, And in A few dayes. Oh, I have seene what bowels of pitty and Compation he had towards mee, that he should give mee such new manifestations of his love that very day.

Well, when the meeting was done, I began to thincke how I should gett home, for *Mr Bunyan* was not to goe by *Edworth* though he came that way. And it was almost night and very Durty, and I had promised my father to come home At night. And my thoughts began to worke, and my heart to be full of feares least I should not get home that night. As I was troubled to get thither, soe I was to get home, but in the time of ye meetin, blessed be god, it was kept out.—Soe I went first to one, and then to Another, to aske who went that way that could cary me some part of the way home; but their was noe body could supply my wants, but A maide that lived at hincksworth, halfe a mile off my fathers, and, the wayes being soe durty and deepe, I was afraid to venture behind her. But I did, and she set mee downe at Sister Prudons gate.

Soe I came home plosshing through the durt over shoes, haveing noe pattings on. I made what hast I could, hopeing I should be at home before my father was A bed; but when I came neere the house, I see noe light in it. Soe I went to the doore, and found it Lockt, wth the key in it. Then my heart began to Ake wth feare; for if I have not beene at home, if my father hath hapned to goe to bed before I came home, he would cary the key to bed wth him, and give me it out at Window. But now I perceived what I was Like to trust too; but however, I went to his Chamber Window, and Called to him.

He asked who was their. 'It is I, father,' said I, 'pray will you let me in; I am come home wett and dirty.'

Said he, 'Where yow have beene all day, goe at Night'; and many such like things, for he was very Angry with me, for rideing behind Mr Bunyan, and said I should never come within his doores Againe, Except I would promise him to leave goeing after that man; for some Enemyes in the towne had set my father Against him wth telling of him of some false reports that was raisd of him; and they affirmed them to my father for truth, and, poore man, he beleeved them because such persons affirmed it.

The narrative goes on to relate how Agnes spent the night in the barn; the following morning she crossed the fields to her brother's house and remained there till the following Sunday; then, after much agony of mind, she surrendered to her father's insistence that she should give up Bunyan and his congregation and returned to her home. The Tuesday after her return her father died of a sudden and mysterious seizure. The clergyman Lane, who had seen her with Bunyan, spread scandal about the relations of pastor and this member of his flock, and a rejected suitor, a lawyer named Feery or Farrow, set in motion the more dangerous and malicious charge that she had poisoned her father, and that Bunyan had furnished her with the means of doing it. A coroner's inquest cleared her name entirely, but she movingly describes her predicament before her innocence was proved. 'And this Alsoe troubled mee, that if I had suffered Another as Inocent as I must have suffred too. . . . But the Lord knew to the Contrary, that neither he nor I was gilty of that wickedness in thought, word, nor deed.'

This is the affair referred to by Bunyan in the passage which first appears in the fifth edition (§§ 306–17) and where he says: 'But that which was reported with the boldest confidence, was, that I had my *Misses*, my *Whores*, my *Bastards*, yea, *two Wives at once*, and the like.' In another manuscript of Agnes Beaumont's narrative (B.M. MS. Egerton 2128) this concluding paragraph is added:

After this Report there was another, raised in another place in the Country, and that was, *Mr. Bunyan was a Widower, and he gave me Councel to poyson my Father so that he might have me to be his Wife, and this we agreed upon as we rid along to Gangy,* and truly this did sometime make me merry, as other things did make me sad, and not long after it was said, *we were married,* but they were mistaken for he had a good Wife before.

Agnes Beaumont's name is the first to be entered in Bunyan's own hand in the *Bedford Church Book*. In 1669 her brother John had been presented by the churchwardens of Edworth for refusing to take the Sacrament at the parish church. Agnes was received into the congregation in November 1672: 'the desire of Sister Behement to walke in fellowshipp wth us was propounded. and was received at the next church-meeting.' Her friend Sister Prudon had joined a few months earlier: 'At an assembly of ye Congregation at Gam: the 7th of ye 4th mo: 72. There was received into fellowship wth this Congregation, Humphrey Thorowgood of Southill; Sister Mattris of Ashwel, & Mary Prutton of Edworth.' 'Railling and other wicked practises', presumably scandal-mongering, are frequently referred to in the *Church Book* at this period. The meeting which caused the trouble took place at Gamlingay on 13 February, when two brethren and one sister were admitted.

Agnes Beaumont was twice married and died at Highgate on 28 November 1720, aged 68 years. She was buried in the Baptist burying ground at Hitchin.

INDEX

Abel, 82.
Alexander, a coppersmith, 108.
Ammon, children of, 51.

Bedford, 14, 18, 19, 79, 116; the Bedford church, 14, 19, 22, 25, 65, 79; Bedford-River (the Ouse), 8.
Beecher, Sir William, 113.
Beelzebub, 117.
Benhadad, 78.
Biblical symbolism:
Adulterer: she who met with, as the soul crying for God's help (Deut. xxii. 25), 35; *Beasts*: clean and unclean ones, as types of the elect and the reprobate (Deut. xiv), 23–24; *Birthright*: as regeneration (Gen. xxvii. 36), 71; *Brass*: gates of, as unbelief (Ps. cvii. 16), 26; *Bread*: the man who went to borrow bread at midnight, as a parable of persistence in prayer (Luke xi. 5–8), 78; *City of God* (Eccles. x. 15), 9; *City of Refuge*: as a type of God's mercy (Joshua xx. 5), 68; *Cymbal*: the tinkling cymbal, as gifts without saving grace (1 Cor. xiii. 1, 2), 91; *Door*: gap in wall, as the entrance to Christ (Matt. vii. 14), 19; *Elders*: round the throne in Apocalypse, as a symbol of Christ's manhood (Rev. v. 6), 38; *Esau*: his selling his birthright, as a type of the sin against the Holy Ghost (Heb. xii. 16, 17), 43–59; *Gideon's fleece*: as a type of doubting God's providence (Judges vi. 36–40), 76; *Goliah*: his head in David's hand, as fears and doubts overcome (1 Sam. xvii. 54), 3; *Honey*: Samson's honey from the carcass of a lion, as the graces to be found under persecution (Judges xiv. 5–8), 1; *Horseleach*: as a mind fixed on eternity (Prov. xxx. 15), 15; *Israelites*: forty years in the wilderness, as the period before conversion (Num. xxxiii. 1, 2), 2; *Job*: as a type of Bunyan's experience, 78, 101; *Kine*: the two milch kine leaving their calves behind them, as a type of Bunyan separated from his family by imprisonment (1 Sam. vi.

10–12), 98; *Land*: as the Christian's heritage of salvation (Lev. xxv. 23), 42; *Lion*: lions' dens or teeth, as persecution (Song of Solomon iv. 8), 1; *Milk and Honey*: as the promise of salvation (Exod. iii. 17), 4; *Peter's sheet*: as short touches of grace (Acts x. 16), 36; *Sea*: the troubled sea, as the uneasy conscience (Isa. lvii. 20, 21), 33; *Sinai*: Moses' stay on, as the period before conversion (Deut. iv. 10, 11), 2; *Spoils*: won in battle, as the type of Bunyan's autobiography (1 Chron. xxvi. 27), 101; *Tombs*: the man with an unclean spirit dwelling among the tombs, as a type of desperation (Mark v. 2–5), 58; *Widow*: the poor widow before the unjust judge (Luke xviii. 1–8), as Bunyan's wife appealing to the assize judges, 126.
Blundale (Blundell), Sir George, 113.
Bunyan, John, his mean parentage and education, 5; terrible dreams as a child, 6; providential escapes from death, 7–8; marriage and outward reformation, 8–9; effect of an awakening sermon on, 9–10; vices and pastimes, 10–14; he gives up his bell-ringing, 13–14; first contact with the Bedford church, 15; relations with the Ranters, 16–17; early Bible reading, 17–19; vision of the Bedford church, 19–20; doubts of his election, 19–23; receives comfort from Scriptural texts, 24–25; meeting with Gifford, 25; his sufferings of conscience, 26–29; a year of temptations, 30–36; becomes a member of the Bedford church, 37; he sees the errors of the Quakers, 39; receives an assurance of his salvation, 39–40; meets with Luther's *Commentary on the Galatians*, 40–41; a second period of temptation to despair, 41–59; an interval of grace, 52–54; his gradual emergence from despair, 59–72; he sees his righteousness in heaven, 72; understands the true nature of Christ, 72–74; analysis of his temptation, 74–77; his reliance on the